VALLEY 1/18/2008
50690010625777
Carey, Percy.
Sentences : [the life of
M.F. Grimm] /

W9-BXL-064

VALLEY COMMUNITY LIBRARY
739 RIVER STREET
PECKVILLE, PA 18452
(570) 489-1765
www.lclshome.org

# Sentences: the Life of M.F. Grimm

VERTIGO
DC COMICS

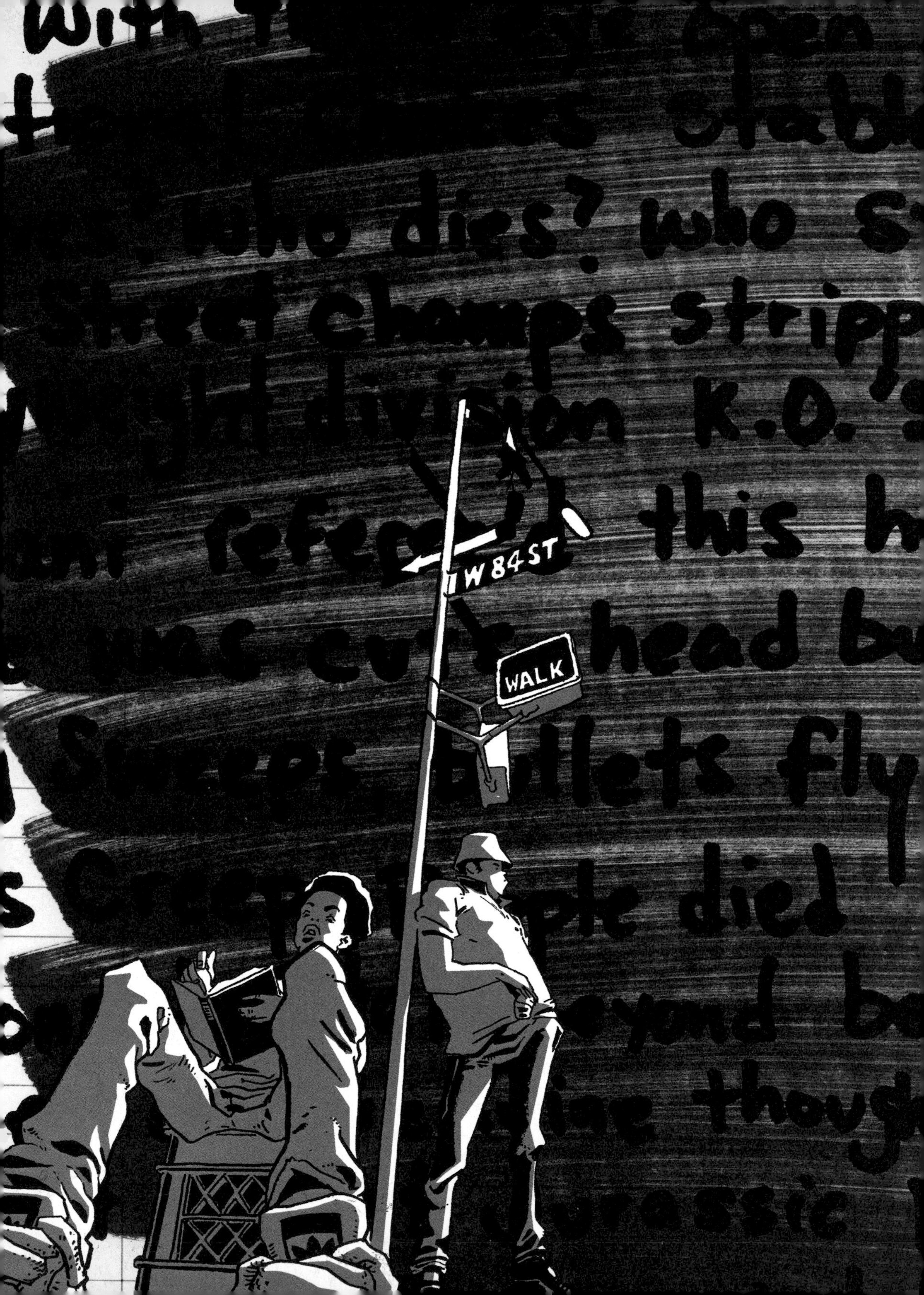

With
open
who dies? who
Street Champs
division K.O.
this
head
bullets fly
died
beyond
W 84 ST
WALK

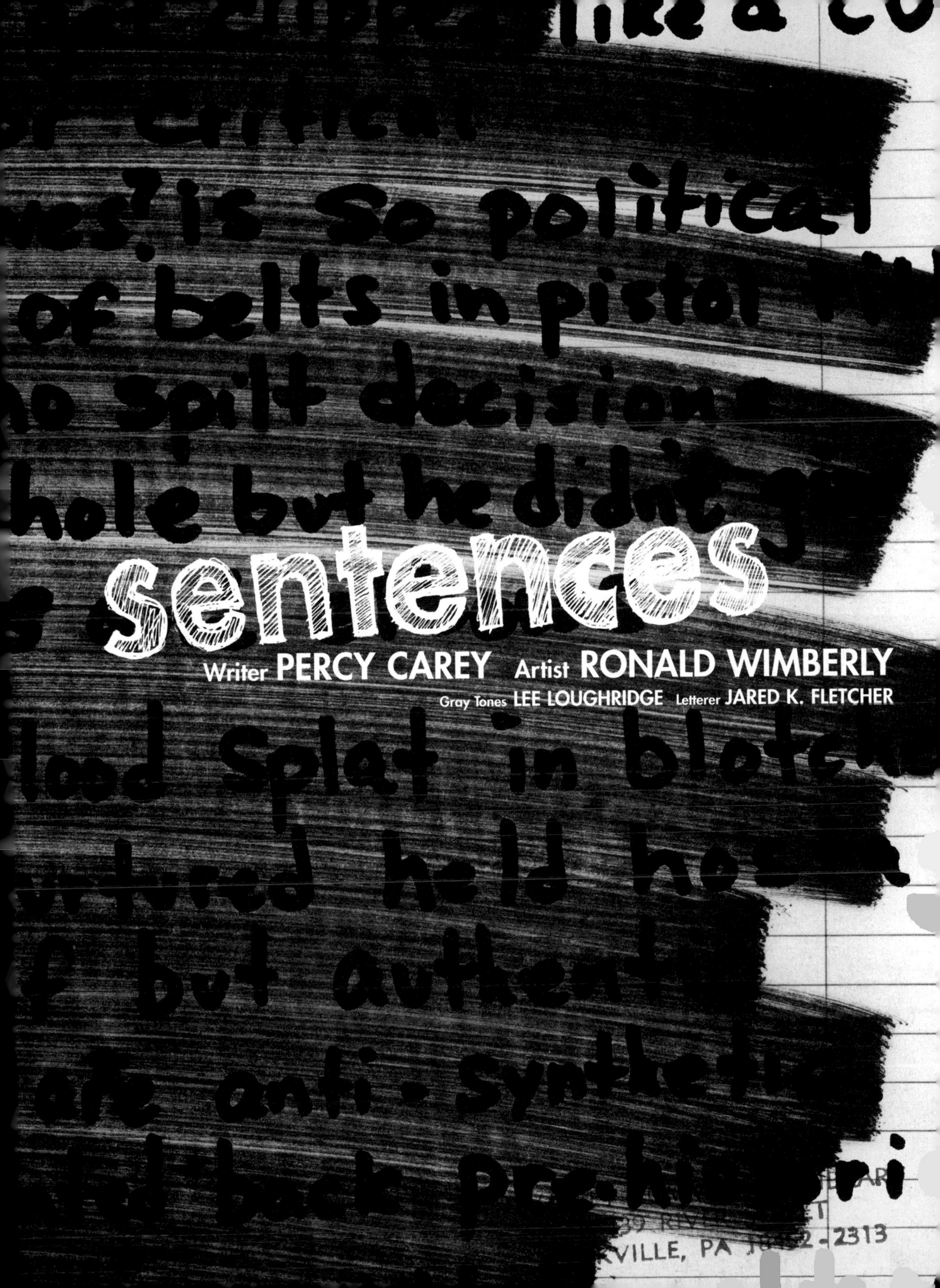
sentences
Writer PERCY CAREY Artist RONALD WIMBERLY
Gray Tones LEE LOUGHRIDGE Letterer JARED K. FLETCHER

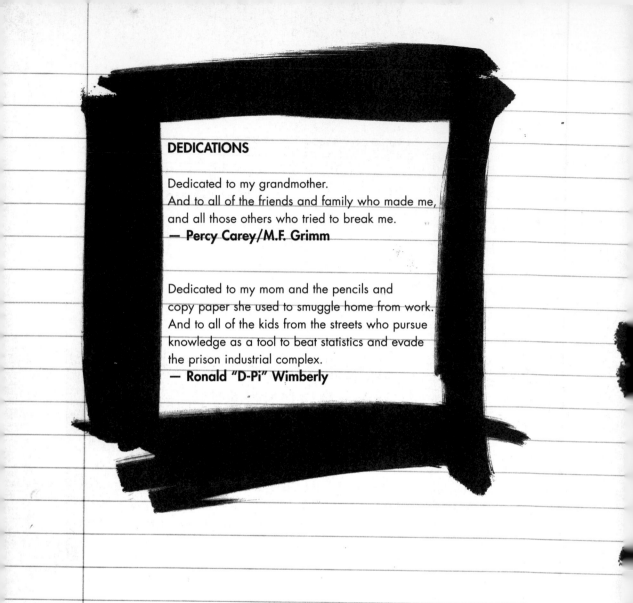

## DEDICATIONS

Dedicated to my grandmother.
And to all of the friends and family who made me,
and all those others who tried to break me.
— **Percy Carey/M.F. Grimm**

Dedicated to my mom and the pencils and
copy paper she used to smuggle home from work.
And to all of the kids from the streets who pursue
knowledge as a tool to beat statistics and evade
the prison industrial complex.
— **Ronald "D-Pi" Wimberly**

**Karen Berger** Sr. VP-Executive Editor   **Casey Seijas** Editor   **Louis Prandi** Art Director   **Paul Levitz** President & Publisher

**Georg Brewer** VP-Design & DC Direct Creative   **Richard Bruning** Sr. VP-Creative Director   **Patrick Caldon** Exec. VP-Finance & Operations

**Chris Caramalis** VP-Finance   **John Cunningham** VP-Marketing   **Terri Cunningham** VP-Managing Editor   **Alison Gill** VP-Manufacturing

**Hank Kanalz** VP-General Manager, WildStorm   **Jim Lee** Editorial Director-WildStorm   **Paula Lowitt** Sr. VP-Business & Legal Affairs

**MaryEllen McLaughlin** VP-Advertising & Custom Publishing   **John Nee** VP-Business Development   **Gregory Noveck** Sr. VP-Creative Affairs

**Sue Pohja** VP-Book Trade Sales   **Cheryl Rubin** Sr. VP-Brand Management   **Jeff Trojan** VP-Business Development, DC Direct   **Bob Wayne** VP-Sales

Cover art and color by Ronald Wimberly.

**SENTENCES: THE LIFE OF M.F. GRIMM** Published by DC Comics, 1700 Broadway, New York, NY 10019. Copyright © 2007 by Percy Carey and DC Comics. All rights reserved. VERTIGO is a trademark of DC Comics. Printed in Canada. First Printing. DC Comics, a Warner Bros. Entertainment Company. HC ISBN: 1-4012-1046-5   978-1-4012-1046-5   SC ISBN: 1-4012-1047-3   978-1-4012-1047-2

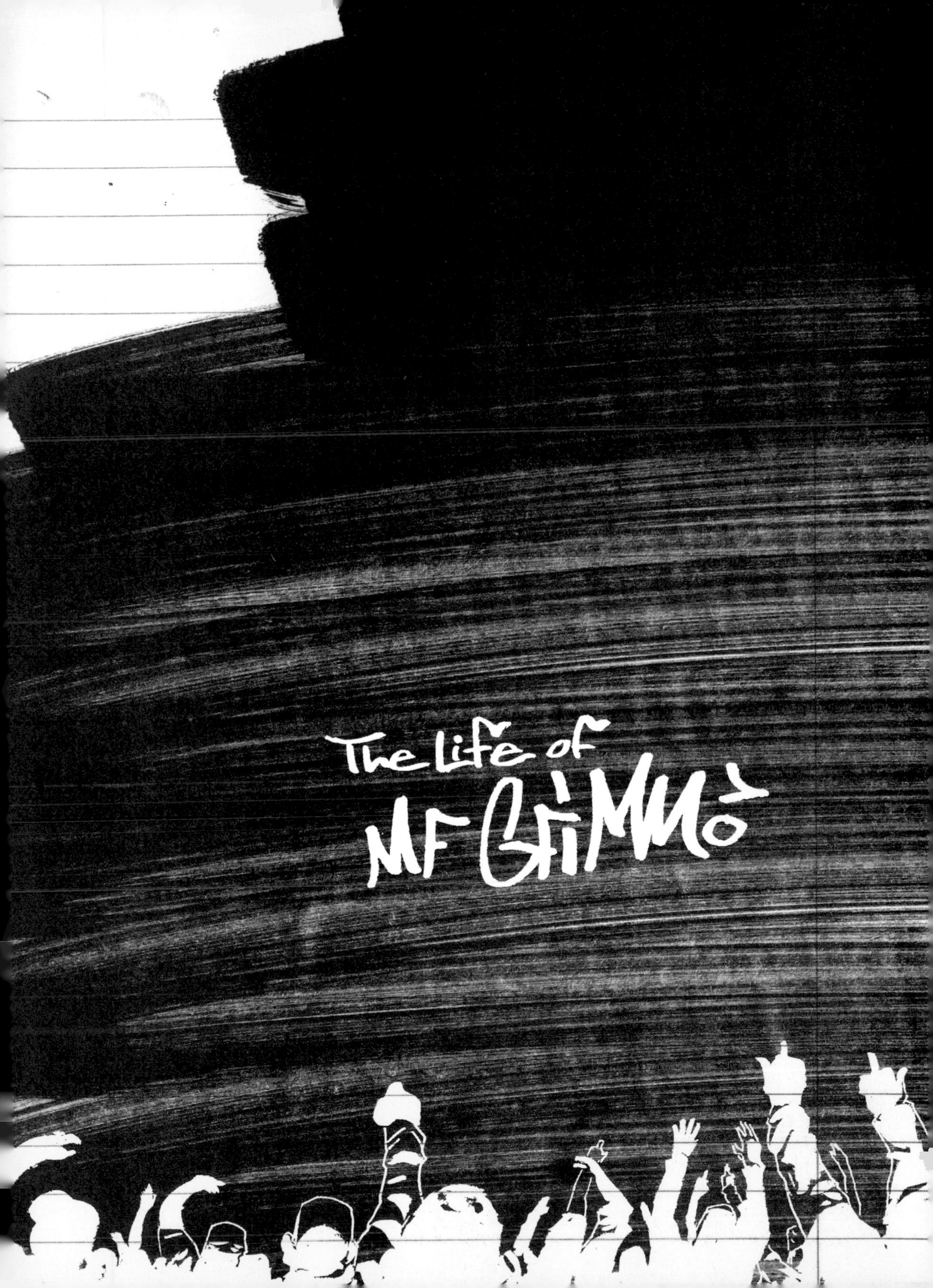
The Life of
MF Grimm

PRELUDE: January 12, 1994, Harlem, New York City.

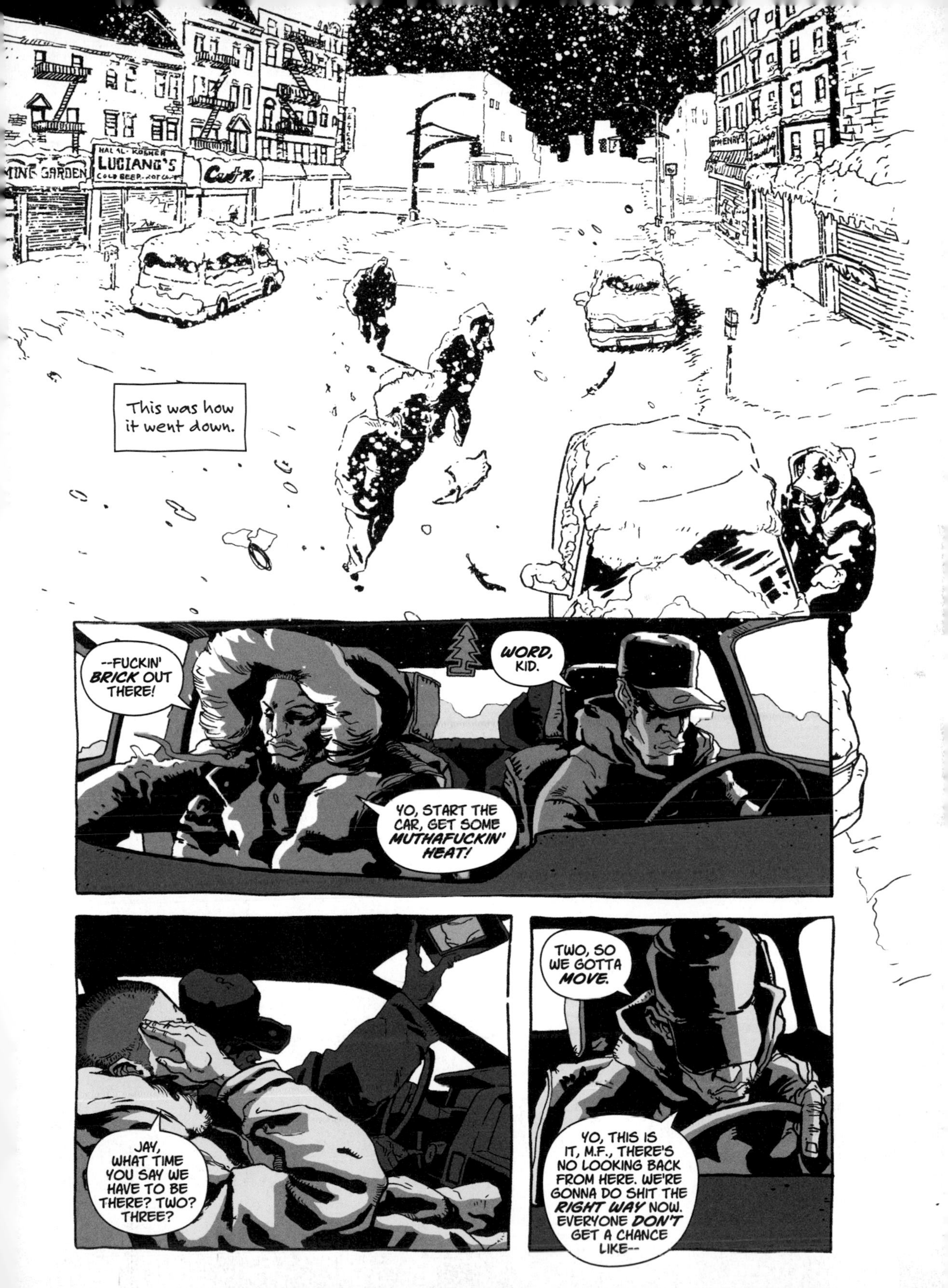
HAL AL-KOSHER
LUCIANO'S
COLD BEER. HOT CAFE
MING GARDEN
This was how it went down.
--FUCKIN' BRICK OUT THERE!
WORD, KID.
YO, START THE CAR, GET SOME MUTHAFUCKIN' HEAT!
JAY, WHAT TIME YOU SAY WE HAVE TO BE THERE? TWO? THREE?
TWO, SO WE GOTTA MOVE.
YO, THIS IS IT, M.F., THERE'S NO LOOKING BACK FROM HERE. WE'RE GONNA DO SHIT THE RIGHT WAY NOW. EVERYONE DON'T GET A CHANCE LIKE--

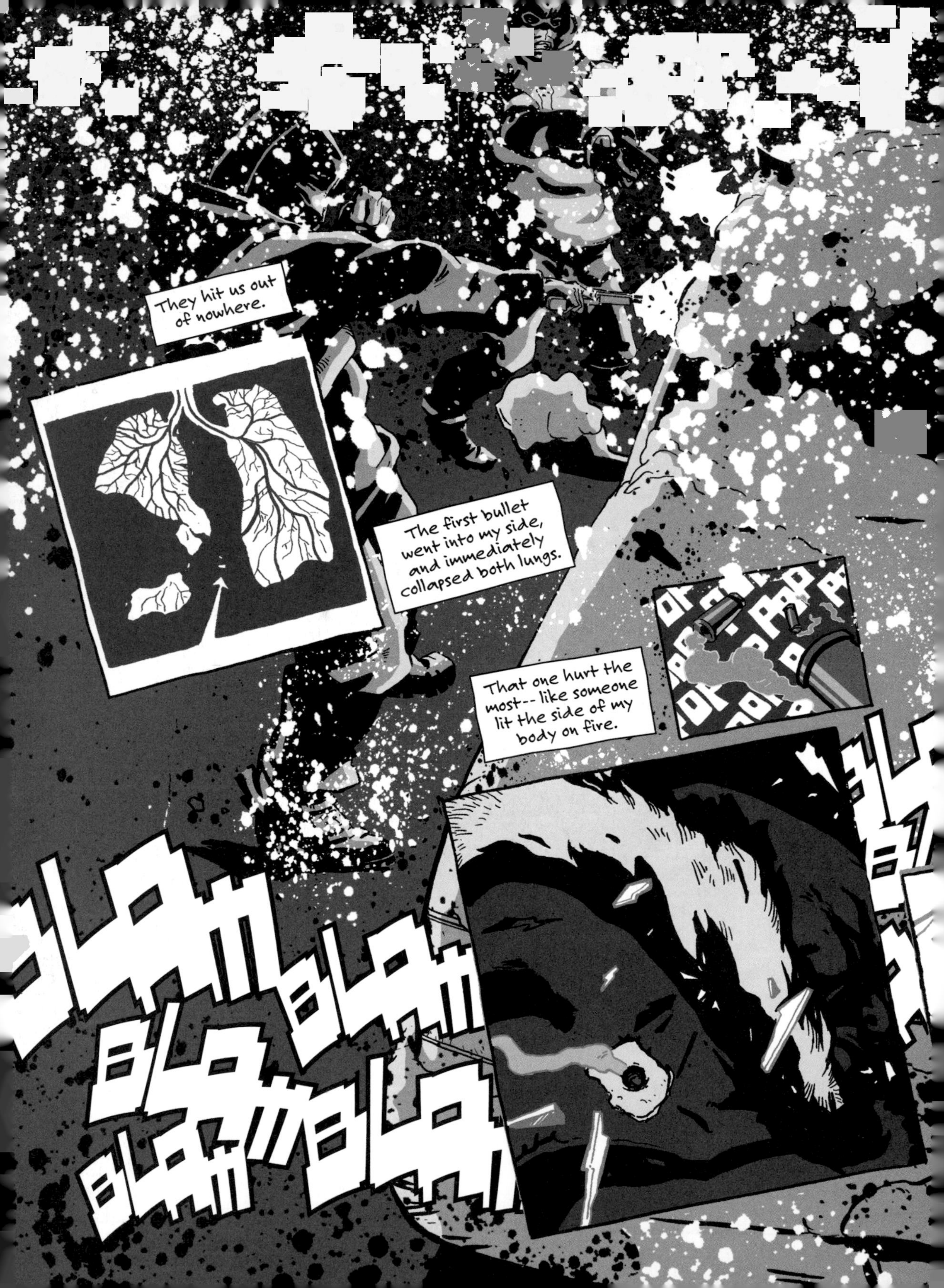
They hit us out of nowhere.
The first bullet went into my side, and immediately collapsed both lungs.
That one hurt the most-- like someone lit the side of my body on fire.
BLAM BLAM
BLAM
BLAM BLAM

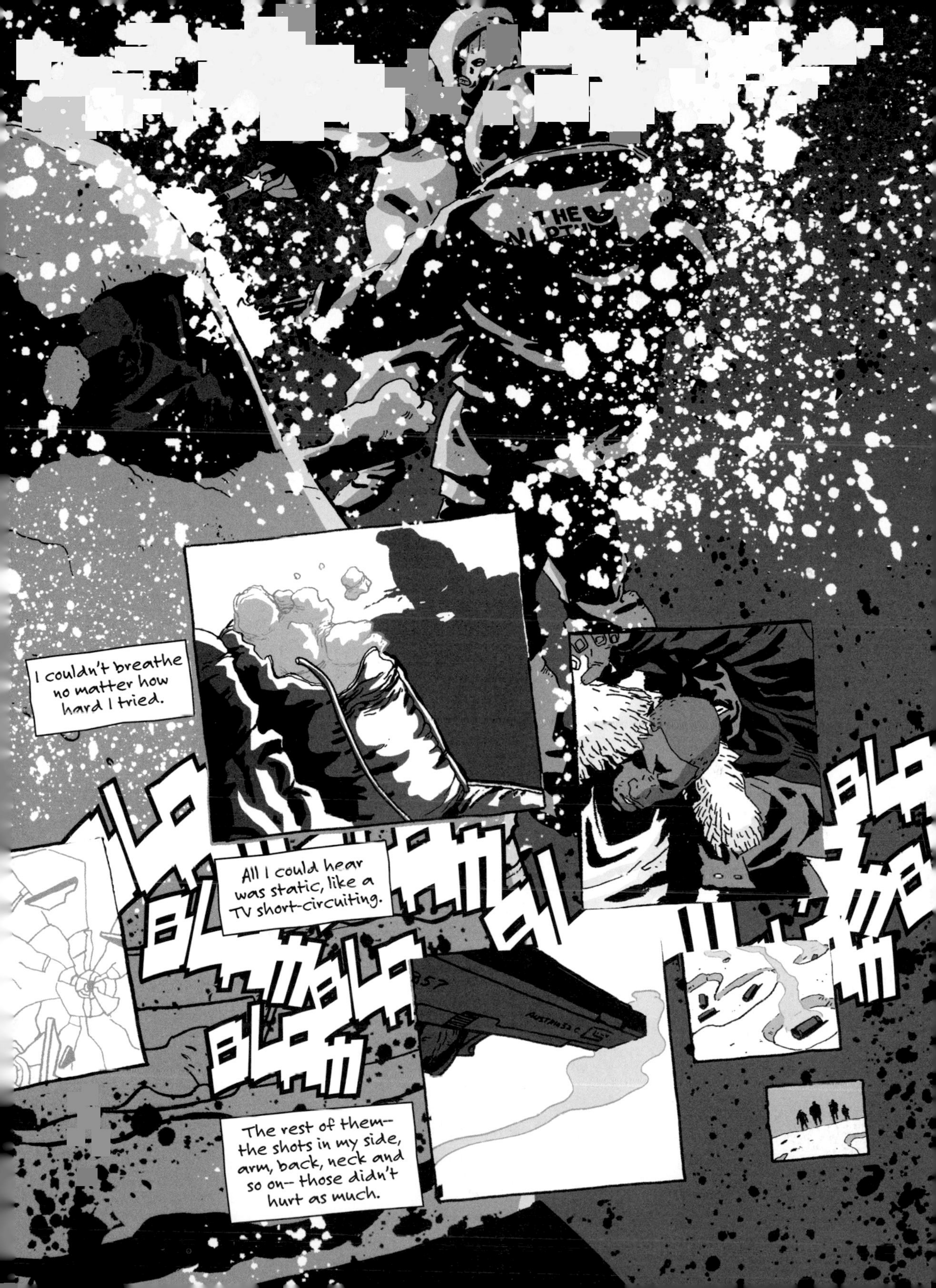
I couldn't breathe no matter how hard I tried.
All I could hear was static, like a TV short-circuiting.
The rest of them— the shots in my side, arm, back, neck and so on— those didn't hurt as much.

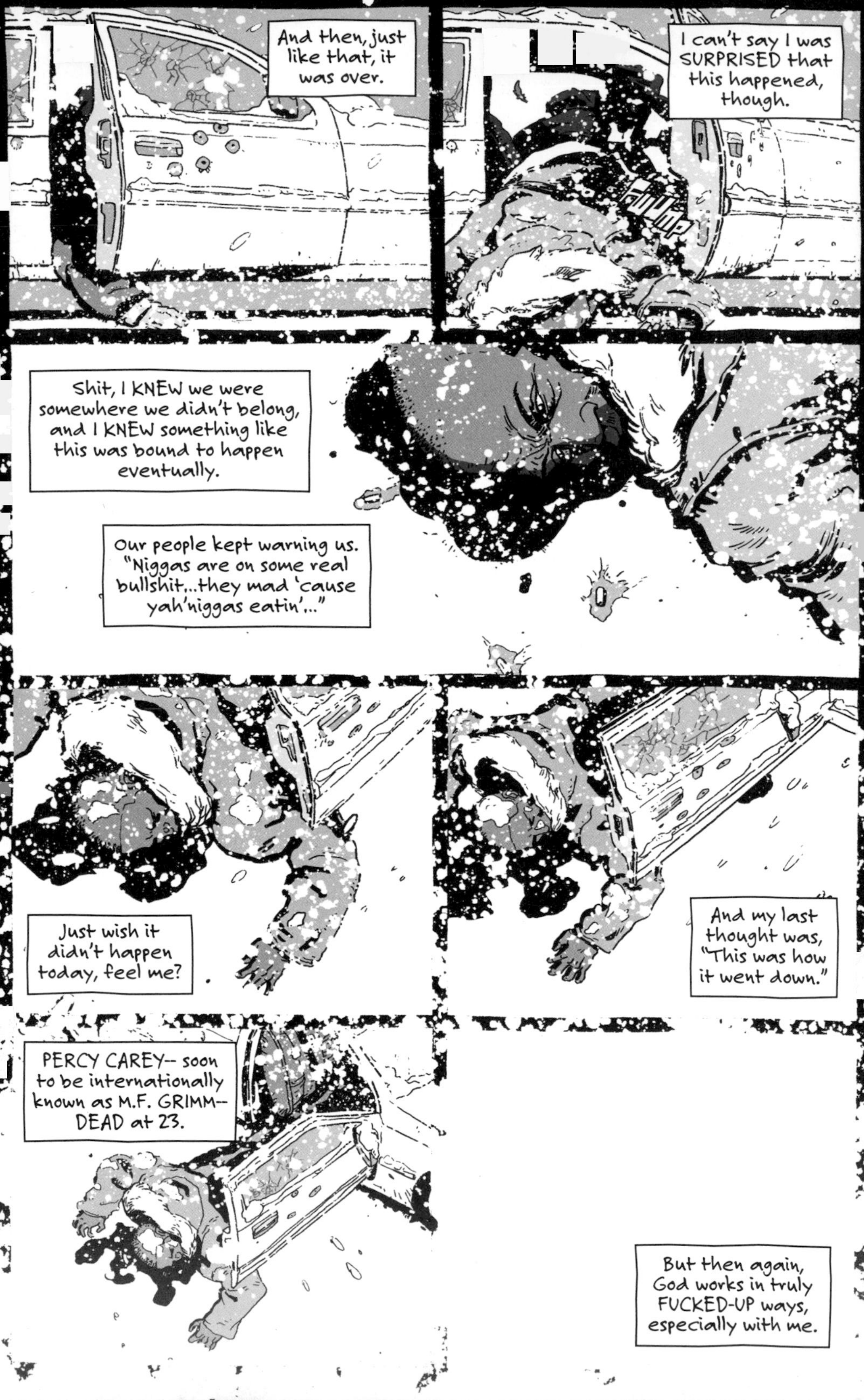
And then, just like that, it was over.
I can't say I was SURPRISED that this happened, though.
Shit, I KNEW we were somewhere we didn't belong, and I KNEW something like this was bound to happen eventually.
Our people kept warning us. "Niggas are on some real bullshit...they mad 'cause yah'niggas eatin'..."
Just wish it didn't happen today, feel me?
And my last thought was, "This was how it went down."
PERCY CAREY-- soon to be internationally known as M.F. GRIMM-- DEAD at 23.
But then again, God works in truly FUCKED-UP ways, especially with me.

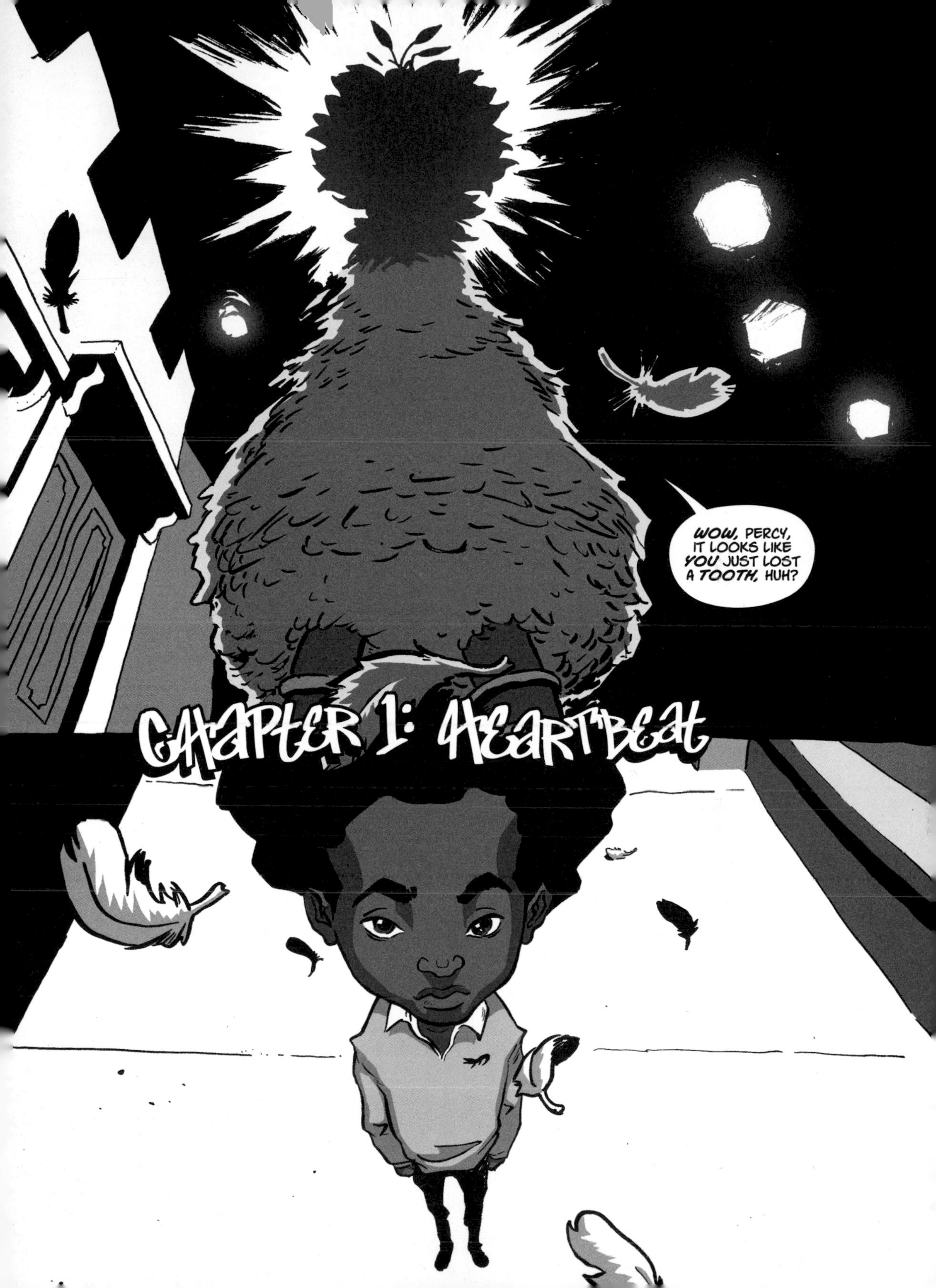
WOW, PERCY, IT LOOKS LIKE YOU JUST LOST A TOOTH, HUH?
CHAPTER 1: HEARTBEAT

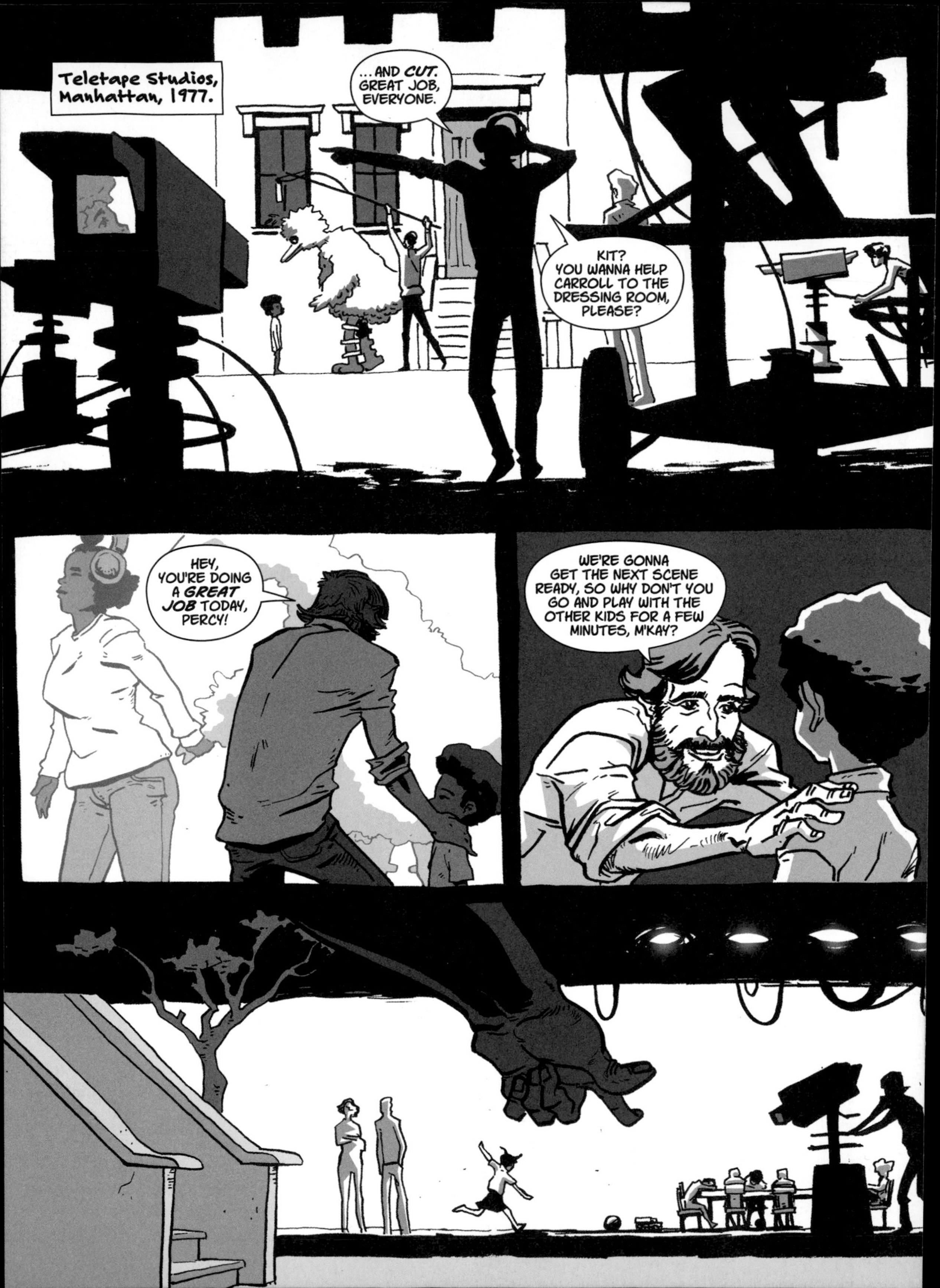
Teletape Studios, Manhattan, 1977.
...AND CUT. GREAT JOB, EVERYONE.
KIT? YOU WANNA HELP CARROLL TO THE DRESSING ROOM, PLEASE?
HEY, YOU'RE DOING A GREAT JOB TODAY, PERCY!
WE'RE GONNA GET THE NEXT SCENE READY, SO WHY DON'T YOU GO AND PLAY WITH THE OTHER KIDS FOR A FEW MINUTES, M'KAY?

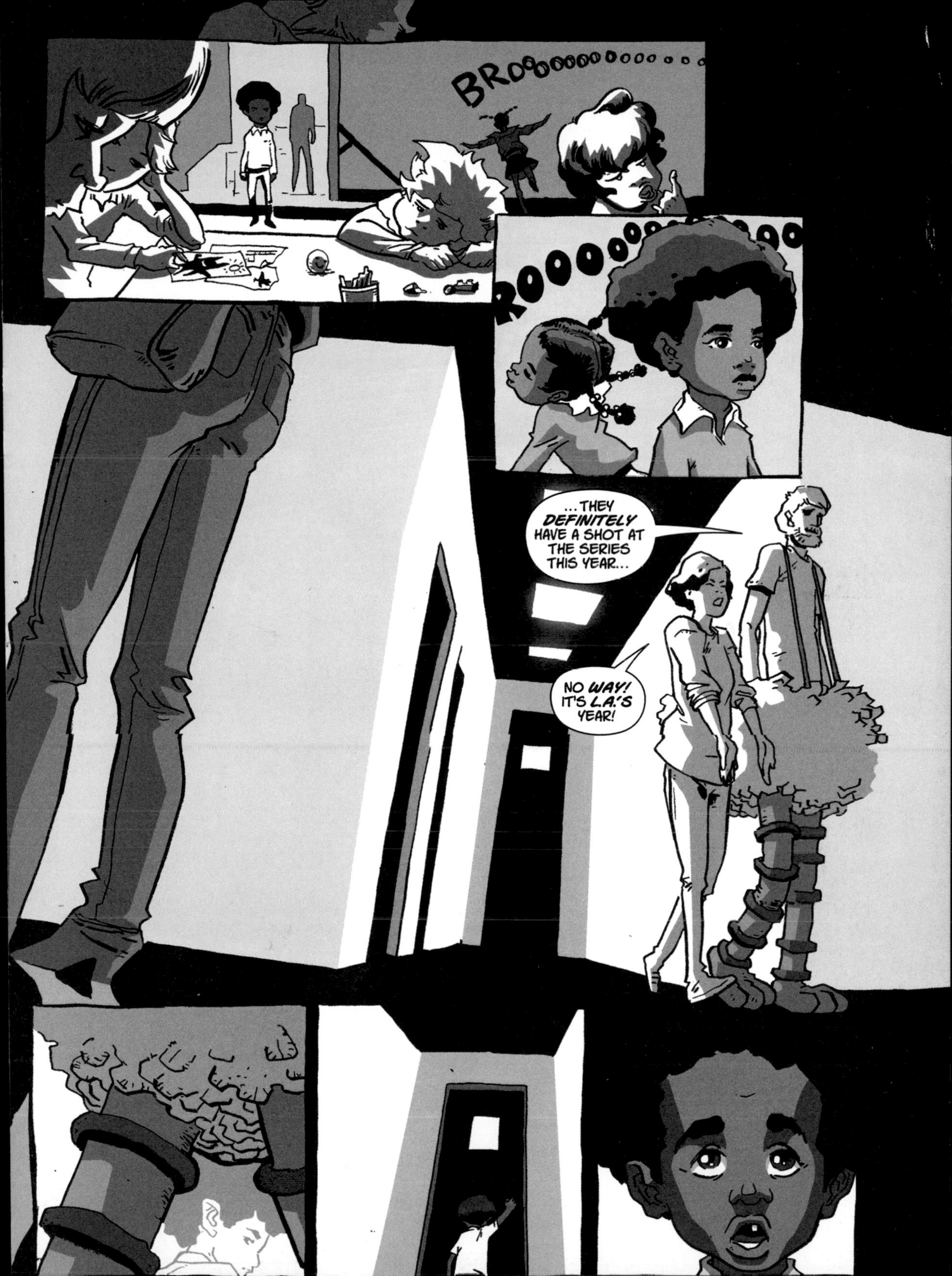
BROOOOOOOOOOOOOO
ROOOOOOOOOOOOO
...THEY DEFINITELY HAVE A SHOT AT THE SERIES THIS YEAR...
NO WAY! IT'S L.A.'S YEAR!

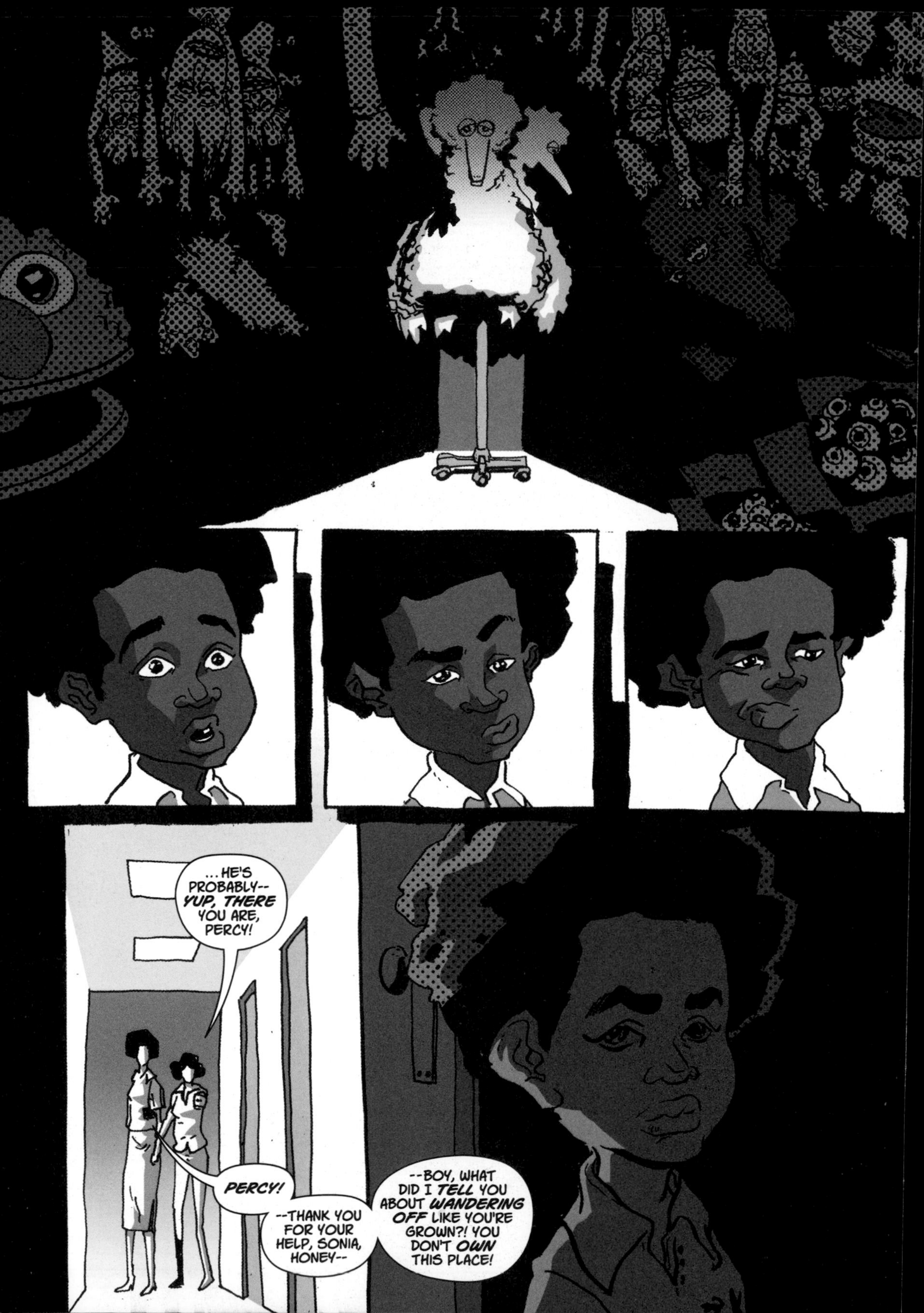
...HE'S PROBABLY-- YUP, THERE YOU ARE, PERCY!
PERCY!
--THANK YOU FOR YOUR HELP, SONIA, HONEY--
--BOY, WHAT DID I TELL YOU ABOUT WANDERING OFF LIKE YOU'RE GROWN?! YOU DON'T OWN THIS PLACE!

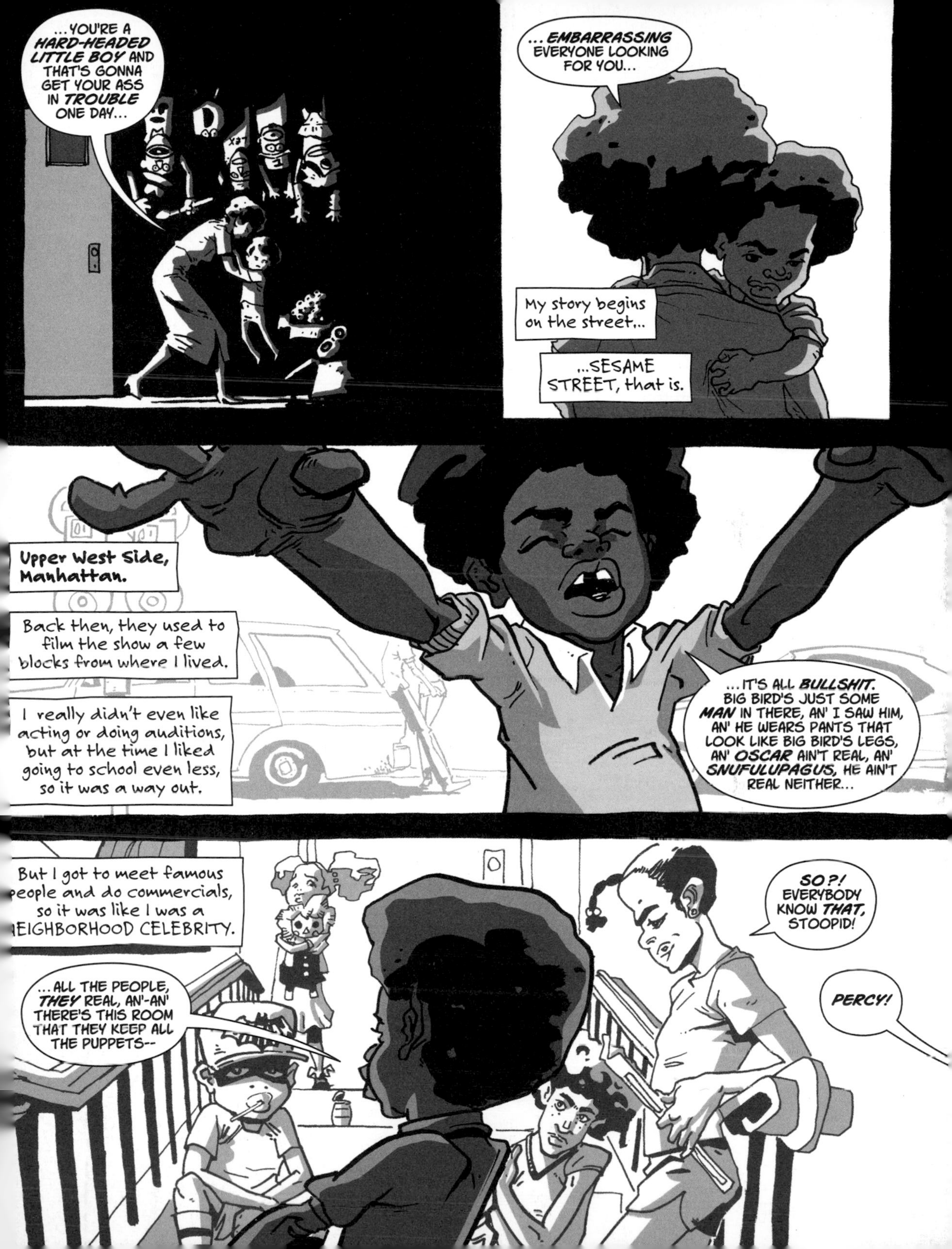
...YOU'RE A HARD-HEADED LITTLE BOY AND THAT'S GONNA GET YOUR ASS IN TROUBLE ONE DAY...
...EMBARRASSING EVERYONE LOOKING FOR YOU...
My story begins on the street...
...SESAME STREET, that is.
Upper West Side, Manhattan.
Back then, they used to film the show a few blocks from where I lived.
I really didn't even like acting or doing auditions, but at the time I liked going to school even less, so it was a way out.
...IT'S ALL BULLSHIT. BIG BIRD'S JUST SOME MAN IN THERE, AN' I SAW HIM, AN' HE WEARS PANTS THAT LOOK LIKE BIG BIRD'S LEGS, AN' OSCAR AIN'T REAL, AN' SNUFULUPAGUS, HE AIN'T REAL NEITHER...
But I got to meet famous people and do commercials, so it was like I was a NEIGHBORHOOD CELEBRITY.
...ALL THE PEOPLE, THEY REAL, AN'-AN' THERE'S THIS ROOM THAT THEY KEEP ALL THE PUPPETS--
SO?! EVERYBODY KNOW THAT, STOOPID!
PERCY!

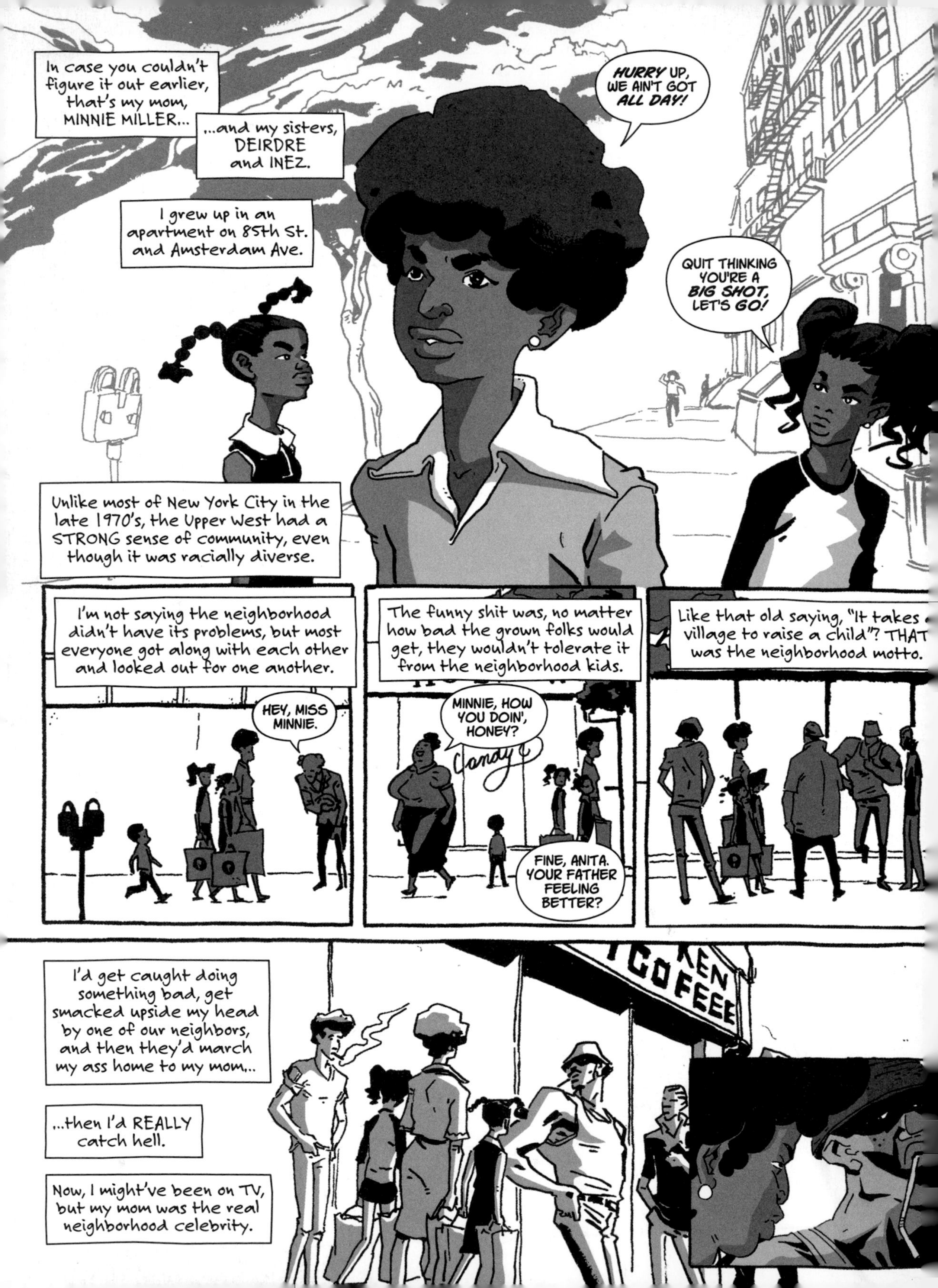
In case you couldn't figure it out earlier, that's my mom, MINNIE MILLER...
...and my sisters, DEIRDRE and INEZ.
HURRY UP, WE AIN'T GOT ALL DAY!
I grew up in an apartment on 85th St. and Amsterdam Ave.
QUIT THINKING YOU'RE A BIG SHOT, LET'S GO!
Unlike most of New York City in the late 1970's, the Upper West had a STRONG sense of community, even though it was racially diverse.
I'm not saying the neighborhood didn't have its problems, but most everyone got along with each other and looked out for one another.
HEY, MISS MINNIE.
The funny shit was, no matter how bad the grown folks would get, they wouldn't tolerate it from the neighborhood kids.
MINNIE, HOW YOU DOIN', HONEY?
Candy
FINE, ANITA. YOUR FATHER FEELING BETTER?
Like that old saying, "It takes a village to raise a child"? THAT was the neighborhood motto.
I'd get caught doing something bad, get smacked upside my head by one of our neighbors, and then they'd march my ass home to my mom...
...then I'd REALLY catch hell.
Now, I might've been on TV, but my mom was the real neighborhood celebrity.
COFFEE

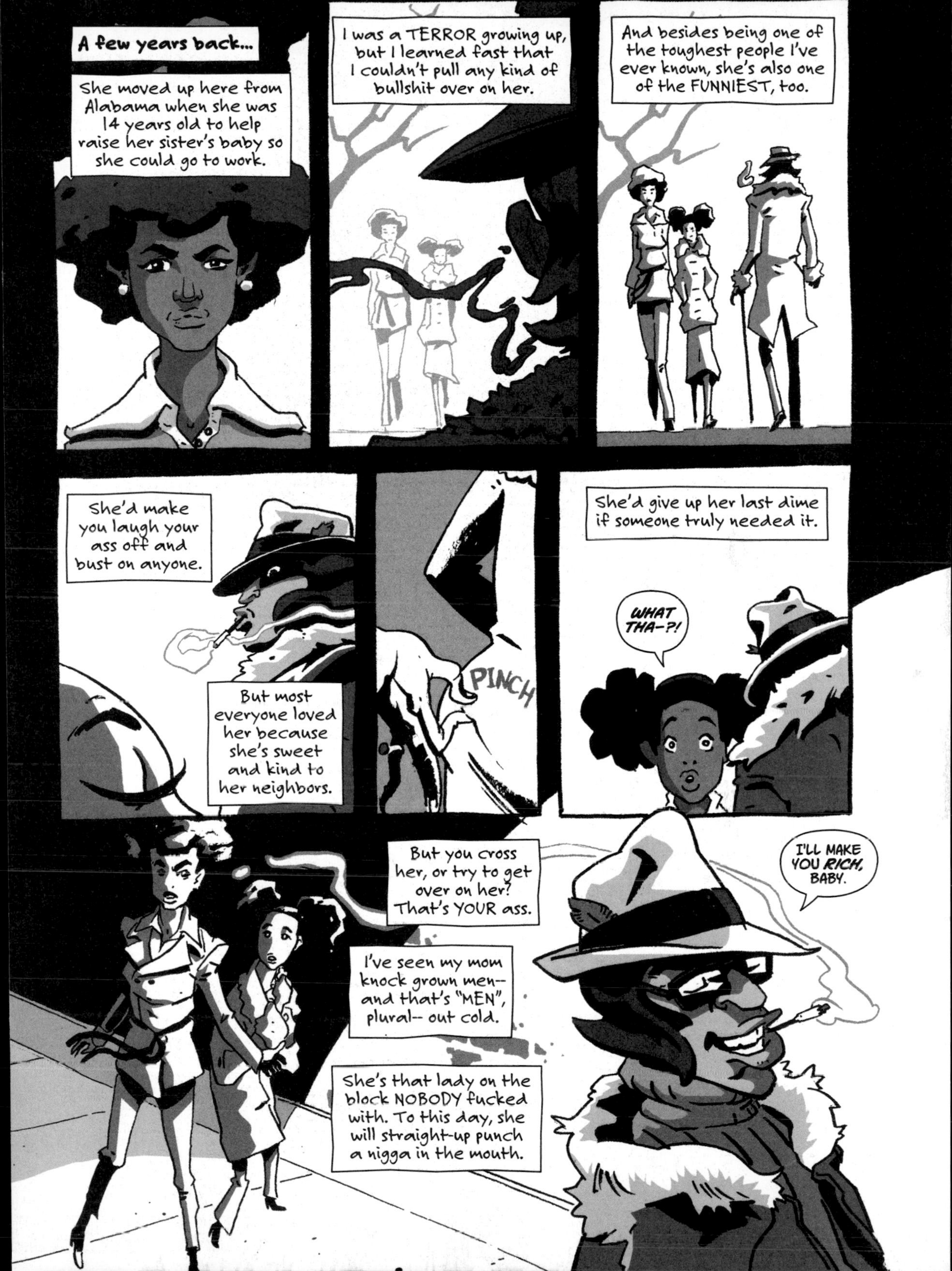
A few years back...
She moved up here from Alabama when she was 14 years old to help raise her sister's baby so she could go to work.
I was a TERROR growing up, but I learned fast that I couldn't pull any kind of bullshit over on her.
And besides being one of the toughest people I've ever known, she's also one of the FUNNIEST, too.
She'd make you laugh your ass off and bust on anyone.
But most everyone loved her because she's sweet and kind to her neighbors.
PINCH
She'd give up her last dime if someone truly needed it.
WHAT THA--?!
But you cross her, or try to get over on her? That's YOUR ass.
I'LL MAKE YOU RICH, BABY.
I've seen my mom knock grown men-- and that's "MEN", plural-- out cold.
She's that lady on the block NOBODY fucked with. To this day, she will straight-up punch a nigga in the mouth.

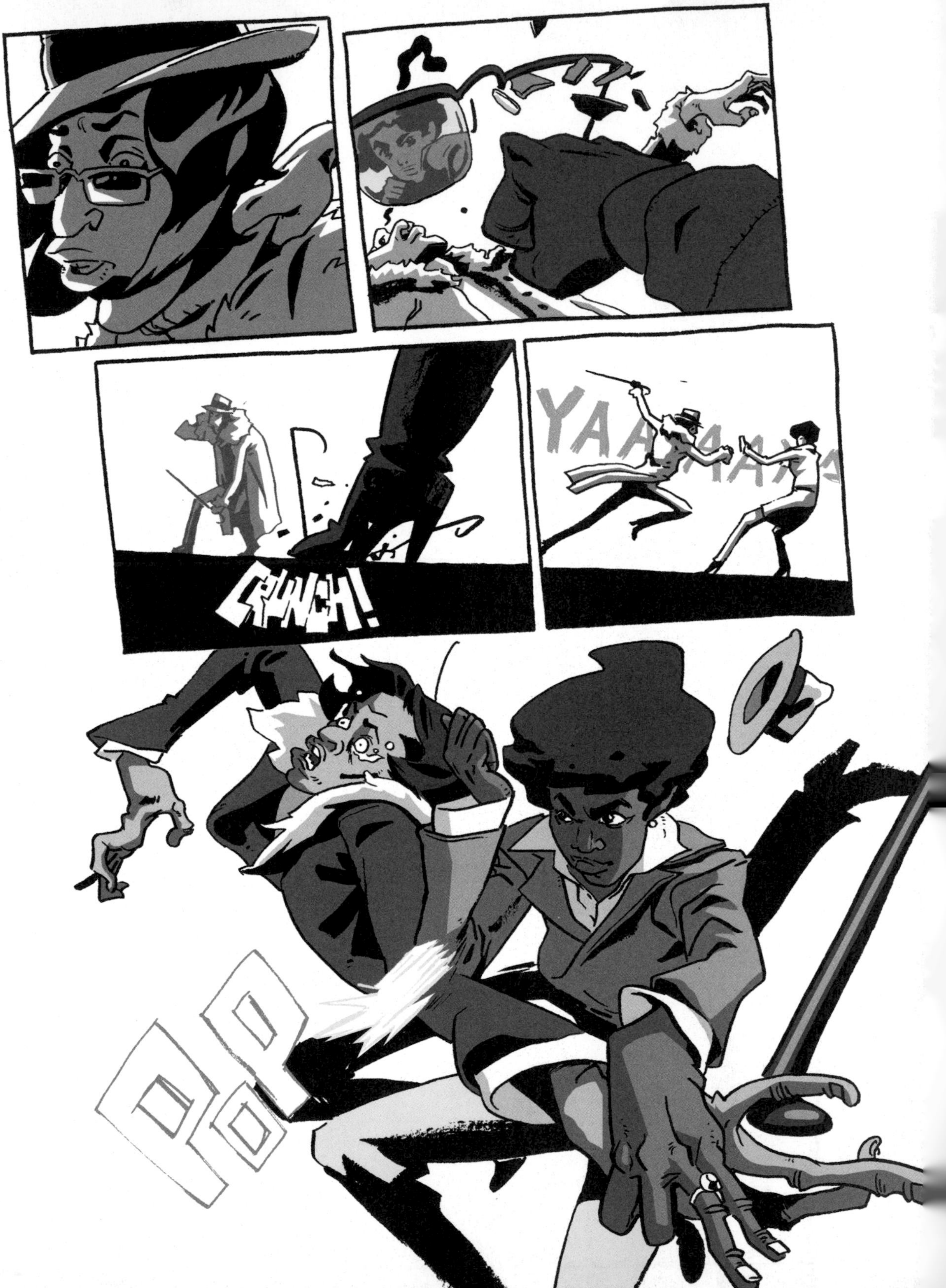

CRUNCH!

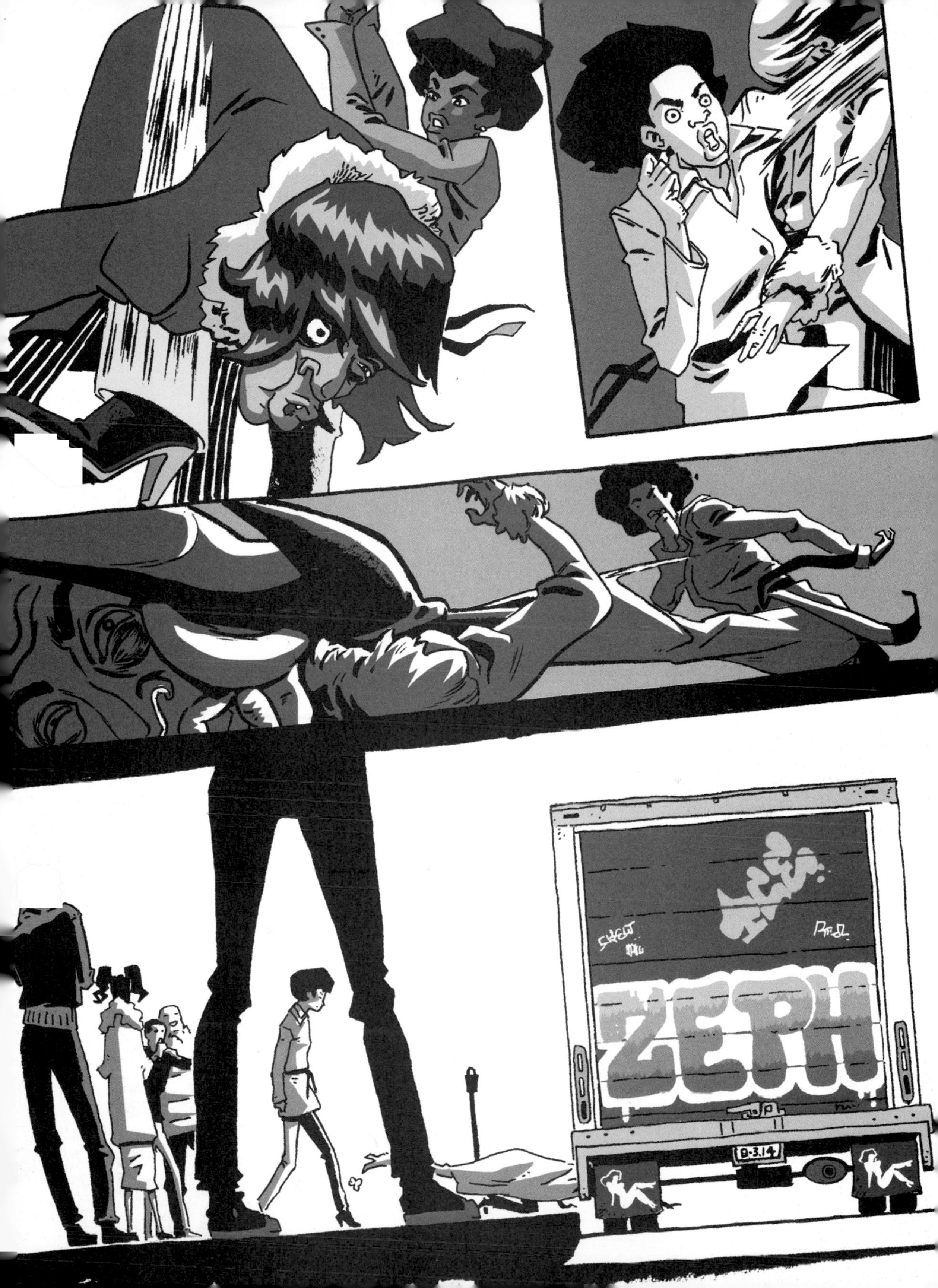
ZERH

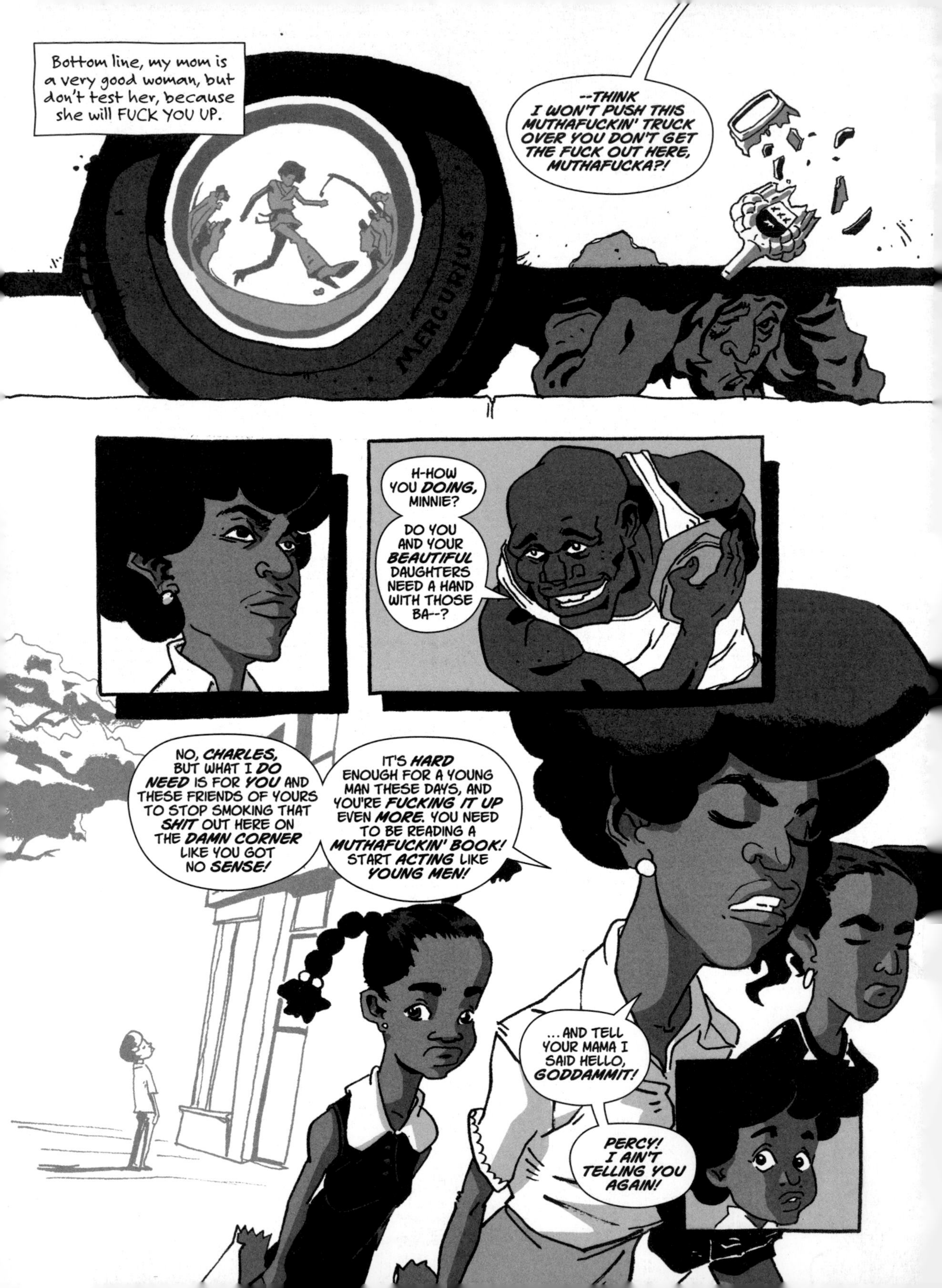
Bottom line, my mom is a very good woman, but don't test her, because she will FUCK YOU UP.
--THINK I WON'T PUSH THIS MUTHAFUCKIN' TRUCK OVER YOU DON'T GET THE FUCK OUT HERE, MUTHAFUCKA?!
MERCURIUS
H-HOW YOU DOING, MINNIE?
DO YOU AND YOUR BEAUTIFUL DAUGHTERS NEED A HAND WITH THOSE BA--?
NO, CHARLES, BUT WHAT I DO NEED IS FOR YOU AND THESE FRIENDS OF YOURS TO STOP SMOKING THAT SHIT OUT HERE ON THE DAMN CORNER LIKE YOU GOT NO SENSE!
IT'S HARD ENOUGH FOR A YOUNG MAN THESE DAYS, AND YOU'RE FUCKING IT UP EVEN MORE. YOU NEED TO BE READING A MUTHAFUCKIN' BOOK! START ACTING LIKE YOUNG MEN!
...AND TELL YOUR MAMA I SAID HELLO, GODDAMMIT!
PERCY! I AIN'T TELLING YOU AGAIN!

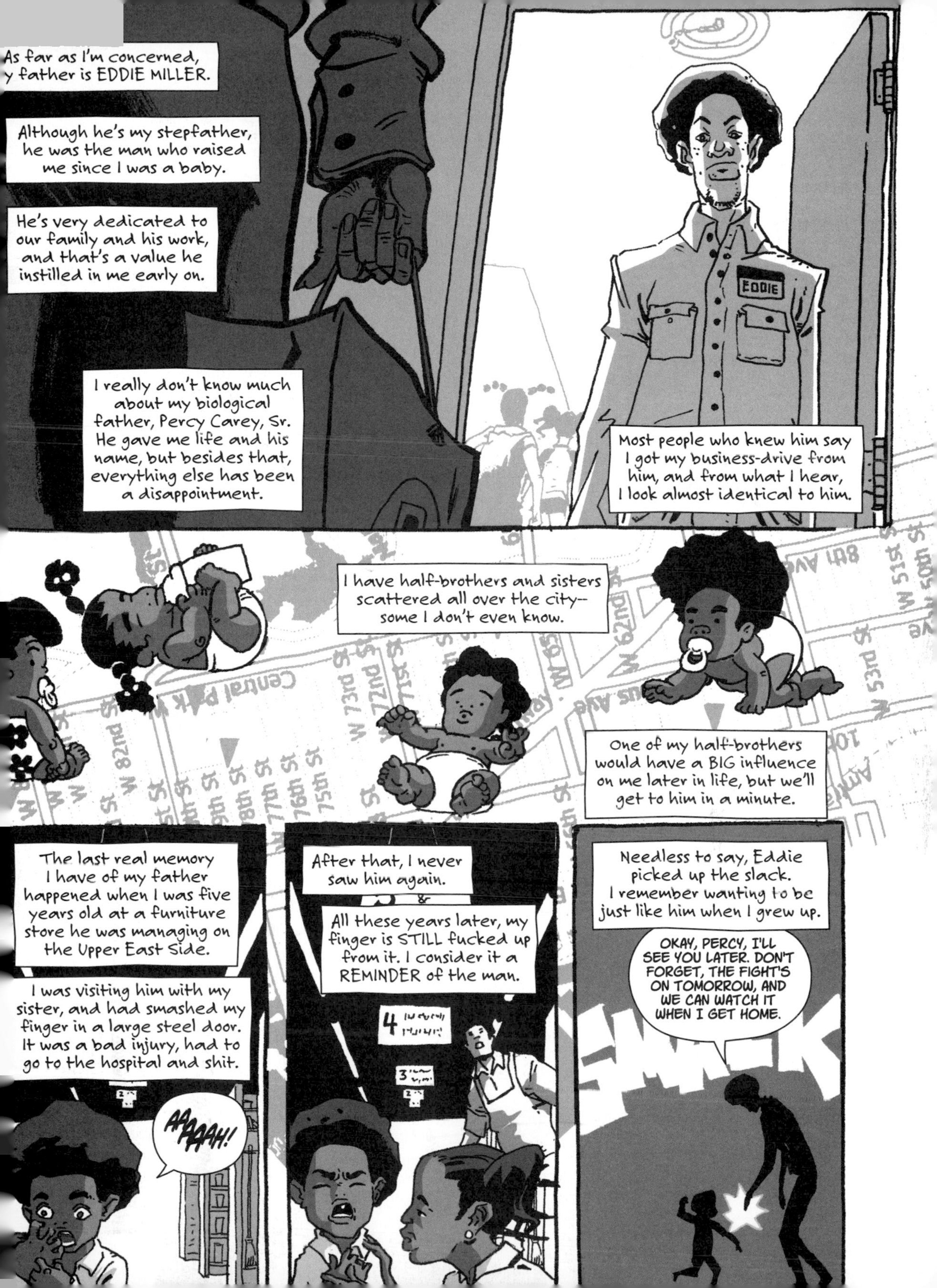
As far as I'm concerned,
y father is EDDIE MILLER.
Although he's my stepfather, he was the man who raised me since I was a baby.
He's very dedicated to our family and his work, and that's a value he instilled in me early on.
EDDIE
I really don't know much about my biological father, Percy Carey, Sr. He gave me life and his name, but besides that, everything else has been a disappointment.
Most people who knew him say I got my business-drive from him, and from what I hear, I look almost identical to him.
I have half-brothers and sisters scattered all over the city-- some I don't even know.
One of my half-brothers would have a BIG influence on me later in life, but we'll get to him in a minute.
The last real memory I have of my father happened when I was five years old at a furniture store he was managing on the Upper East Side.
I was visiting him with my sister, and had smashed my finger in a large steel door. It was a bad injury, had to go to the hospital and shit.
AAAAAH!
After that, I never saw him again.
All these years later, my finger is STILL fucked up from it. I consider it a REMINDER of the man.
Needless to say, Eddie picked up the slack. I remember wanting to be just like him when I grew up.
OKAY, PERCY, I'LL SEE YOU LATER. DON'T FORGET, THE FIGHT'S ON TOMORROW, AND WE CAN WATCH IT WHEN I GET HOME.
SMACK

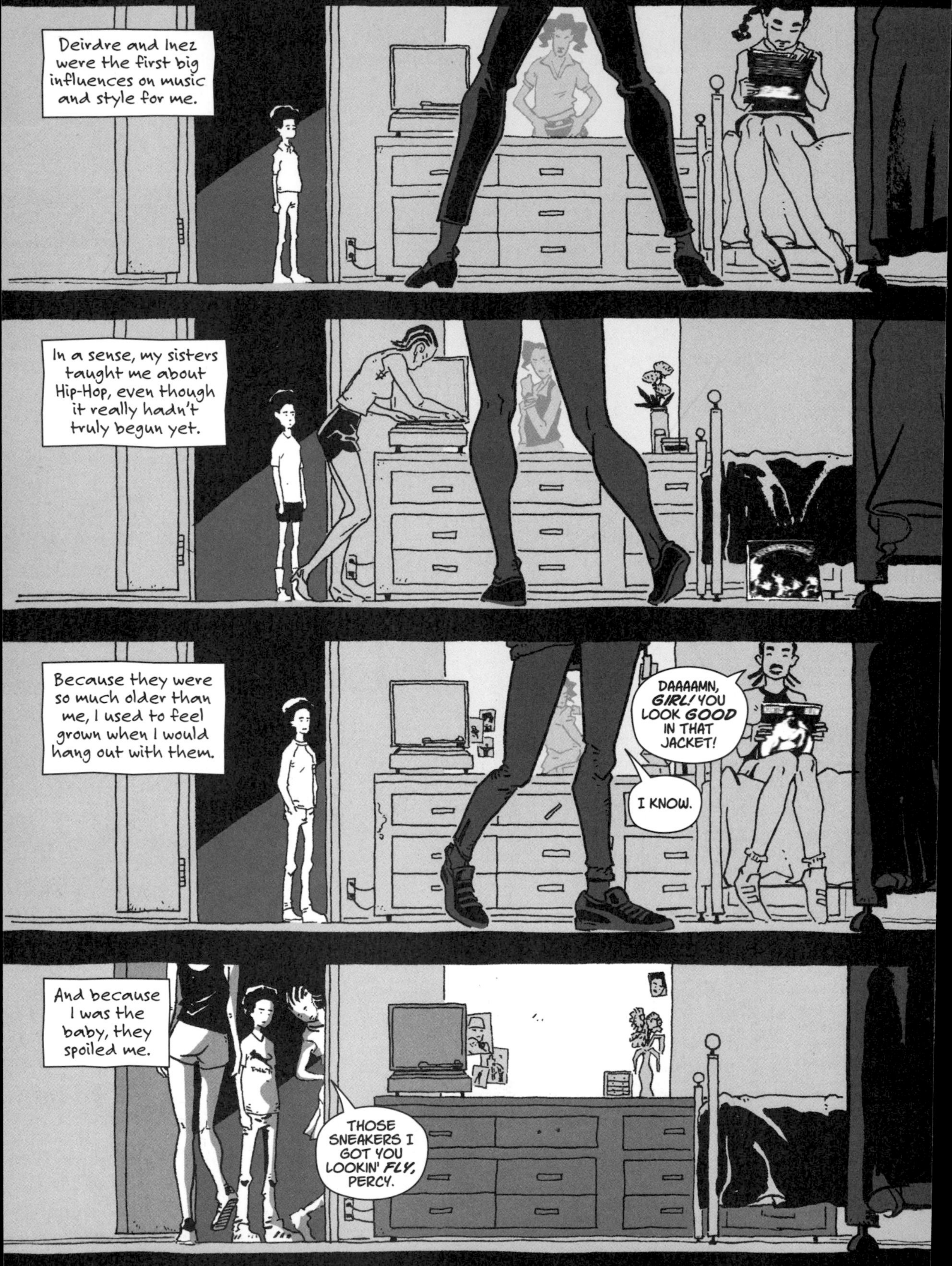
Deirdre and Inez were the first big influences on music and style for me.
In a sense, my sisters taught me about Hip-Hop, even though it really hadn't truly begun yet.
Because they were so much older than me, I used to feel grown when I would hang out with them.
DAAAAMN, GIRL! YOU LOOK GOOD IN THAT JACKET!
I KNOW.
And because I was the baby, they spoiled me.
THOSE SNEAKERS I GOT YOU LOOKIN' FLY, PERCY.

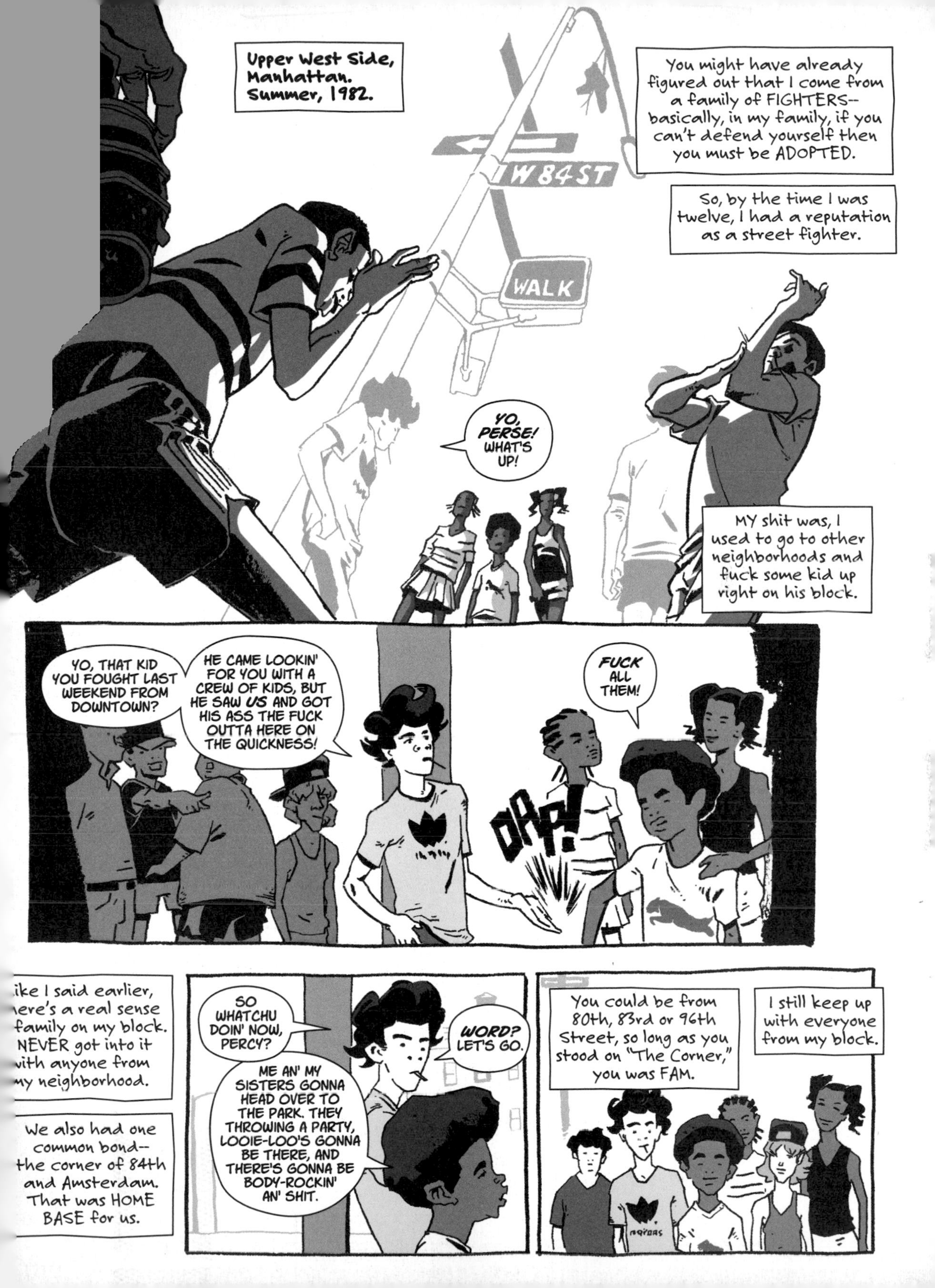

Upper West Side, Manhattan. Summer, 1982.
W 84 ST
WALK
You might have already figured out that I come from a family of FIGHTERS-- basically, in my family, if you can't defend yourself then you must be ADOPTED.
So, by the time I was twelve, I had a reputation as a street fighter.
YO, PERSE! WHAT'S UP!
MY shit was, I used to go to other neighborhoods and fuck some kid up right on his block.
YO, THAT KID YOU FOUGHT LAST WEEKEND FROM DOWNTOWN?
HE CAME LOOKIN' FOR YOU WITH A CREW OF KIDS, BUT HE SAW US AND GOT HIS ASS THE FUCK OUTTA HERE ON THE QUICKNESS!
FUCK ALL THEM!
DAP!
ike I said earlier, ere's a real sense family on my block. NEVER got into it with anyone from my neighborhood.
We also had one common bond-- the corner of 84th and Amsterdam. That was HOME BASE for us.
SO WHATCHU DOIN' NOW, PERCY?
ME AN' MY SISTERS GONNA HEAD OVER TO THE PARK. THEY THROWING A PARTY, LOOIE-LOO'S GONNA BE THERE, AND THERE'S GONNA BE BODY-ROCKIN' AN' SHIT.
WORD? LET'S GO.
You could be from 80th, 83rd or 96th Street, so long as you stood on "The Corner," you was FAM.
I still keep up with everyone from my block.

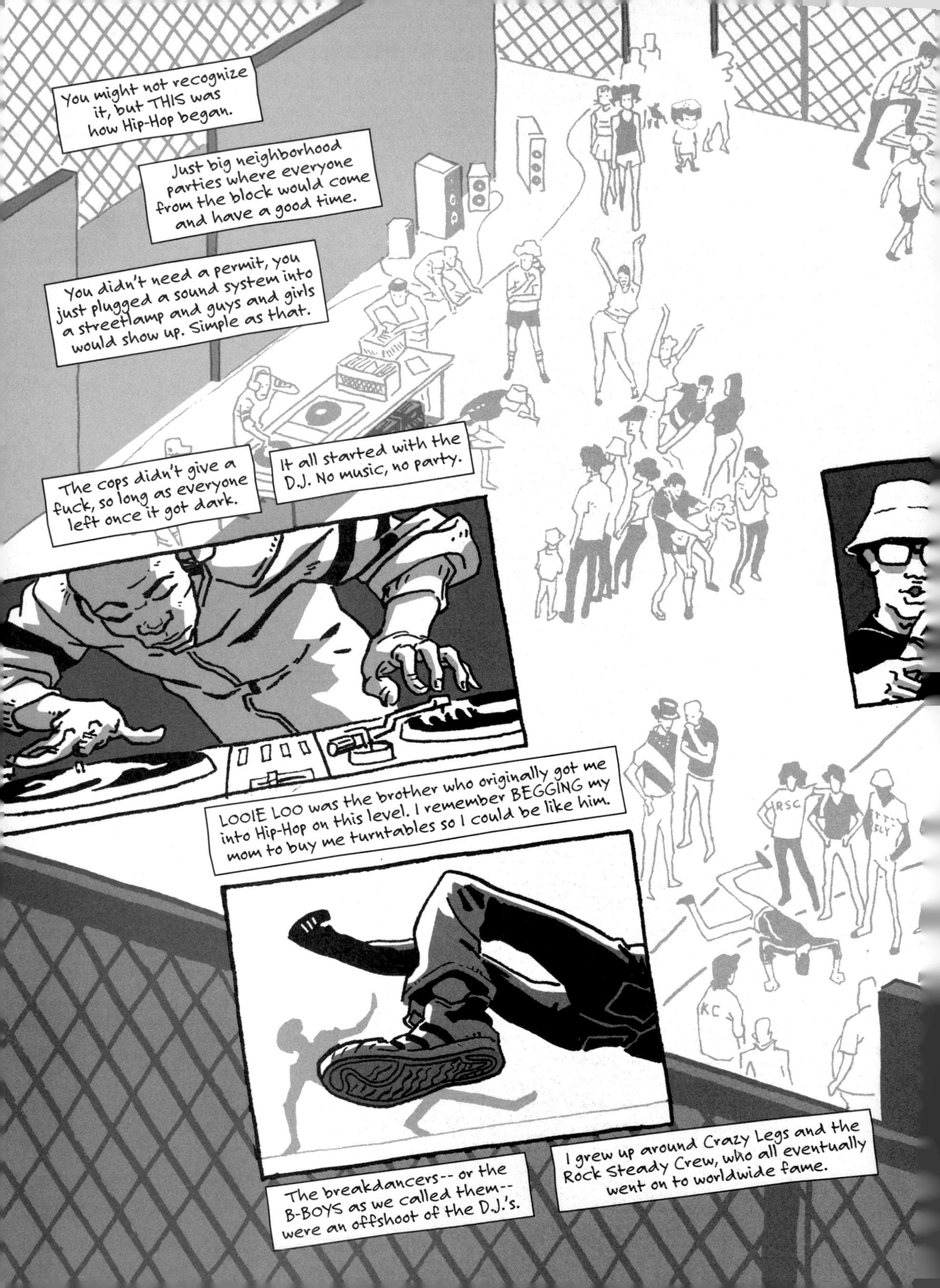

You might not recognize it, but THIS was how Hip-Hop began.
Just big neighborhood parties where everyone from the block would come and have a good time.
You didn't need a permit, you just plugged a sound system into a streetlamp and guys and girls would show up. Simple as that.
The cops didn't give a fuck, so long as everyone left once it got dark.
It all started with the D.J. No music, no party.
LOOIE LOO was the brother who originally got me into Hip-Hop on this level. I remember BEGGING my mom to buy me turntables so I could be like him.
RSC
KC
The breakdancers-- or the B-BOYS as we called them-- were an offshoot of the D.J.'s.
I grew up around Crazy Legs and the Rock Steady Crew, who all eventually went on to worldwide fame.

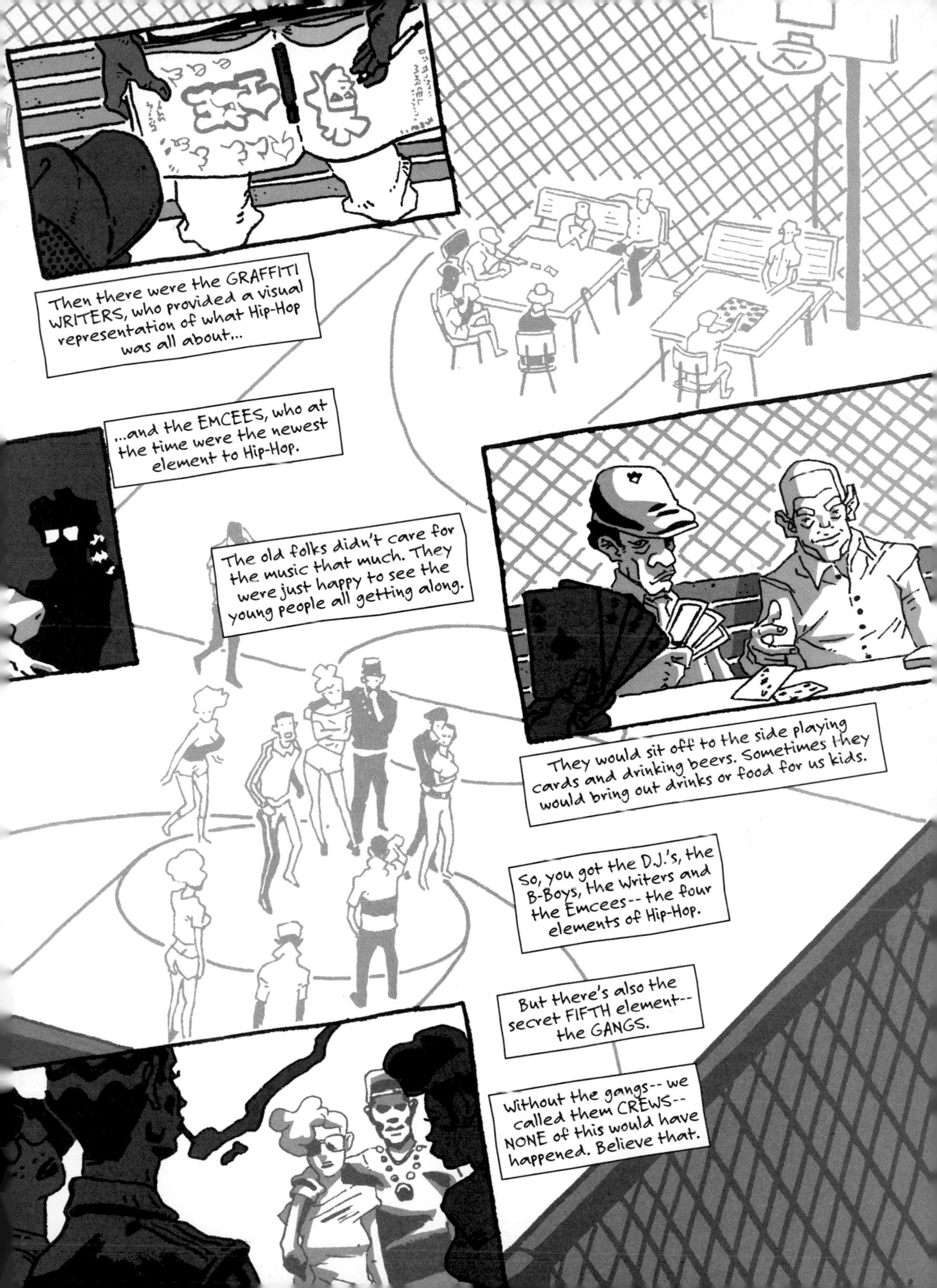
Then there were the GRAFFITI WRITERS, who provided a visual representation of what Hip-Hop was all about...
...and the EMCEES, who at the time were the newest element to Hip-Hop.
The old folks didn't care for the music that much. They the were just happy to see the young people all getting along.
They would sit off to the side playing cards and drinking beers. Sometimes they would bring out drinks or food for us kids.
So, you got the D.J.'s, the B-Boys, the Writers and the Emcees-- the four elements of Hip-Hop.
But there's also the secret FIFTH element-- the GANGS.
Without the gangs-- we called them CREWS-- NONE of this would have happened. Believe that.

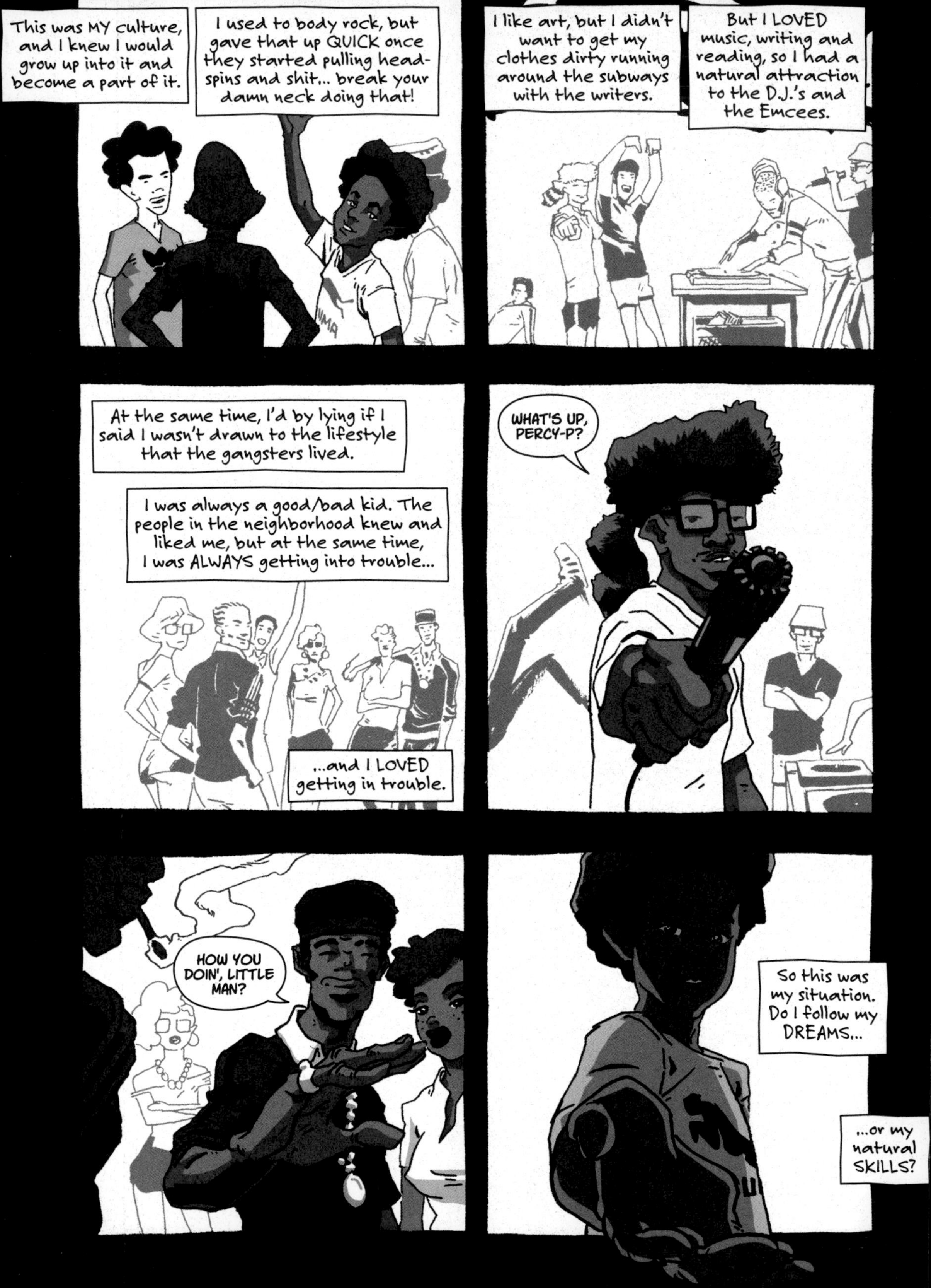
This was MY culture, and I knew I would grow up into it and become a part of it.
I used to body rock, but gave that up QUICK once they started pulling head-spins and shit... break your damn neck doing that!
I like art, but I didn't want to get my clothes dirty running around the subways with the writers.
But I LOVED music, writing and reading, so I had a natural attraction to the D.J.'s and the Emcees.
At the same time, I'd by lying if I said I wasn't drawn to the lifestyle that the gangsters lived.
I was always a good/bad kid. The people in the neighborhood knew and liked me, but at the same time, I was ALWAYS getting into trouble...
...and I LOVED getting in trouble.
WHAT'S UP, PERCY-P?
HOW YOU DOIN', LITTLE MAN?
So this was my situation. Do I follow my DREAMS...
...or my natural SKILLS?

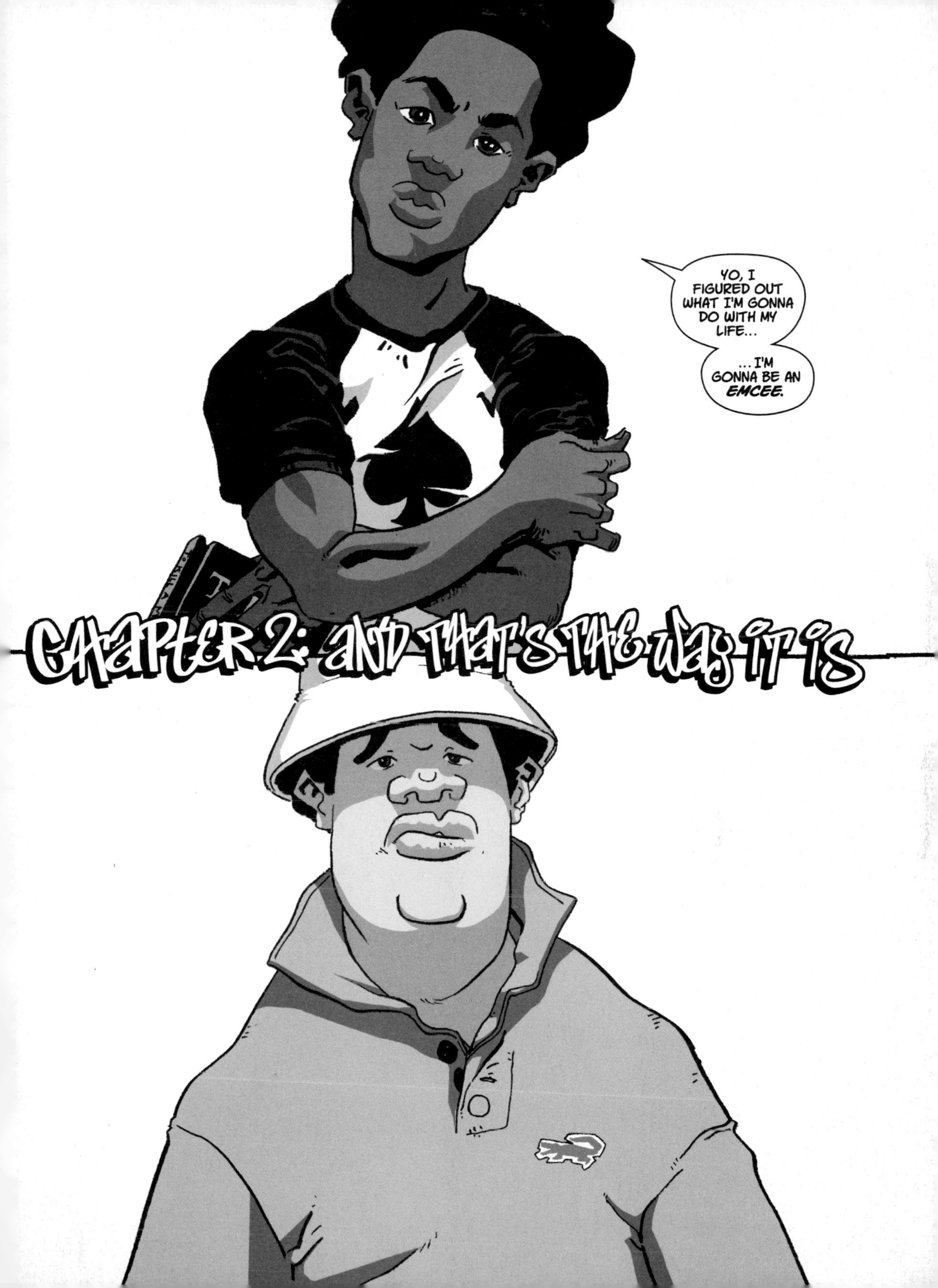
YO, I FIGURED OUT WHAT I'M GONNA DO WITH MY LIFE...
...I'M GONNA BE AN *EMCEE.*
CHAPTER 2: AND THAT'S THE WAY IT IS

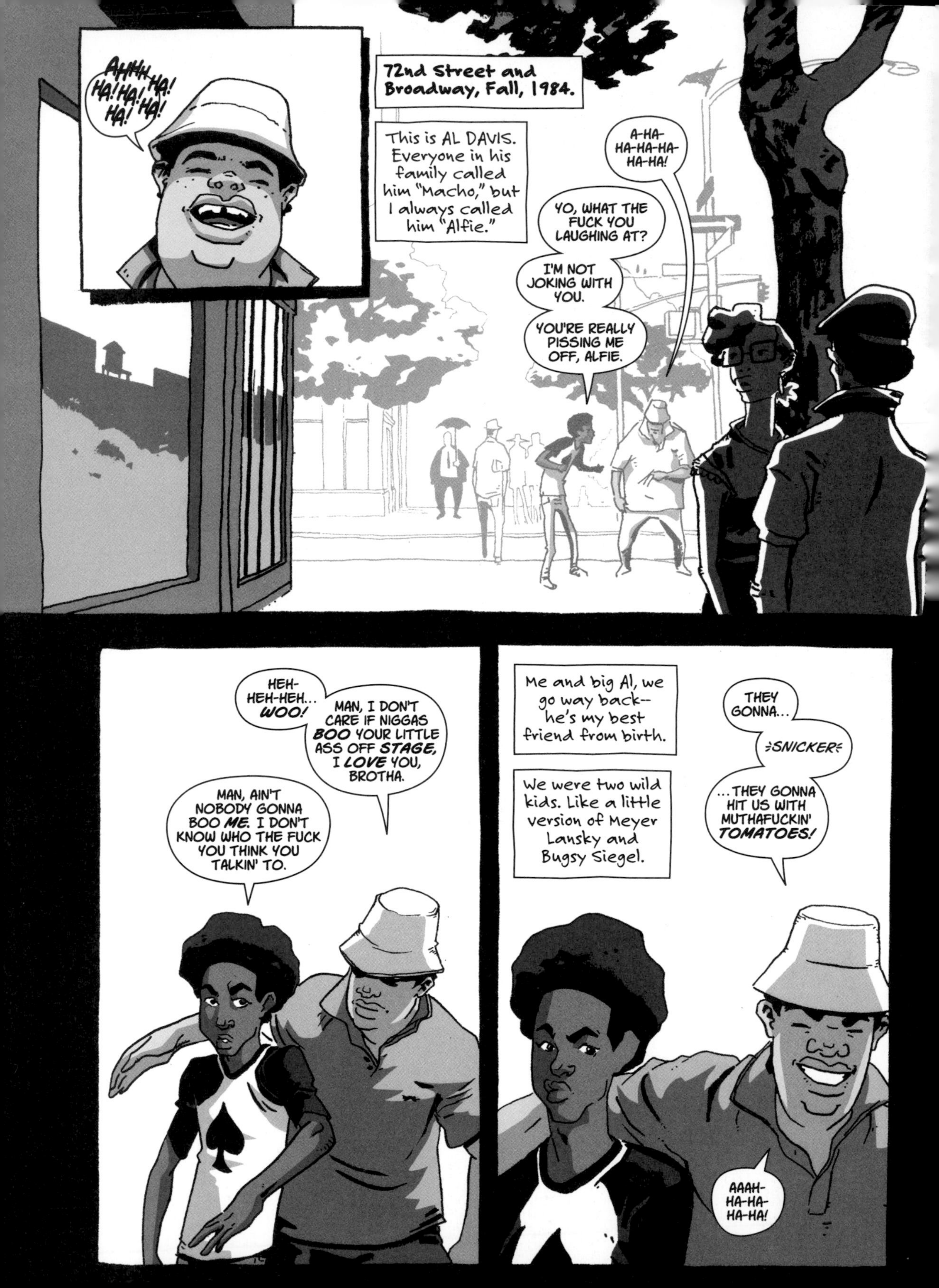
AHHH HA! HA! HA! HA! HA!
72nd Street and Broadway, Fall, 1984.
This is AL DAVIS. Everyone in his family called him "Macho," but I always called him "Alfie."
A-HA-HA-HA-HA-HA-HA!
YO, WHAT THE FUCK YOU LAUGHING AT?
I'M NOT JOKING WITH YOU.
YOU'RE REALLY PISSING ME OFF, ALFIE.
HEH-HEH-HEH... WOO!
MAN, I DON'T CARE IF NIGGAS BOO YOUR LITTLE ASS OFF STAGE, I LOVE YOU, BROTHA.
MAN, AIN'T NOBODY GONNA BOO ME. I DON'T KNOW WHO THE FUCK YOU THINK YOU TALKIN' TO.
Me and big Al, we go way back--he's my best friend from birth.
We were two wild kids. Like a little version of Meyer Lansky and Bugsy Siegel.
THEY GONNA...
SNICKER
...THEY GONNA HIT US WITH MUTHAFUCKIN' TOMATOES!
AAAH-HA-HA-HA-HA!

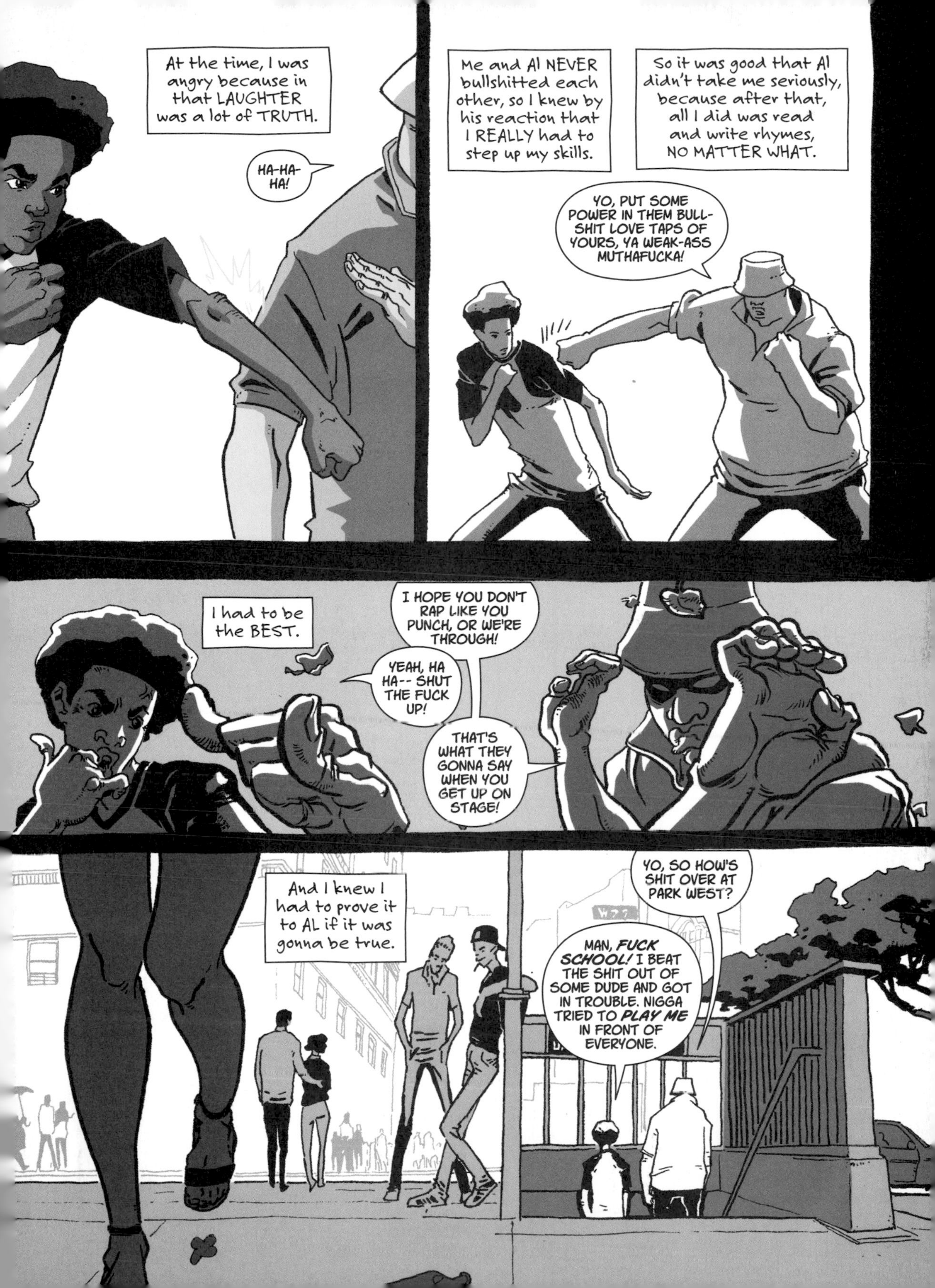
At the time, I was angry because in that LAUGHTER was a lot of TRUTH.
HA-HA-HA!
Me and Al NEVER bullshitted each other, so I knew by his reaction that I REALLY had to step up my skills.
So it was good that Al didn't take me seriously, because after that, all I did was read and write rhymes, NO MATTER WHAT.
YO, PUT SOME POWER IN THEM BULL-SHIT LOVE TAPS OF YOURS, YA WEAK-ASS MUTHAFUCKA!
I had to be the BEST.
I HOPE YOU DON'T RAP LIKE YOU PUNCH, OR WE'RE THROUGH!
YEAH, HA HA-- SHUT THE FUCK UP!
THAT'S WHAT THEY GONNA SAY WHEN YOU GET UP ON STAGE!
And I knew I had to prove it to AL if it was gonna be true.
YO, SO HOW'S SHIT OVER AT PARK WEST?
MAN, FUCK SCHOOL! I BEAT THE SHIT OUT OF SOME DUDE AND GOT IN TROUBLE. NIGGA TRIED TO PLAY ME IN FRONT OF EVERYONE.

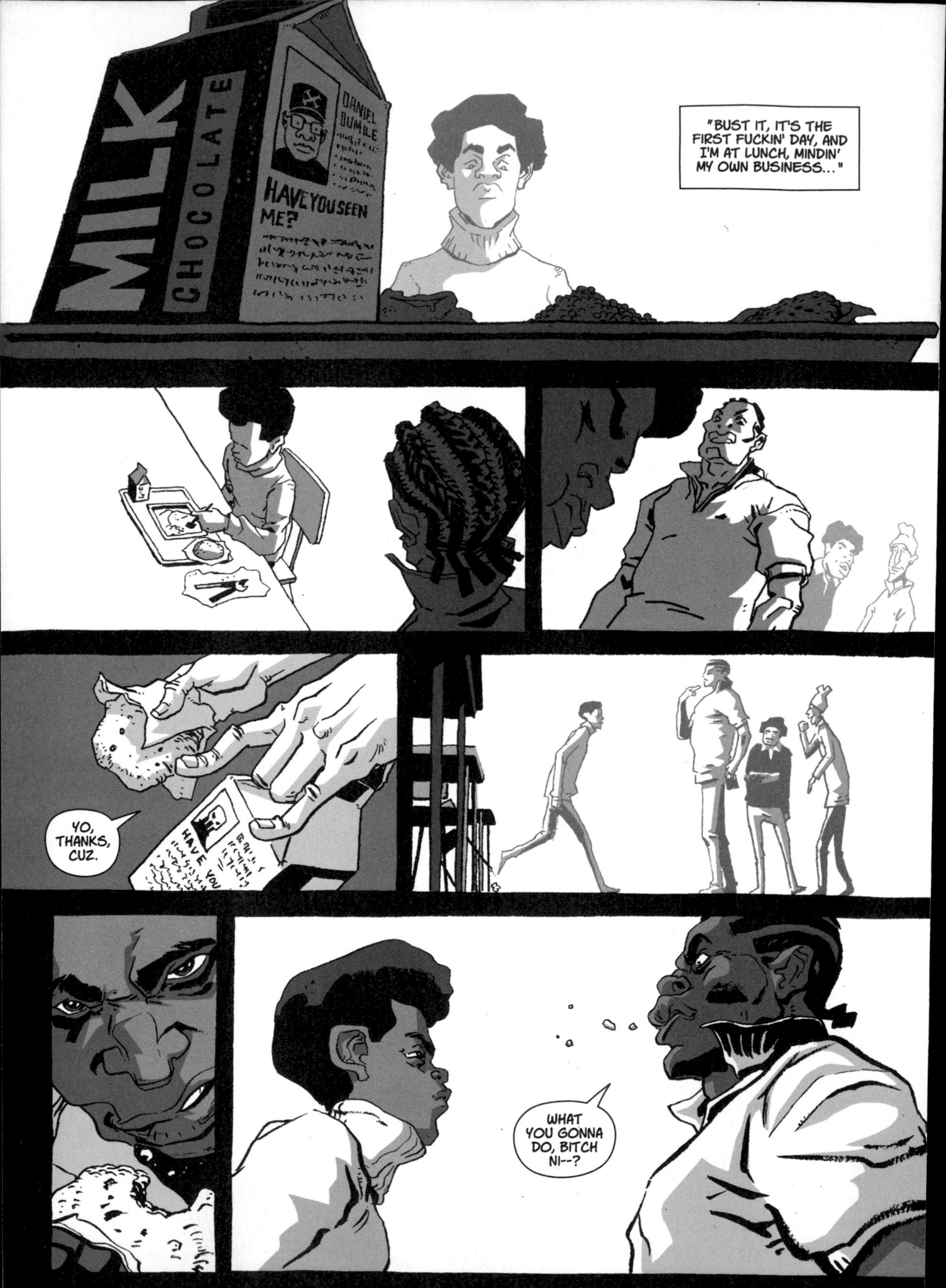
MILK
CHOCOLATE
DANIEL DUMILE
HAVE YOU SEEN ME?
"BUST IT, IT'S THE FIRST FUCKIN' DAY, AND I'M AT LUNCH, MINDIN' MY OWN BUSINESS..."
YO, THANKS, CUZ.
WHAT YOU GONNA DO, BITCH NI--?

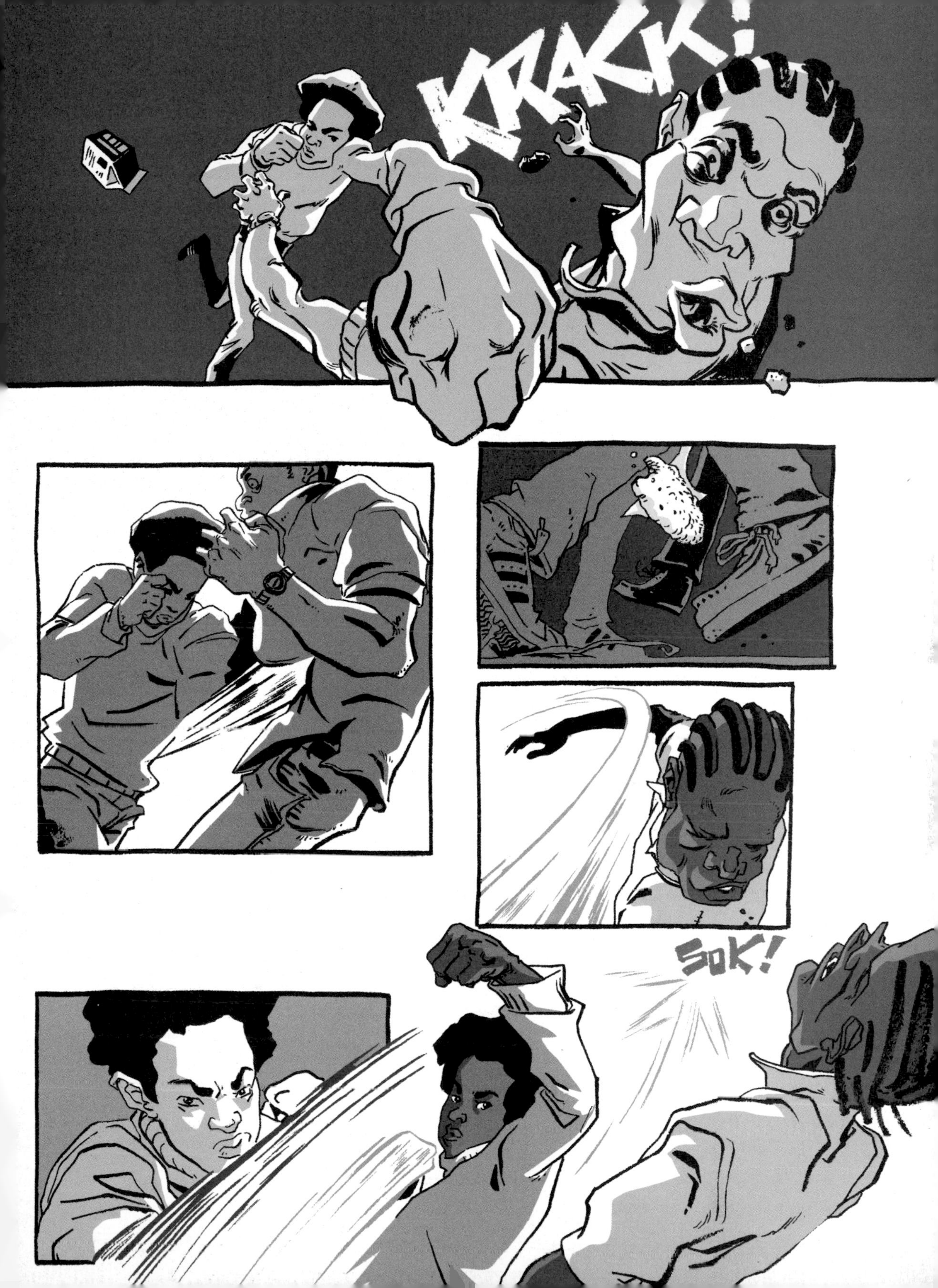
KRACK!
SOK!

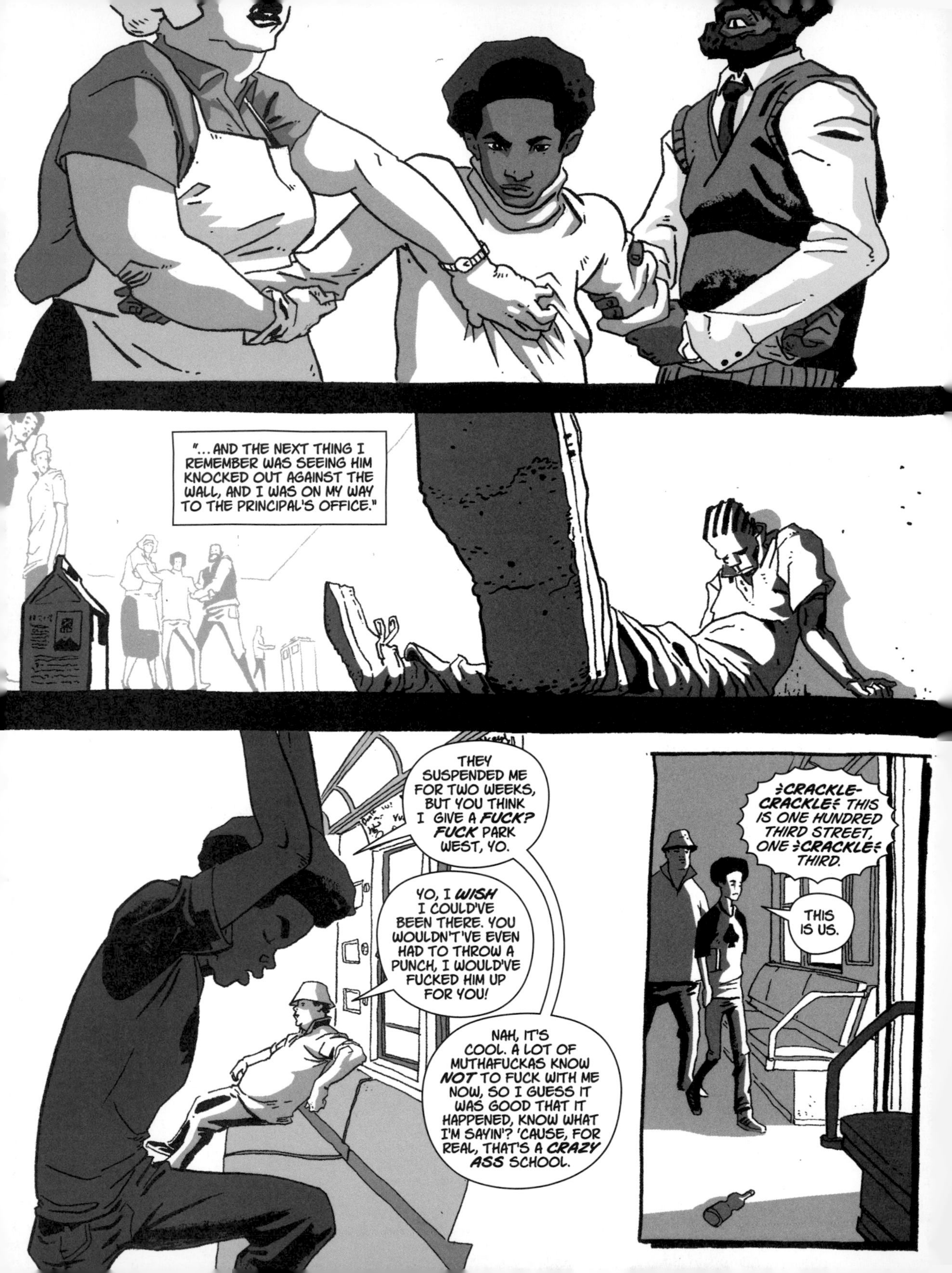
"...AND THE NEXT THING I REMEMBER WAS SEEING HIM KNOCKED OUT AGAINST THE WALL, AND I WAS ON MY WAY TO THE PRINCIPAL'S OFFICE."
THEY SUSPENDED ME FOR TWO WEEKS, BUT YOU THINK I GIVE A FUCK? FUCK PARK WEST, YO.
YO, I WISH I COULD'VE BEEN THERE. YOU WOULDN'T'VE EVEN HAD TO THROW A PUNCH, I WOULD'VE FUCKED HIM UP FOR YOU!
NAH, IT'S COOL. A LOT OF MUTHAFUCKAS KNOW NOT TO FUCK WITH ME NOW, SO I GUESS IT WAS GOOD THAT IT HAPPENED, KNOW WHAT I'M SAYIN'? 'CAUSE, FOR REAL, THAT'S A CRAZY ASS SCHOOL.
CRACKLE-CRACKLE THIS IS ONE HUNDRED THIRD STREET, ONE CRACKLE THIRD.
THIS IS US.

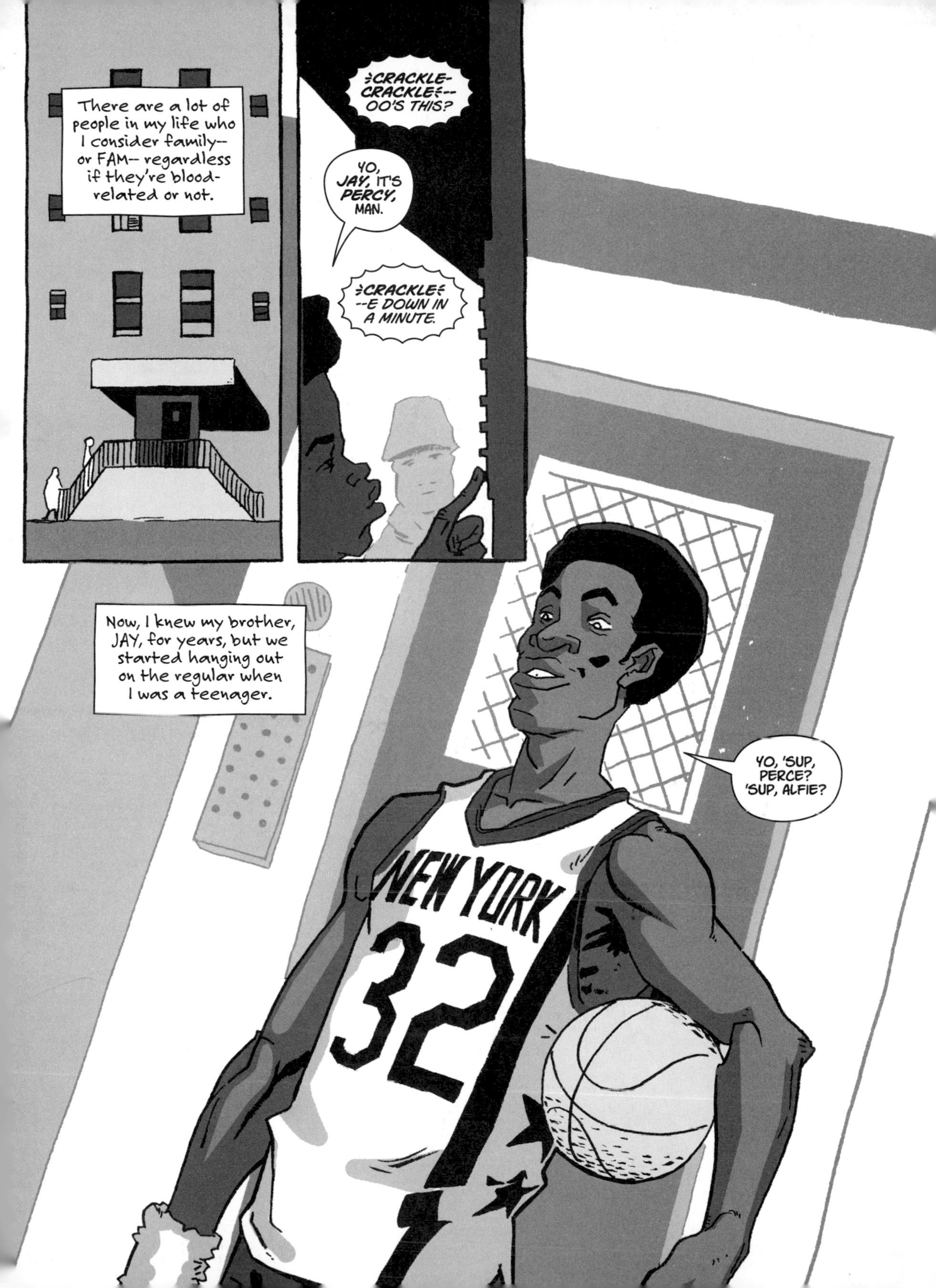
There are a lot of people in my life who I consider family-- or FAM-- regardless if they're blood-related or not.
⸗CRACKLE-CRACKLE⸗--OO'S THIS?
YO, JAY, IT'S PERCY, MAN.
⸗CRACKLE⸗--E DOWN IN A MINUTE.
Now, I knew my brother, JAY, for years, but we started hanging out on the regular when I was a teenager.
YO, 'SUP, PERCE? 'SUP, ALFIE?
NEW YORK
32

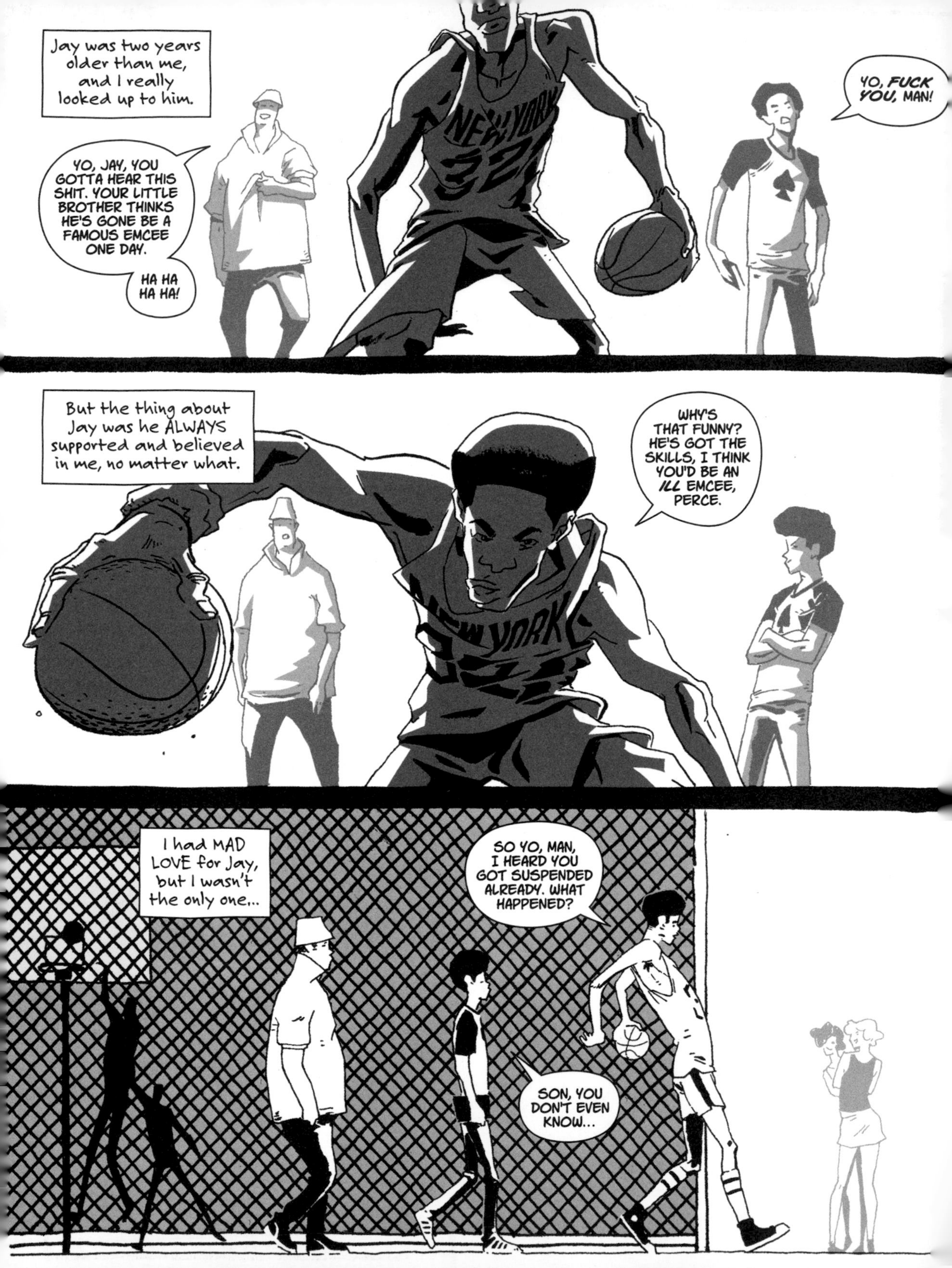
Jay was two years older than me, and I really looked up to him.
YO, JAY, YOU GOTTA HEAR THIS SHIT. YOUR LITTLE BROTHER THINKS HE'S GONE BE A FAMOUS EMCEE ONE DAY.
HA HA HA HA!
YO, FUCK YOU, MAN!
NEW YORK 32
But the thing about Jay was he ALWAYS supported and believed in me, no matter what.
WHY'S THAT FUNNY? HE'S GOT THE SKILLS, I THINK YOU'D BE AN ILL EMCEE, PERCE.
NEW YORK
I had MAD LOVE for Jay, but I wasn't the only one...
SO YO, MAN, I HEARD YOU GOT SUSPENDED ALREADY. WHAT HAPPENED?
SON, YOU DON'T EVEN KNOW...

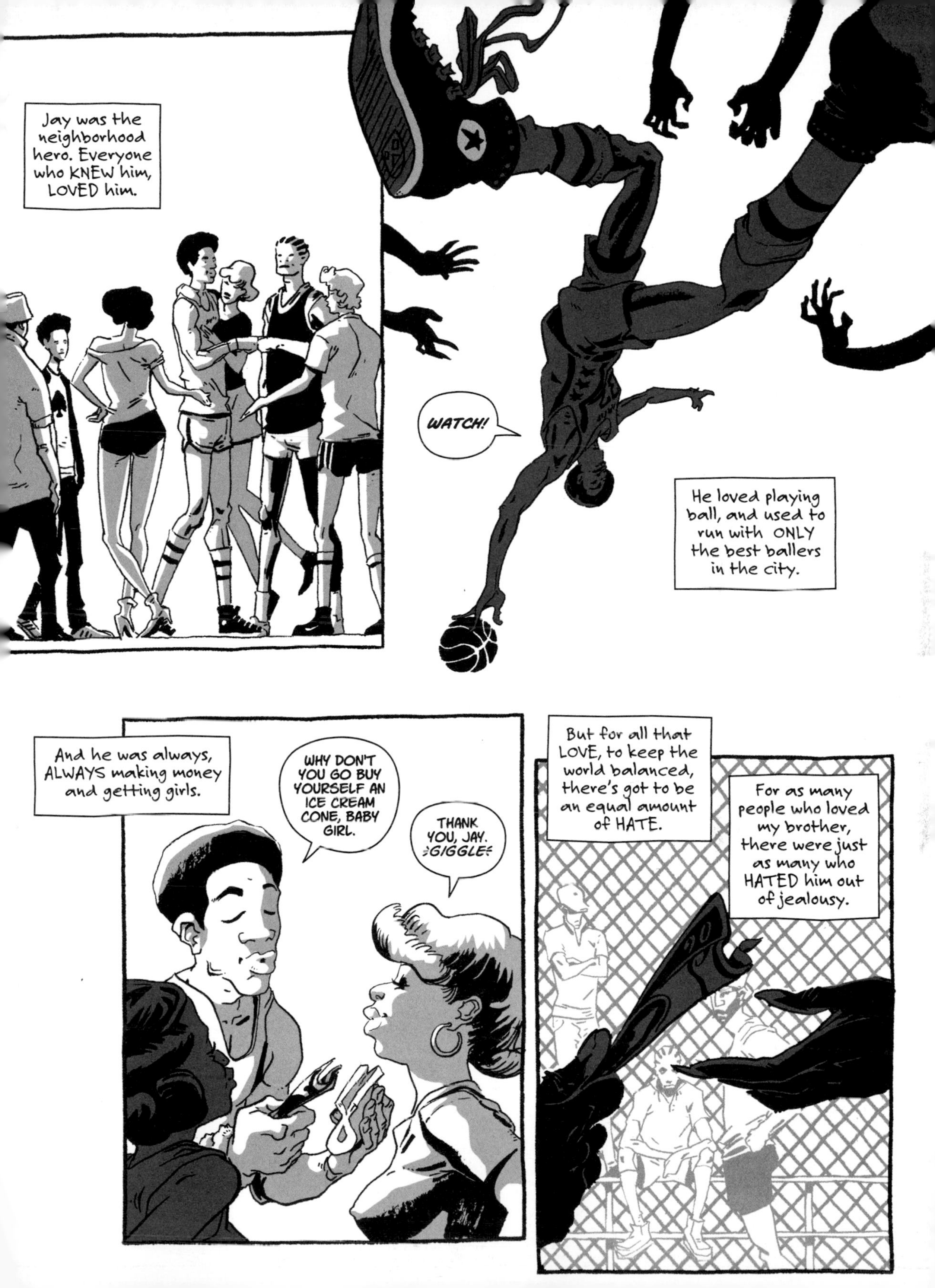
Jay was the neighborhood hero. Everyone who KNEW him, LOVED him.
WATCH!
He loved playing ball, and used to run with ONLY the best ballers in the city.
And he was always, ALWAYS making money and getting girls.
WHY DON'T YOU GO BUY YOURSELF AN ICE CREAM CONE, BABY GIRL.
THANK YOU, JAY. *GIGGLE*
But for all that LOVE, to keep the world balanced, there's got to be an equal amount of HATE.
For as many people who loved my brother, there were just as many who HATED him out of jealousy.

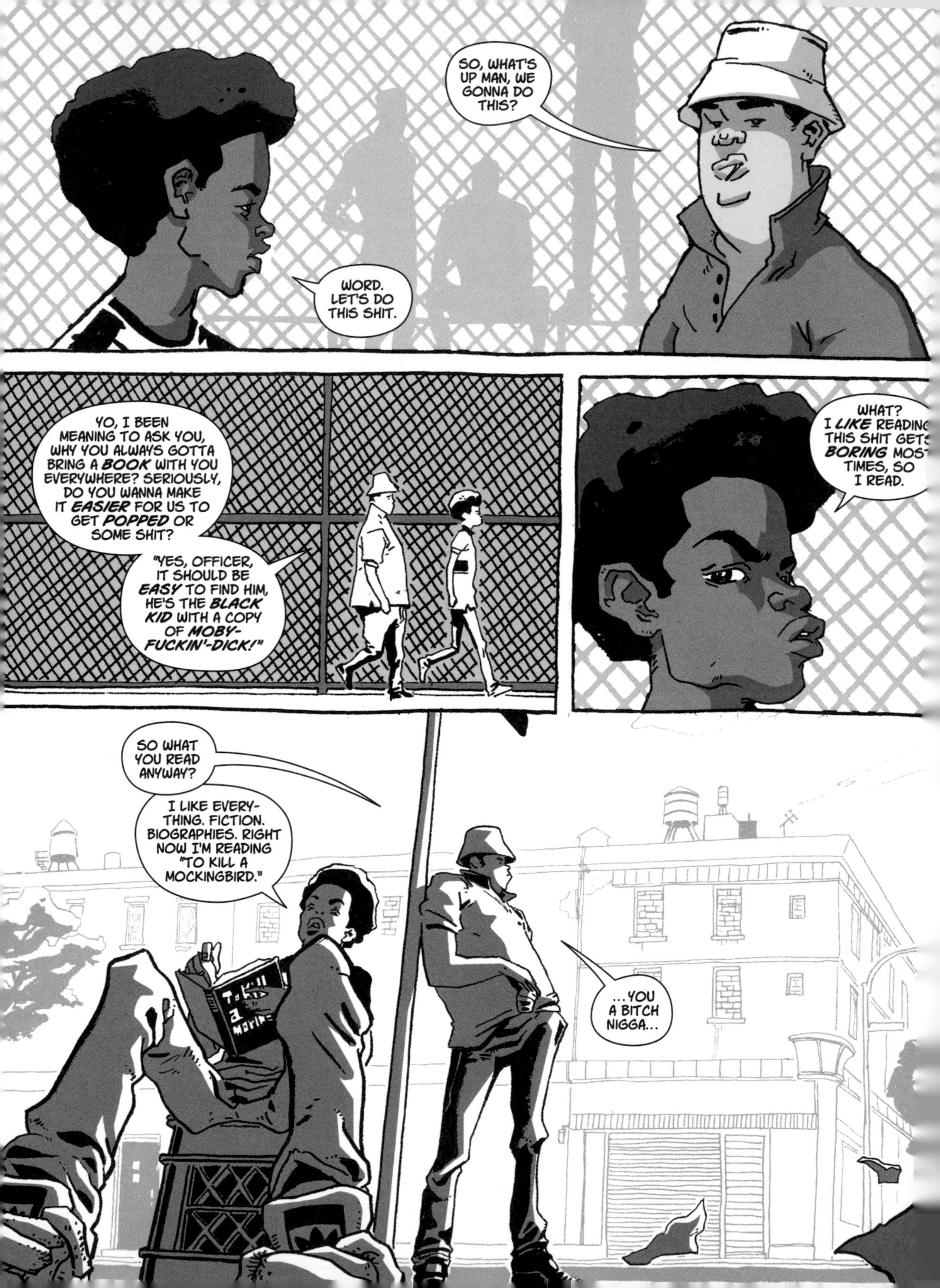
SO, WHAT'S UP MAN, WE GONNA DO THIS?
WORD. LET'S DO THIS SHIT.
YO, I BEEN MEANING TO ASK YOU, WHY YOU ALWAYS GOTTA BRING A BOOK WITH YOU EVERYWHERE? SERIOUSLY, DO YOU WANNA MAKE IT EASIER FOR US TO GET POPPED OR SOME SHIT?
"YES, OFFICER, IT SHOULD BE EASY TO FIND HIM, HE'S THE BLACK KID WITH A COPY OF MOBY-FUCKIN'-DICK!"
WHAT? I LIKE READING. THIS SHIT GETS BORING MOST TIMES, SO I READ.
SO WHAT YOU READ ANYWAY?
I LIKE EVERY-THING. FICTION. BIOGRAPHIES. RIGHT NOW I'M READING "TO KILL A MOCKINGBIRD."
...YOU A BITCH NIGGA...

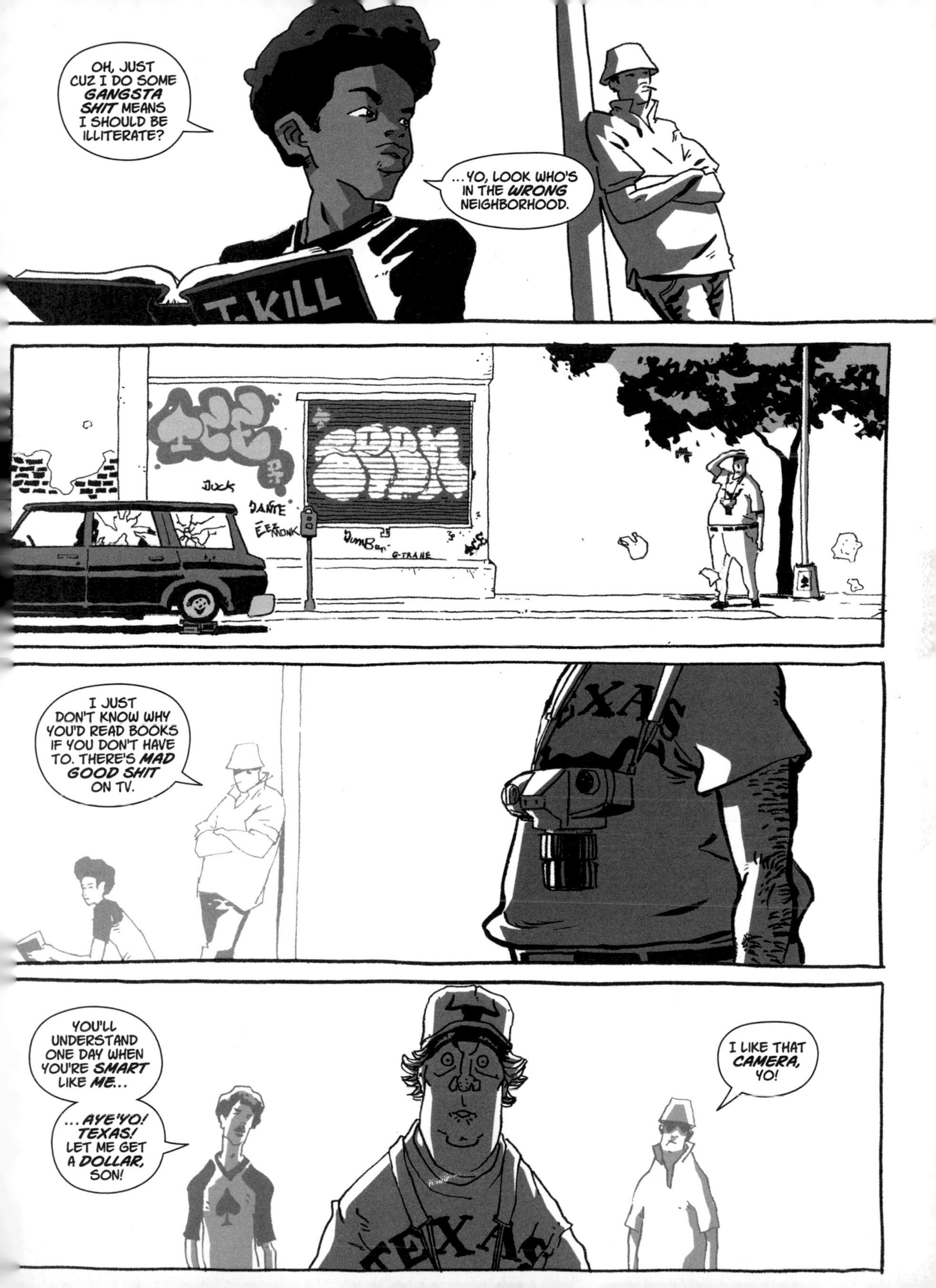

OH, JUST CUZ I DO SOME *GANGSTA SHIT* MEANS I SHOULD BE ILLITERATE?
...YO, LOOK WHO'S IN THE *WRONG* NEIGHBORHOOD.
I JUST DON'T KNOW WHY YOU'D READ BOOKS IF YOU DON'T HAVE TO. THERE'S *MAD GOOD SHIT* ON TV.
YOU'LL UNDERSTAND ONE DAY WHEN YOU'RE *SMART* LIKE *ME*...
...*AYE'YO! TEXAS!* LET ME GET A *DOLLAR,* SON!
I LIKE THAT *CAMERA,* YO!

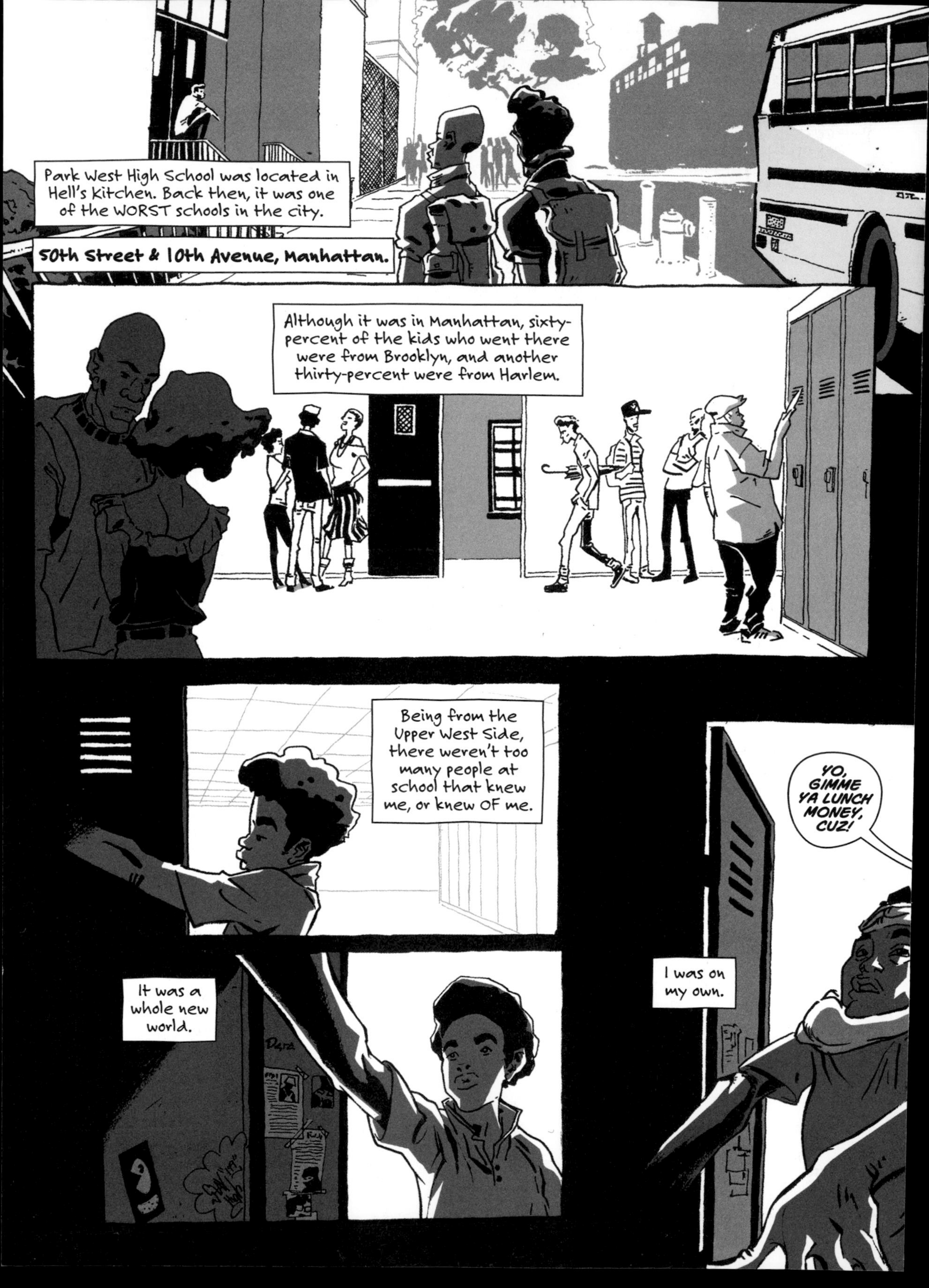

Park West High School was located in Hell's Kitchen. Back then, it was one of the WORST schools in the city.
50th Street & 10th Avenue, Manhattan.
Although it was in Manhattan, sixty-percent of the kids who went there were from Brooklyn, and another thirty-percent were from Harlem.
Being from the Upper West Side, there weren't too many people at school that knew me, or knew OF me.
YO, GIMME YA LUNCH MONEY, CUZ!
It was a whole new world.
I was on my own.

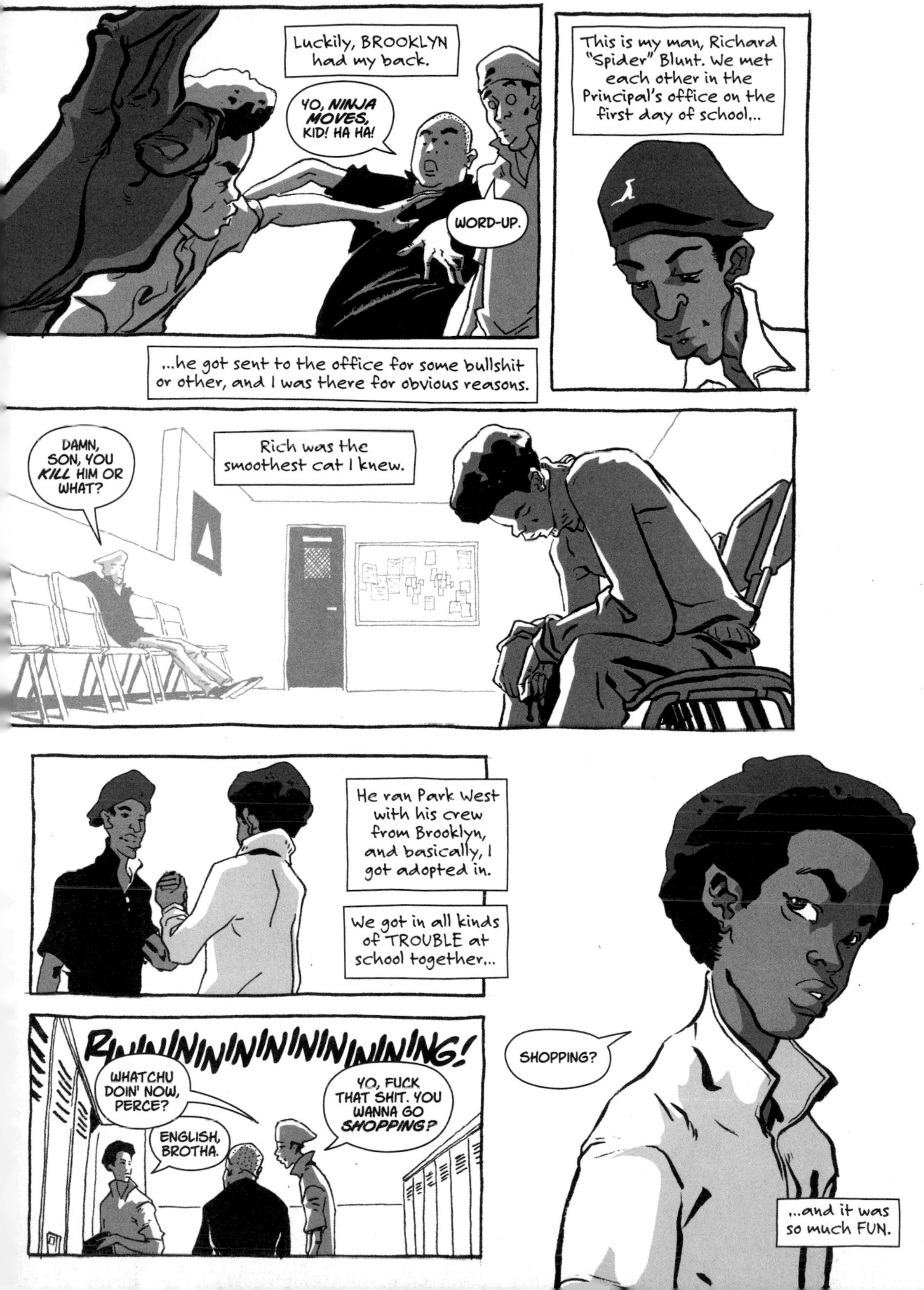
Luckily, BROOKLYN had my back.
YO, NINJA MOVES, KID! HA HA!
WORD-UP.
This is my man, Richard "Spider" Blunt. We met each other in the Principal's office on the first day of school,...
...he got sent to the office for some bullshit or other, and I was there for obvious reasons.
DAMN, SON, YOU KILL HIM OR WHAT?
Rich was the smoothest cat I knew.
He ran Park West with his crew from Brooklyn, and basically, I got adopted in.
We got in all kinds of TROUBLE at school together...
RINININININININININING!
WHATCHU DOIN' NOW, PERCE?
ENGLISH, BROTHA.
YO, FUCK THAT SHIT. YOU WANNA GO SHOPPING?
SHOPPING?
...and it was so much FUN.

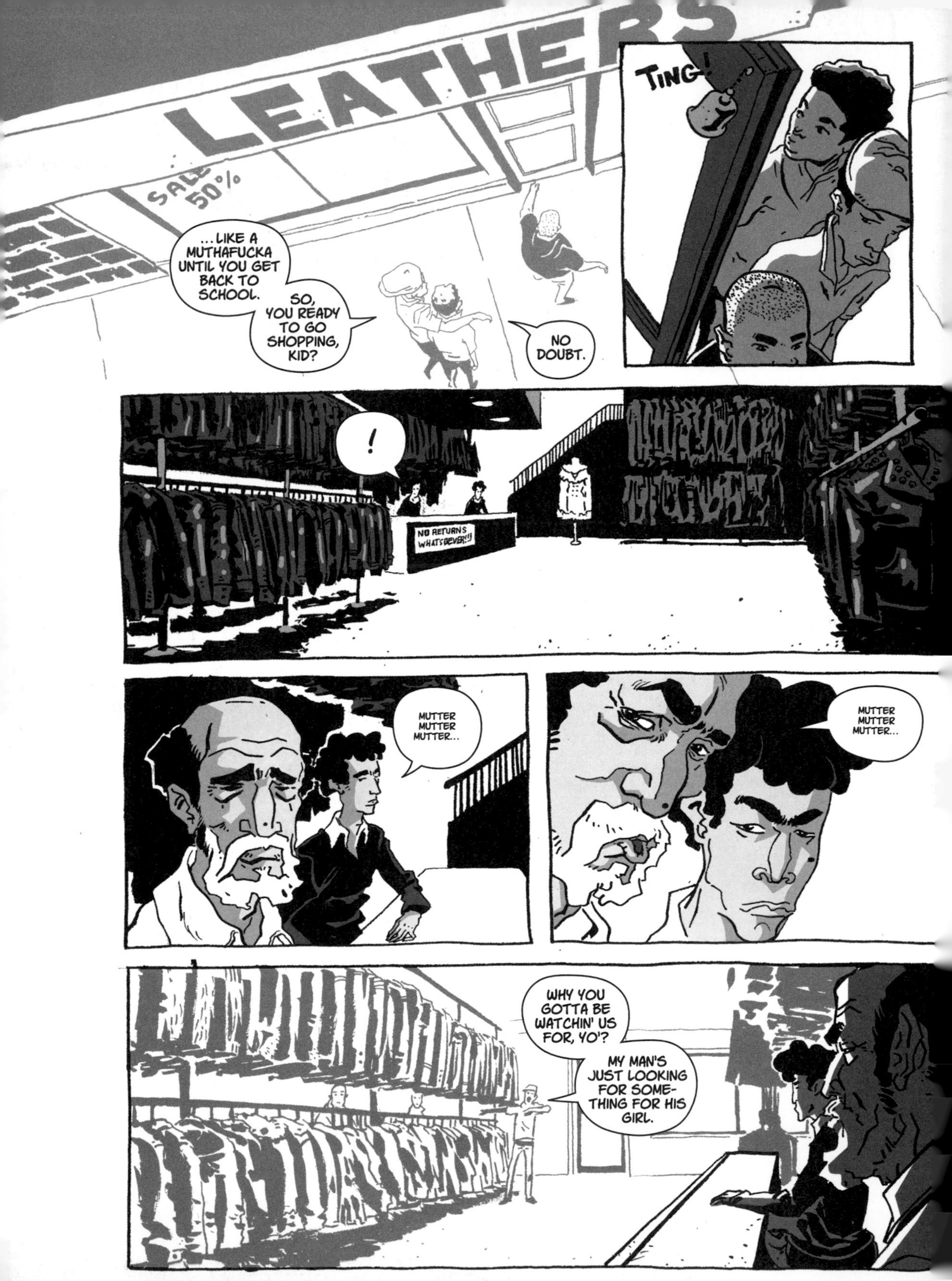
LEATHERS
SALE 50%
...LIKE A MUTHAFUCKA UNTIL YOU GET BACK TO SCHOOL.
SO, YOU READY TO GO SHOPPING, KID?
NO DOUBT.
TING!
!
NO RETURNS WHATSOEVER!!!
MUTTER MUTTER MUTTER...
MUTTER MUTTER MUTTER...
WHY YOU GOTTA BE WATCHIN' US FOR, YO'?
MY MAN'S JUST LOOKING FOR SOME-THING FOR HIS GIRL.

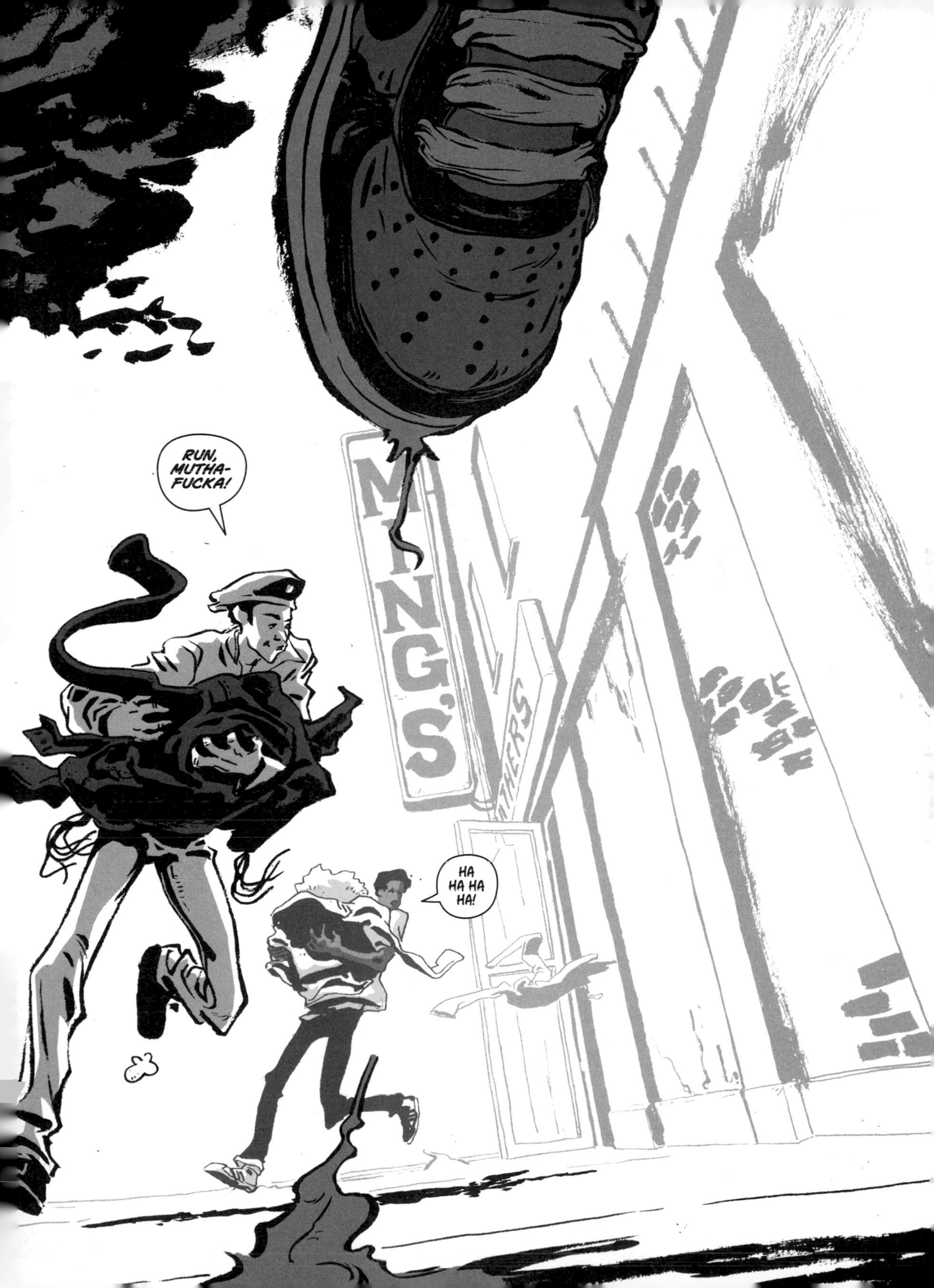

RUN, MUTHA-FUCKA!
HA HA HA HA!
MING'S

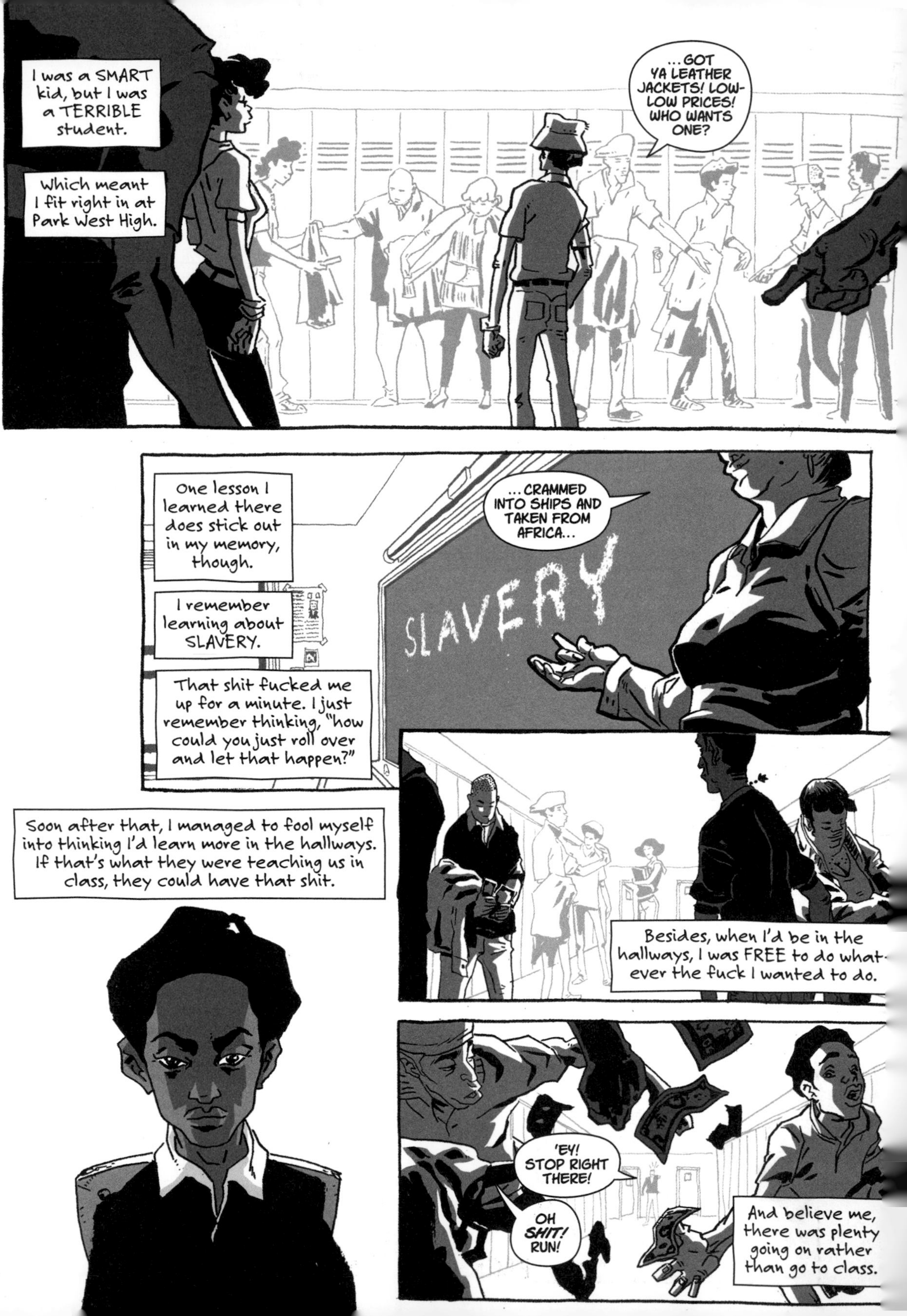

I was a SMART kid, but I was a TERRIBLE student.
Which meant I fit right in at Park West High.
...GOT YA LEATHER JACKETS! LOW-LOW PRICES! WHO WANTS ONE?
One lesson I learned there does stick out in my memory, though.
I remember learning about SLAVERY.
That shit fucked me up for a minute. I just remember thinking, "how could you just roll over and let that happen?"
...CRAMMED INTO SHIPS AND TAKEN FROM AFRICA...
SLAVERY
Soon after that, I managed to fool myself into thinking I'd learn more in the hallways. If that's what they were teaching us in class, they could have that shit.
Besides, when I'd be in the hallways, I was FREE to do whatever the fuck I wanted to do.
'EY! STOP RIGHT THERE!
OH SHIT! RUN!
And believe me, there was plenty going on rather than go to class.

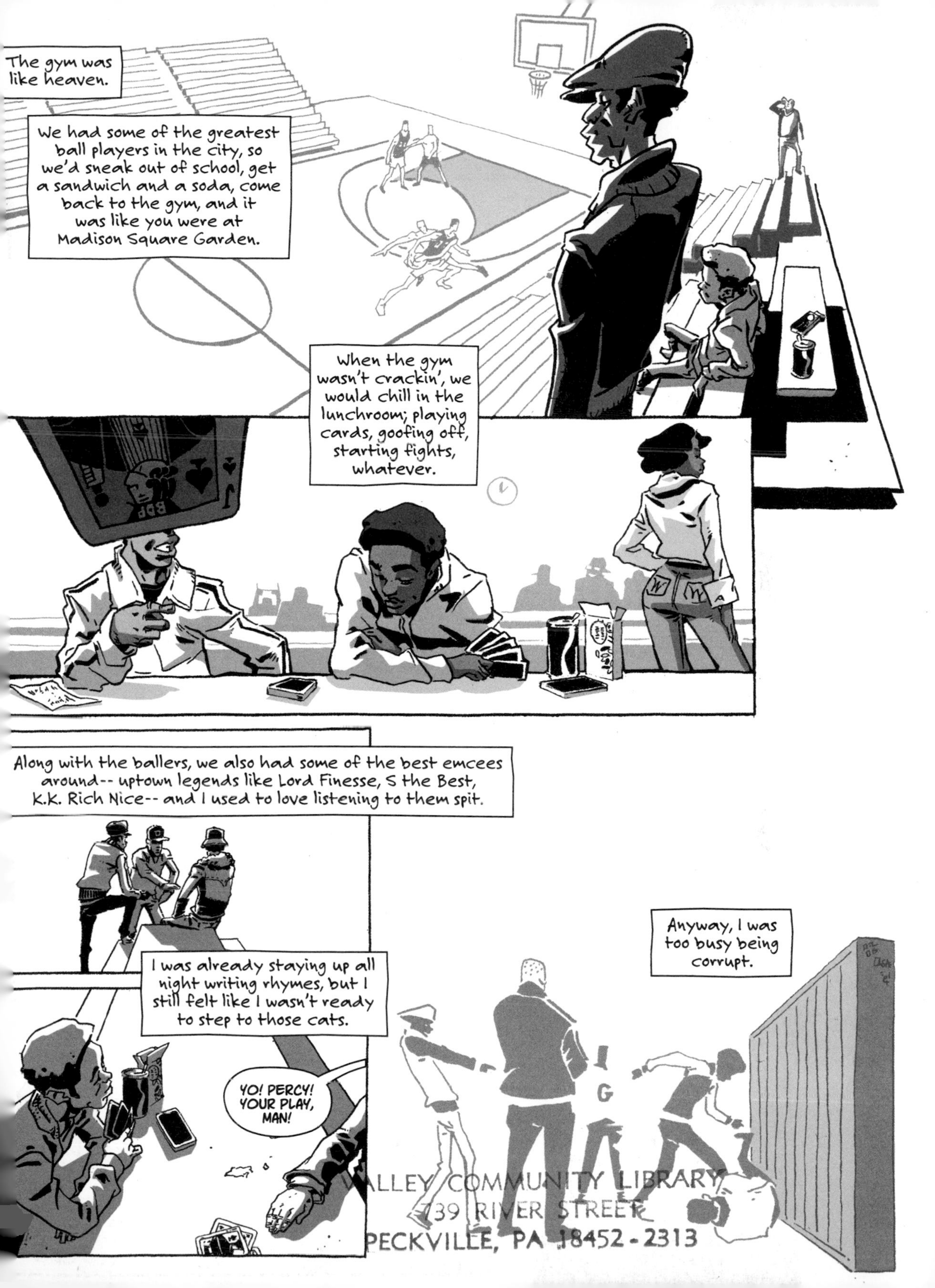
The gym was like heaven.
We had some of the greatest ball players in the city, so we'd sneak out of school, get a sandwich and a soda, come back to the gym, and it was like you were at Madison Square Garden.
When the gym wasn't crackin', we would chill in the lunchroom; playing cards, goofing off, starting fights, whatever.
Along with the ballers, we also had some of the best emcees around-- uptown legends like Lord Finesse, S the Best, K.K. Rich Nice-- and I used to love listening to them spit.
I was already staying up all night writing rhymes, but I still felt like I wasn't ready to step to those cats.
YO! PERCY! YOUR PLAY, MAN!
Anyway, I was too busy being corrupt.

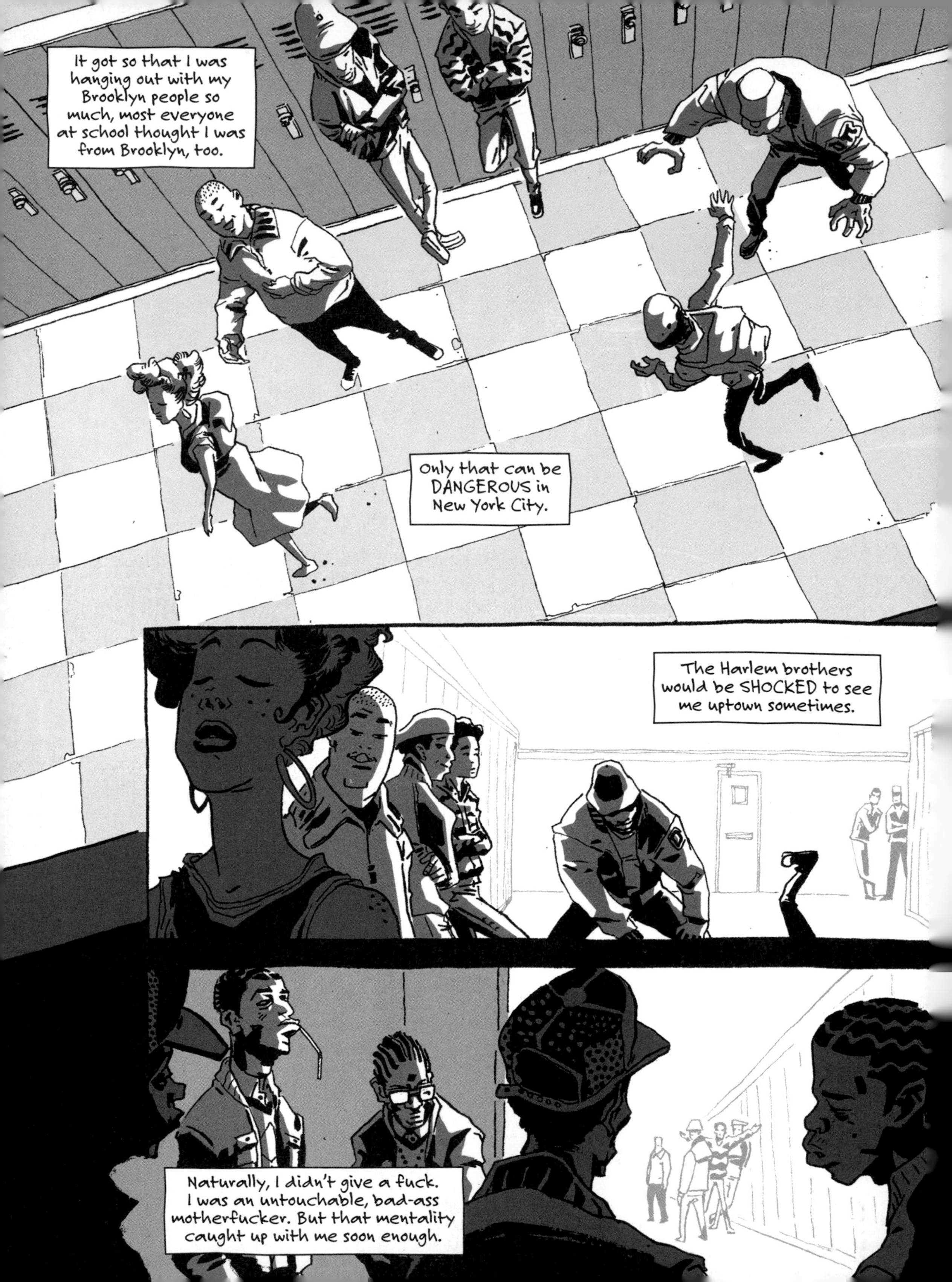

It got so that I was hanging out with my Brooklyn people so much, most everyone at school thought I was from Brooklyn, too.
Only that can be DANGEROUS in New York City.
The Harlem brothers would be SHOCKED to see me uptown sometimes.
Naturally, I didn't give a fuck. I was an untouchable, bad-ass motherfucker. But that mentality caught up with me soon enough.

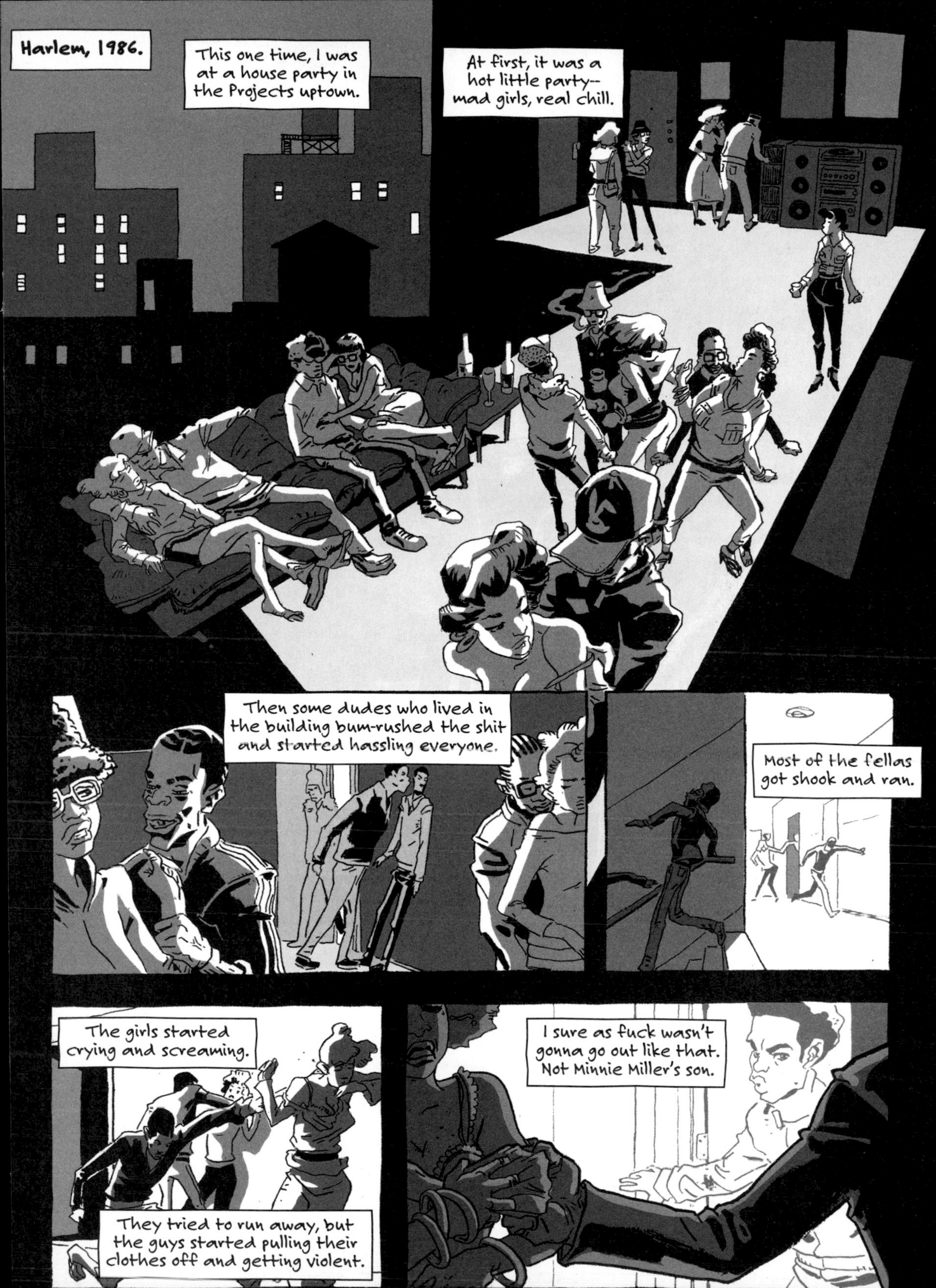
Harlem, 1986.
This one time, I was at a house party in the Projects uptown.
At first, it was a hot little party-- mad girls, real chill.
Then some dudes who lived in the building bum-rushed the shit and started hassling everyone.
Most of the fellas got shook and ran.
The girls started crying and screaming.
They tried to run away, but the guys started pulling their clothes off and getting violent.
I sure as fuck wasn't gonna go out like that. Not Minnie Miller's son.

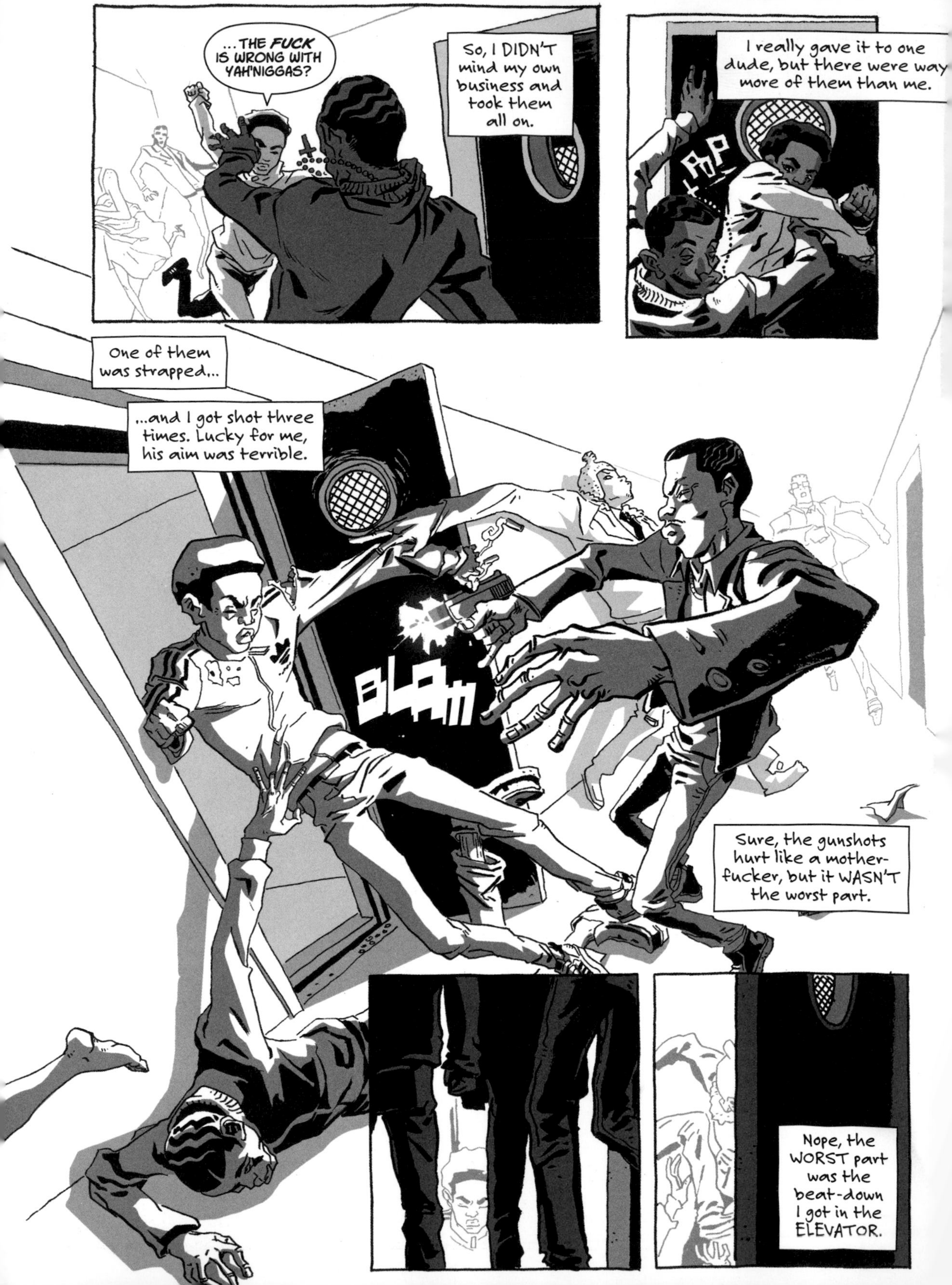

...THE *FUCK* IS WRONG WITH YAH'NIGGAS?
So, I DIDN'T mind my own business and took them all on.
I really gave it to one dude, but there were way more of them than me.
One of them was strapped...
...and I got shot three times. Lucky for me, his aim was terrible.
BLAM
Sure, the gunshots hurt like a mother-fucker, but it WASN'T the worst part.
Nope, the WORST part was the beat-down I got in the ELEVATOR.

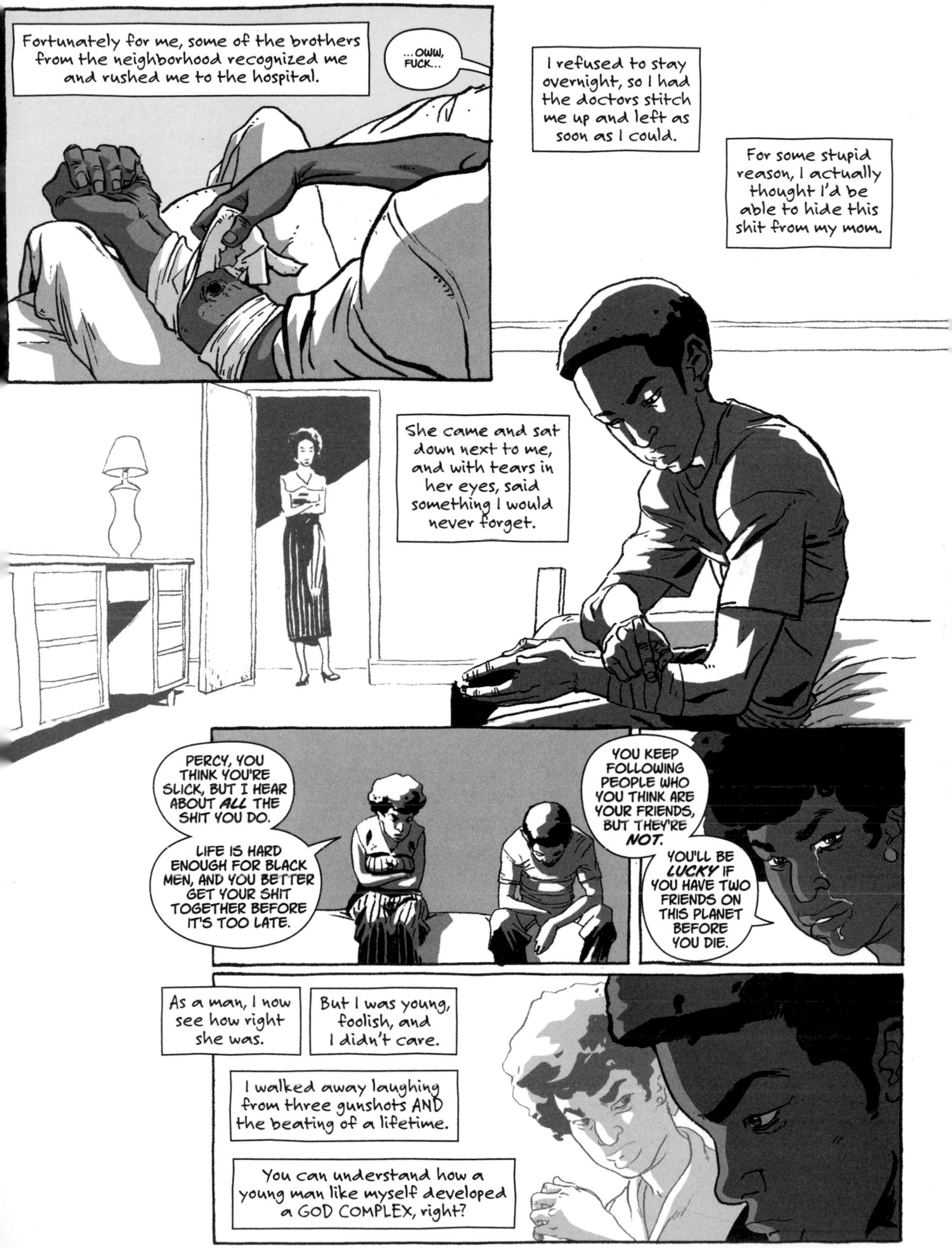
Fortunately for me, some of the brothers from the neighborhood recognized me and rushed me to the hospital.
...OWW, FUCK...
I refused to stay overnight, so I had the doctors stitch me up and left as soon as I could.
For some stupid reason, I actually thought I'd be able to hide this shit from my mom.
She came and sat down next to me, and with tears in her eyes, said something I would never forget.
PERCY, YOU THINK YOU'RE SLICK, BUT I HEAR ABOUT ALL THE SHIT YOU DO.
LIFE IS HARD ENOUGH FOR BLACK MEN, AND YOU BETTER GET YOUR SHIT TOGETHER BEFORE IT'S TOO LATE.
YOU KEEP FOLLOWING PEOPLE WHO YOU THINK ARE YOUR FRIENDS, BUT THEY'RE NOT.
YOU'LL BE LUCKY IF YOU HAVE TWO FRIENDS ON THIS PLANET BEFORE YOU DIE.
As a man, I now see how right she was.
But I was young, foolish, and I didn't care.
I walked away laughing from three gunshots AND the beating of a lifetime.
You can understand how a young man like myself developed a GOD COMPLEX, right?

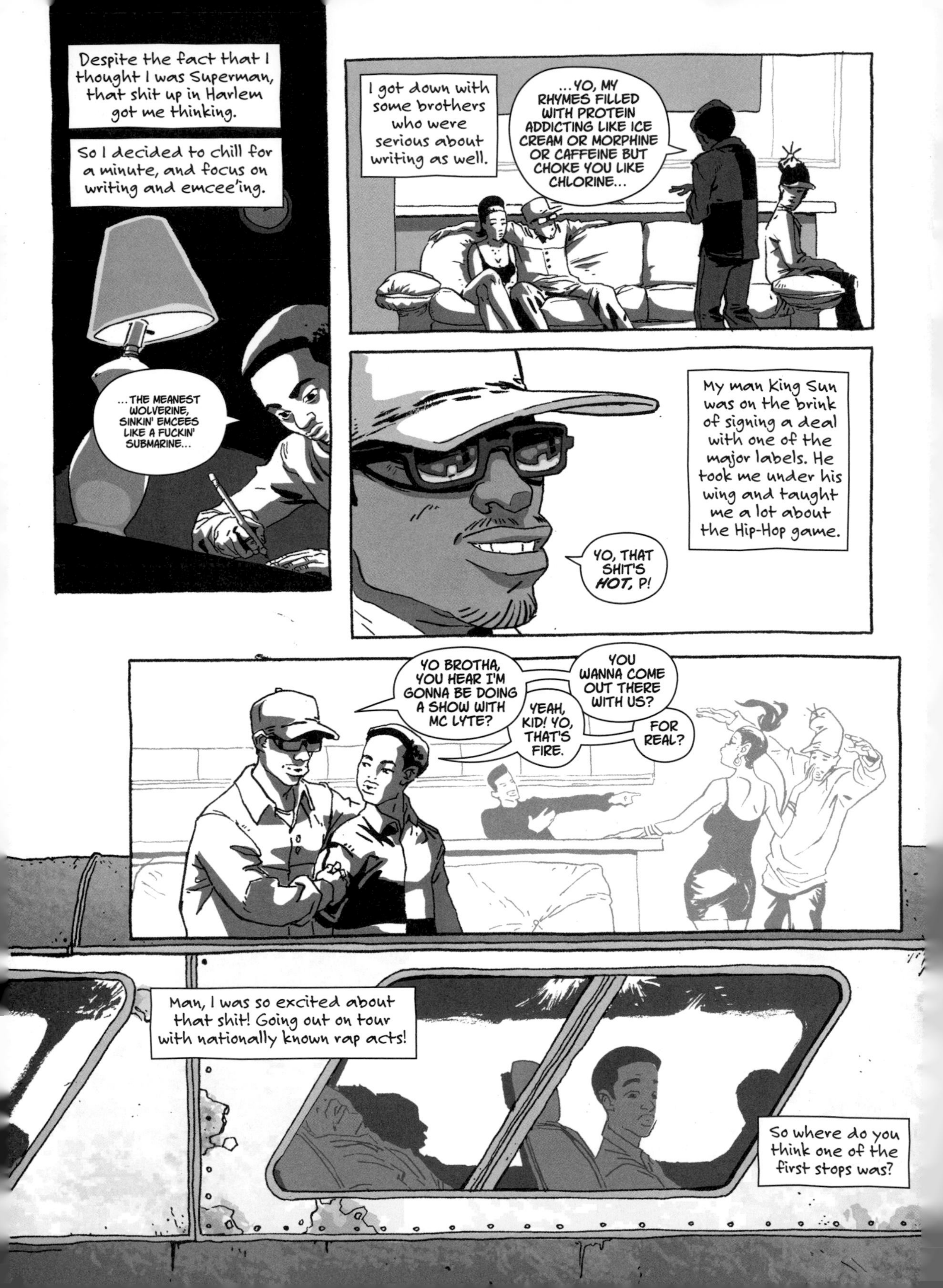
Despite the fact that I thought I was Superman, that shit up in Harlem got me thinking.
So I decided to chill for a minute, and focus on writing and emcee'ing.
...THE MEANEST WOLVERINE, SINKIN' EMCEES LIKE A FUCKIN' SUBMARINE...
I got down with some brothers who were serious about writing as well.
...YO, MY RHYMES FILLED WITH PROTEIN ADDICTING LIKE ICE CREAM OR MORPHINE OR CAFFEINE BUT CHOKE YOU LIKE CHLORINE...
My man King Sun was on the brink of signing a deal with one of the major labels. He took me under his wing and taught me a lot about the Hip-Hop game.
YO, THAT SHIT'S HOT, P!
YO BROTHA, YOU HEAR I'M GONNA BE DOING A SHOW WITH MC LYTE?
YEAH, KID! YO, THAT'S FIRE.
YOU WANNA COME OUT THERE WITH US?
FOR REAL?
Man, I was so excited about that shit! Going out on tour with nationally known rap acts!
So where do you think one of the first stops was?

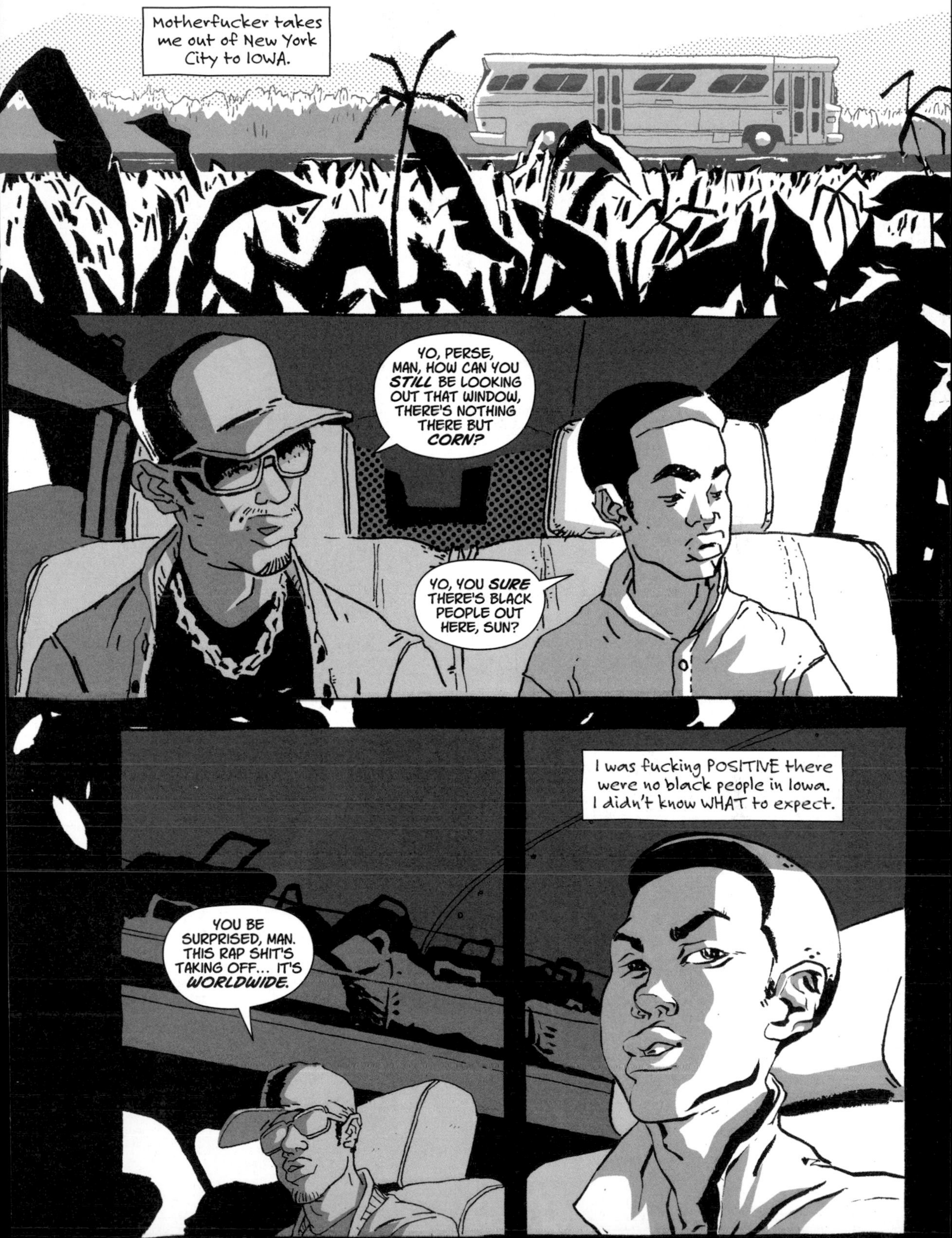
Motherfucker takes me out of New York City to IOWA.
YO, PERSE, MAN, HOW CAN YOU STILL BE LOOKING OUT THAT WINDOW, THERE'S NOTHING THERE BUT CORN?
YO, YOU SURE THERE'S BLACK PEOPLE OUT HERE, SUN?
YOU BE SURPRISED, MAN. THIS RAP SHIT'S TAKING OFF... IT'S WORLDWIDE.
I was fucking POSITIVE there were no black people in Iowa. I didn't know WHAT to expect.

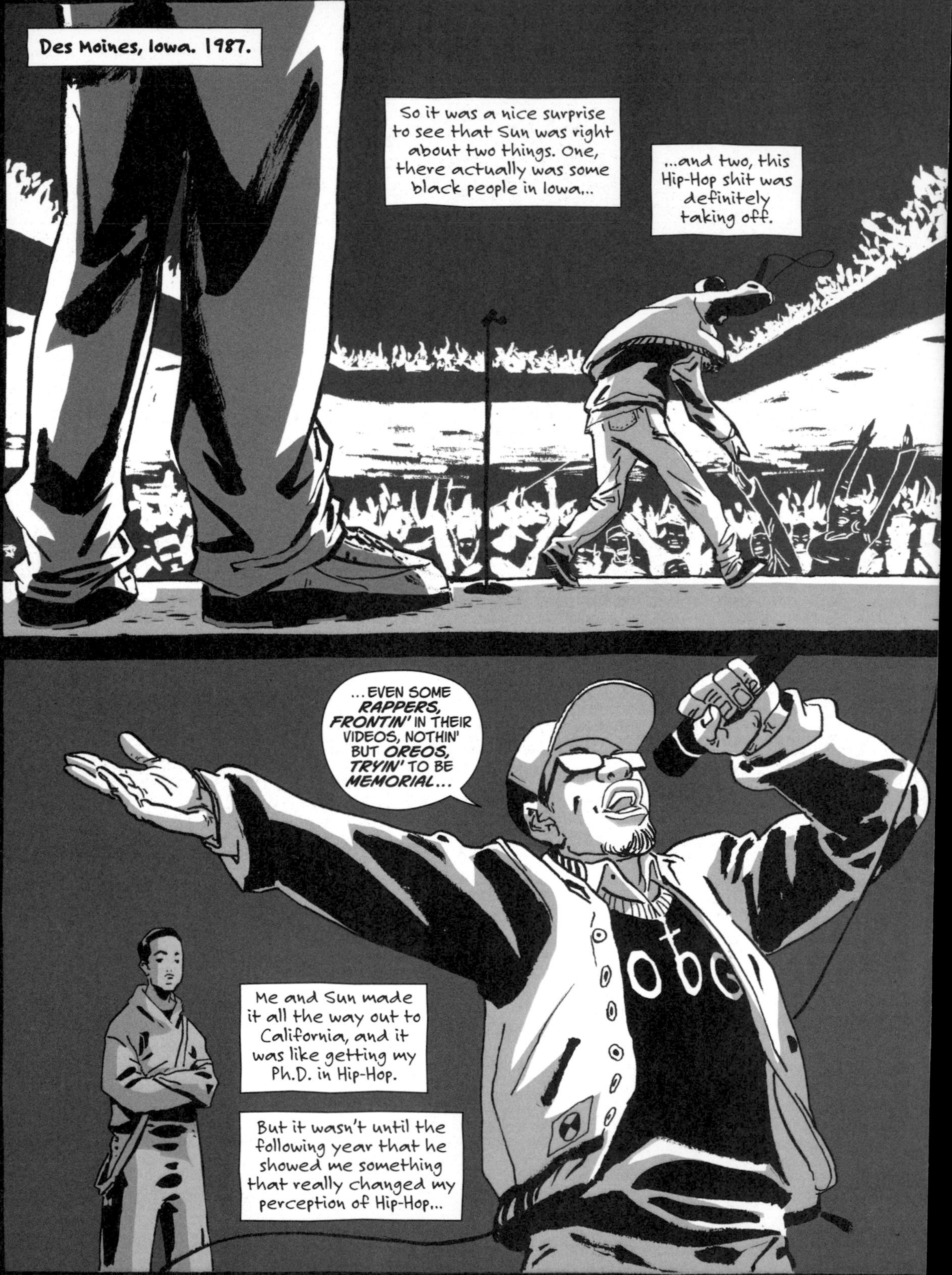

Des Moines, Iowa. 1987.
So it was a nice surprise to see that Sun was right about two things. One, there actually was some black people in Iowa...
...and two, this Hip-Hop shit was definitely taking off.
...EVEN SOME RAPPERS, FRONTIN' IN THEIR VIDEOS, NOTHIN' BUT OREOS, TRYIN' TO BE MEMORIAL...
Me and Sun made it all the way out to California, and it was like getting my Ph.D. in Hip-Hop.
But it wasn't until the following year that he showed me something that really changed my perception of Hip-Hop...

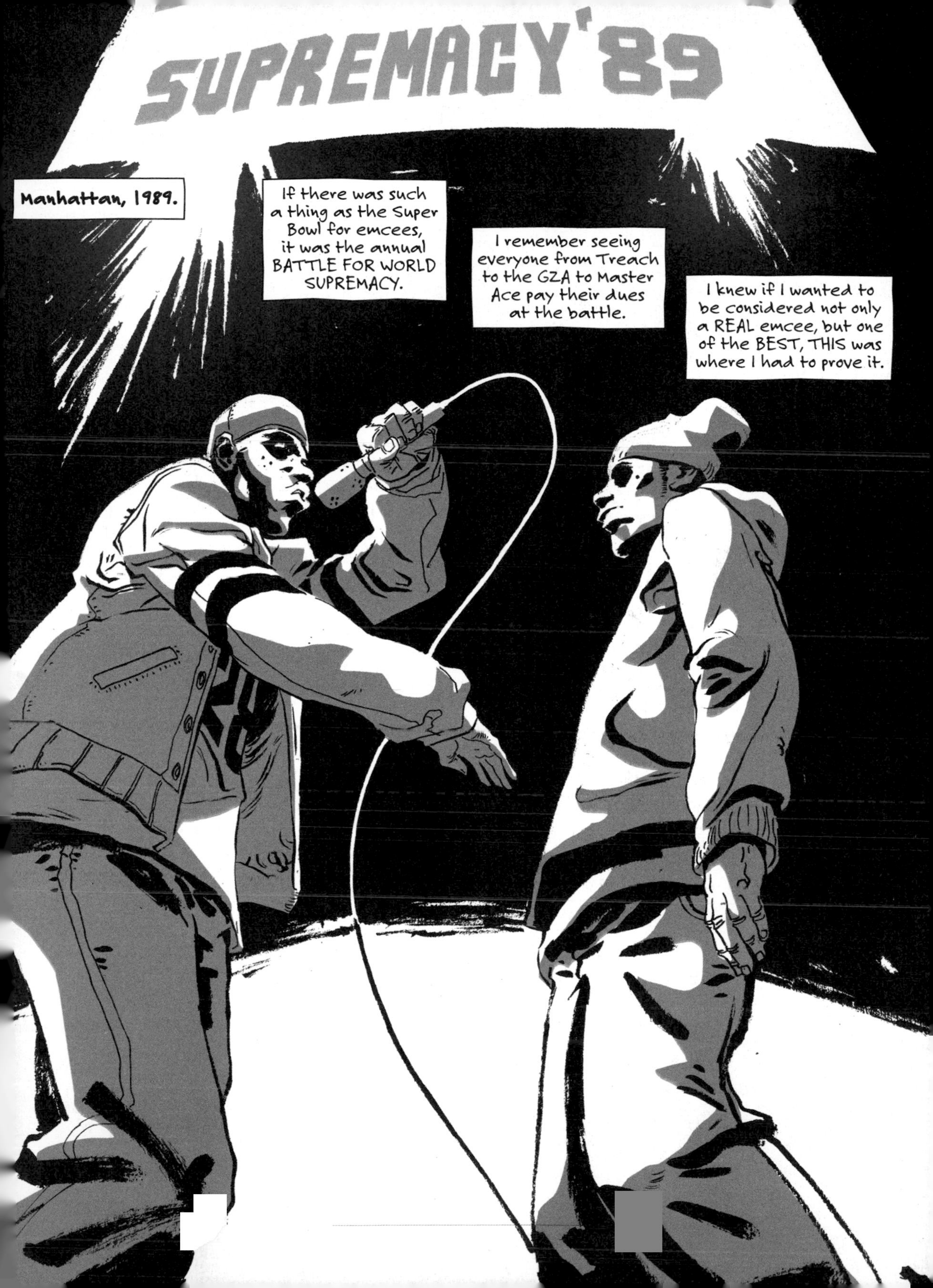
SUPREMACY '89
Manhattan, 1989.
If there was such a thing as the Super Bowl for emcees, it was the annual BATTLE FOR WORLD SUPREMACY.
I remember seeing everyone from Treach to the GZA to Master Ace pay their dues at the battle.
I knew if I wanted to be considered not only a REAL emcee, but one of the BEST, THIS was where I had to prove it.

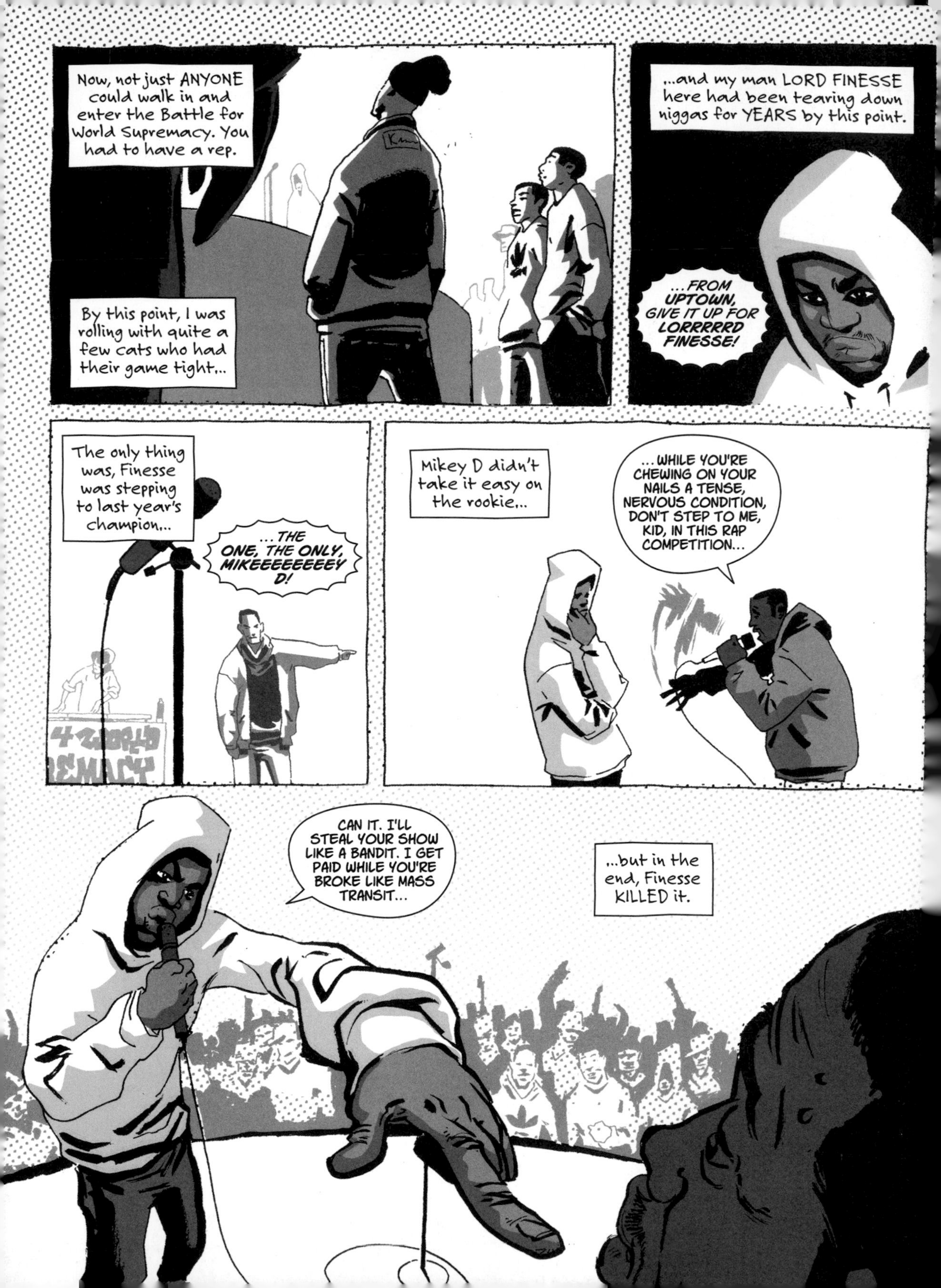
Now, not just ANYONE could walk in and enter the Battle for World Supremacy. You had to have a rep.
By this point, I was rolling with quite a few cats who had their game tight...
...and my man LORD FINESSE here had been tearing down niggas for YEARS by this point.
...FROM UPTOWN, GIVE IT UP FOR LORRRRRD FINESSE!
The only thing was, Finesse was stepping to last year's champion...
...THE ONE, THE ONLY, MIKEEEEEEEEEY D!
Mikey D didn't take it easy on the rookie...
...WHILE YOU'RE CHEWING ON YOUR NAILS A TENSE, NERVOUS CONDITION, DON'T STEP TO ME, KID, IN THIS RAP COMPETITION...
CAN IT. I'LL STEAL YOUR SHOW LIKE A BANDIT. I GET PAID WHILE YOU'RE BROKE LIKE MASS TRANSIT...
...but in the end, Finesse KILLED it.

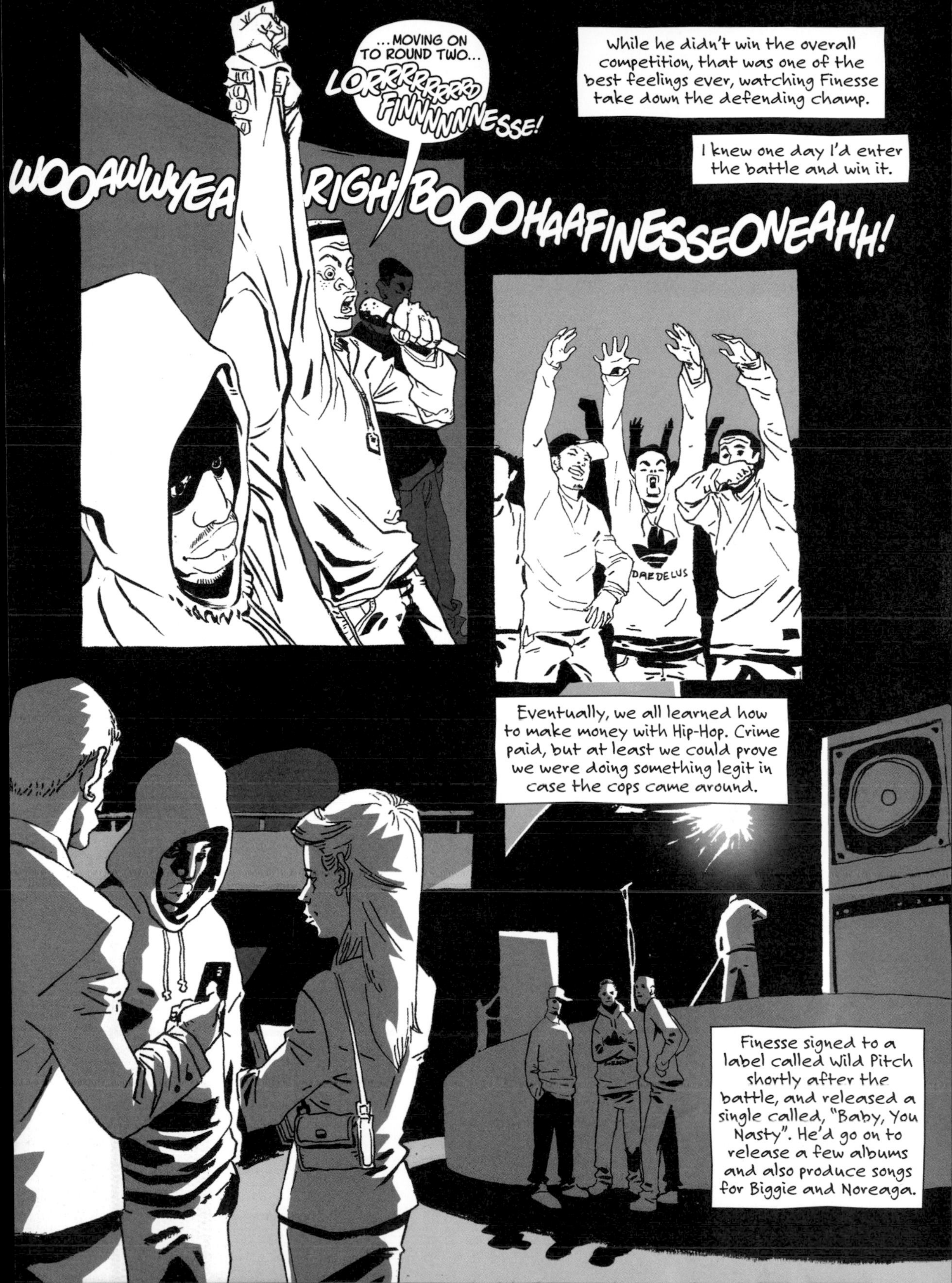
...MOVING ON TO ROUND TWO...
LORRRRRRRRD FINNNNNNESSE!
While he didn't win the overall competition, that was one of the best feelings ever, watching Finesse take down the defending champ.
I knew one day I'd enter the battle and win it.
WOOAWWYEA ARIGH BOOOHAAFINESSEONEAHH!
DAEDELUS
Eventually, we all learned how to make money with Hip-Hop. Crime paid, but at least we could prove we were doing something legit in case the cops came around.
Finesse signed to a label called Wild Pitch shortly after the battle, and released a single called, "Baby, You Nasty". He'd go on to release a few albums and also produce songs for Biggie and Noreaga.

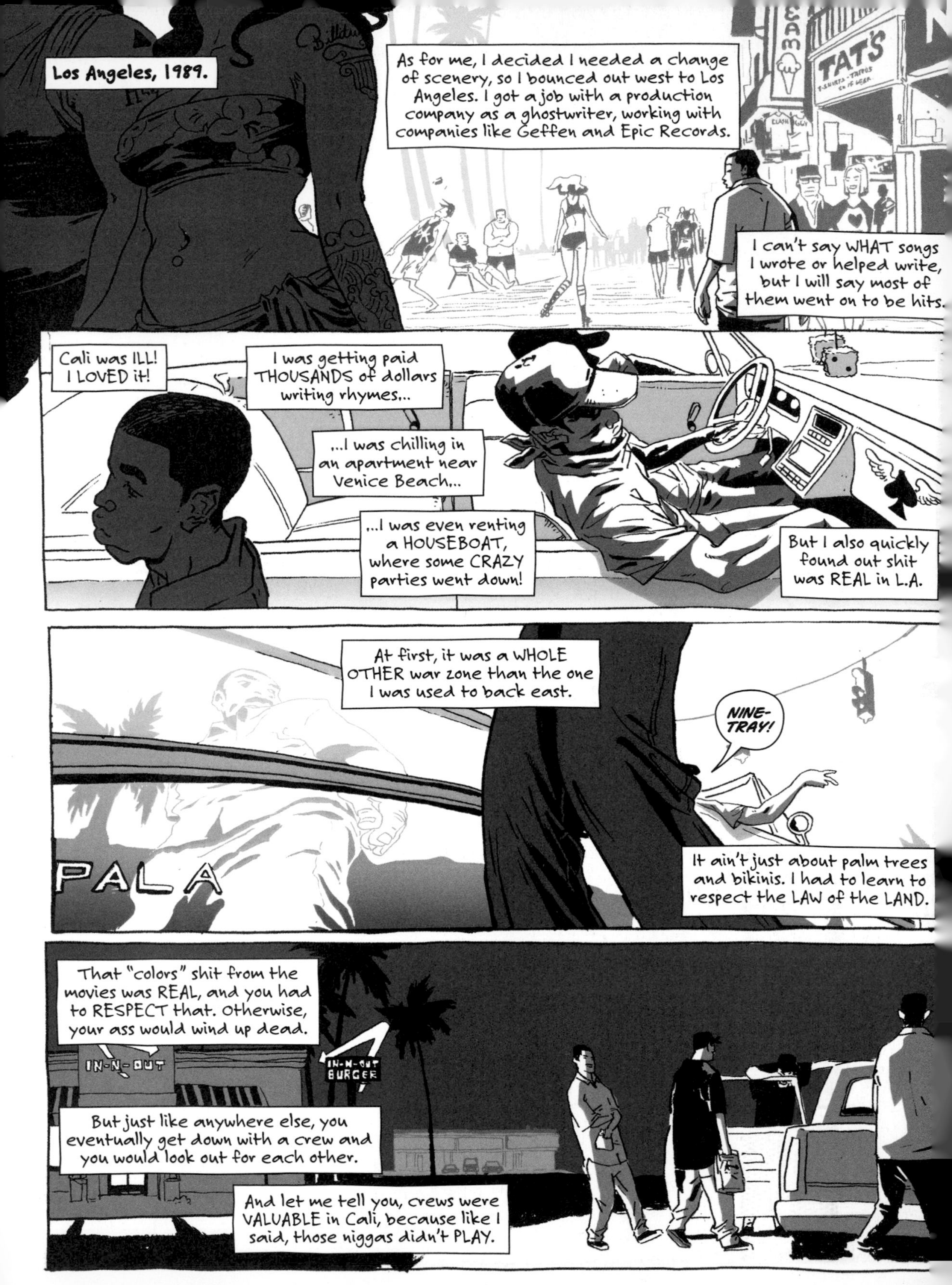

Los Angeles, 1989.
As for me, I decided I needed a change of scenery, so I bounced out west to Los Angeles. I got a job with a production company as a ghostwriter, working with companies like Geffen and Epic Records.
TAT'S
I can't say WHAT songs I wrote or helped write, but I will say most of them went on to be hits.
Cali was ILL! I LOVED it!
I was getting paid THOUSANDS of dollars writing rhymes...
...I was chilling in an apartment near Venice Beach...
...I was even renting a HOUSEBOAT, where some CRAZY parties went down!
But I also quickly found out shit was REAL in L.A.
At first, it was a WHOLE OTHER war zone than the one I was used to back east.
NINE-TRAY!
PALA
It ain't just about palm trees and bikinis. I had to learn to respect the LAW of the LAND.
That "colors" shit from the movies was REAL, and you had to RESPECT that. Otherwise, your ass would wind up dead.
IN-N-OUT
IN-N-OUT BURGER
But just like anywhere else, you eventually get down with a crew and you would look out for each other.
And let me tell you, crews were VALUABLE in Cali, because like I said, those niggas didn't PLAY.

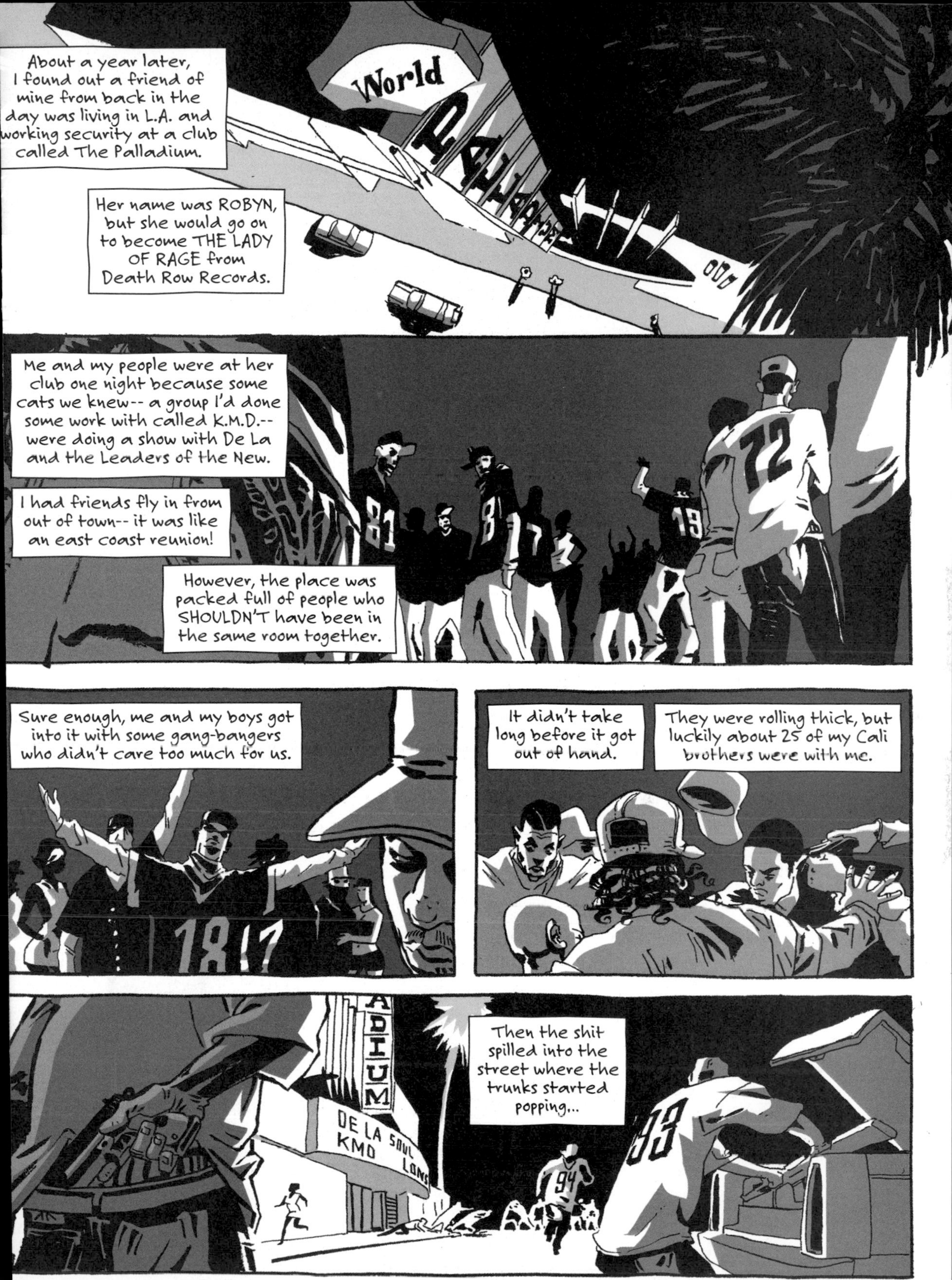

About a year later, I found out a friend of mine from back in the day was living in L.A. and working security at a club called The Palladium.
Her name was ROBYN, but she would go on to become THE LADY OF RAGE from Death Row Records.
World
Me and my people were at her club one night because some cats we knew-- a group I'd done some work with called K.M.D.-- were doing a show with De La and the Leaders of the New.
I had friends fly in from out of town-- it was like an east coast reunion!
However, the place was packed full of people who SHOULDN'T have been in the same room together.
Sure enough, me and my boys got into it with some gang-bangers who didn't care too much for us.
It didn't take long before it got out of hand.
They were rolling thick, but luckily about 25 of my Cali brothers were with me.
Then the shit spilled into the street where the trunks started popping...
DE LA SOUL
KMD

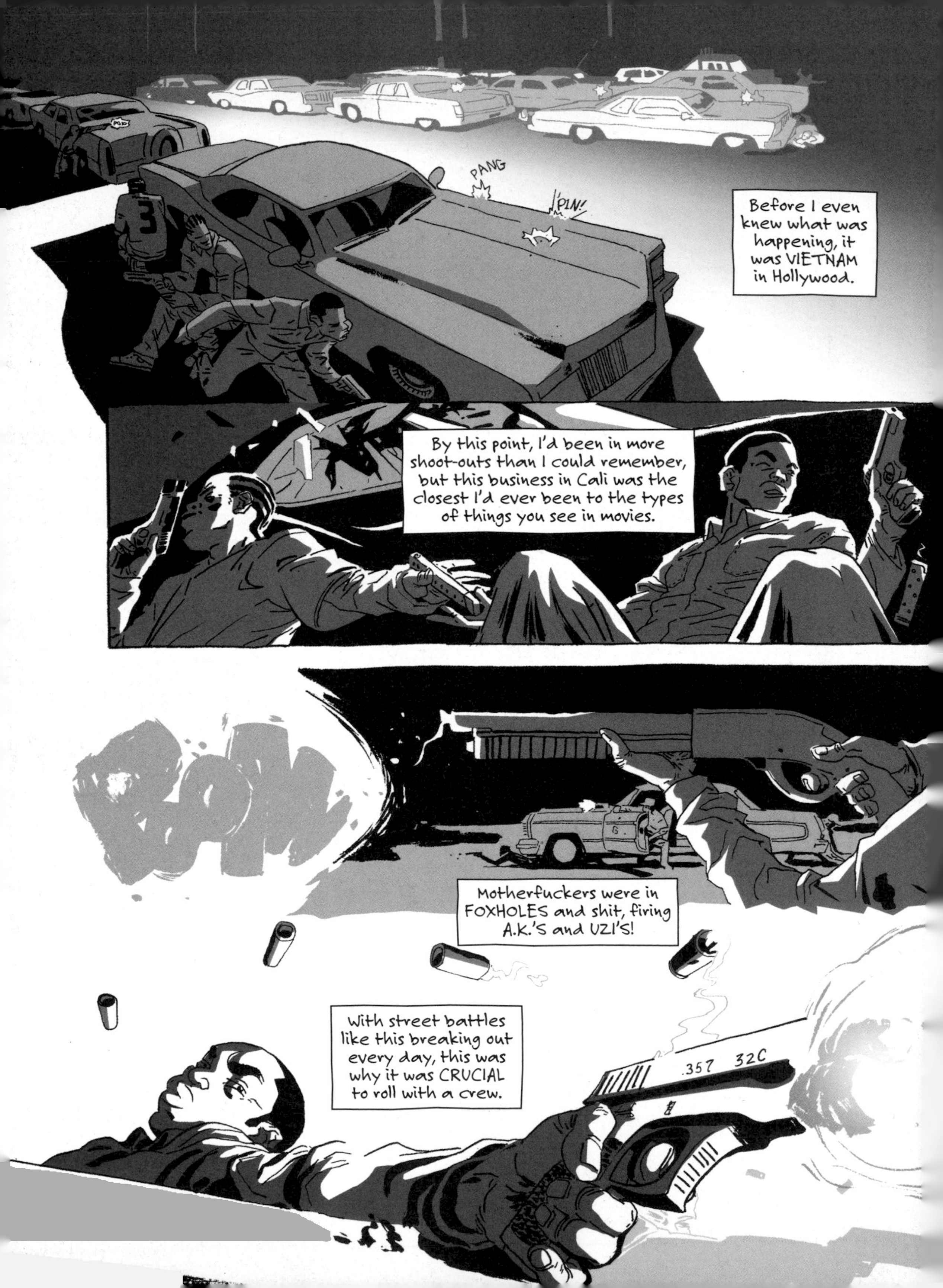
PANG
PIN!
Before I even knew what was happening, it was VIETNAM in Hollywood.
By this point, I'd been in more shoot-outs than I could remember, but this business in Cali was the closest I'd ever been to the types of things you see in movies.
Motherfuckers were in FOXHOLES and shit, firing A.K.'S and UZI'S!
With street battles like this breaking out every day, this was why it was CRUCIAL to roll with a crew.
.357 32C

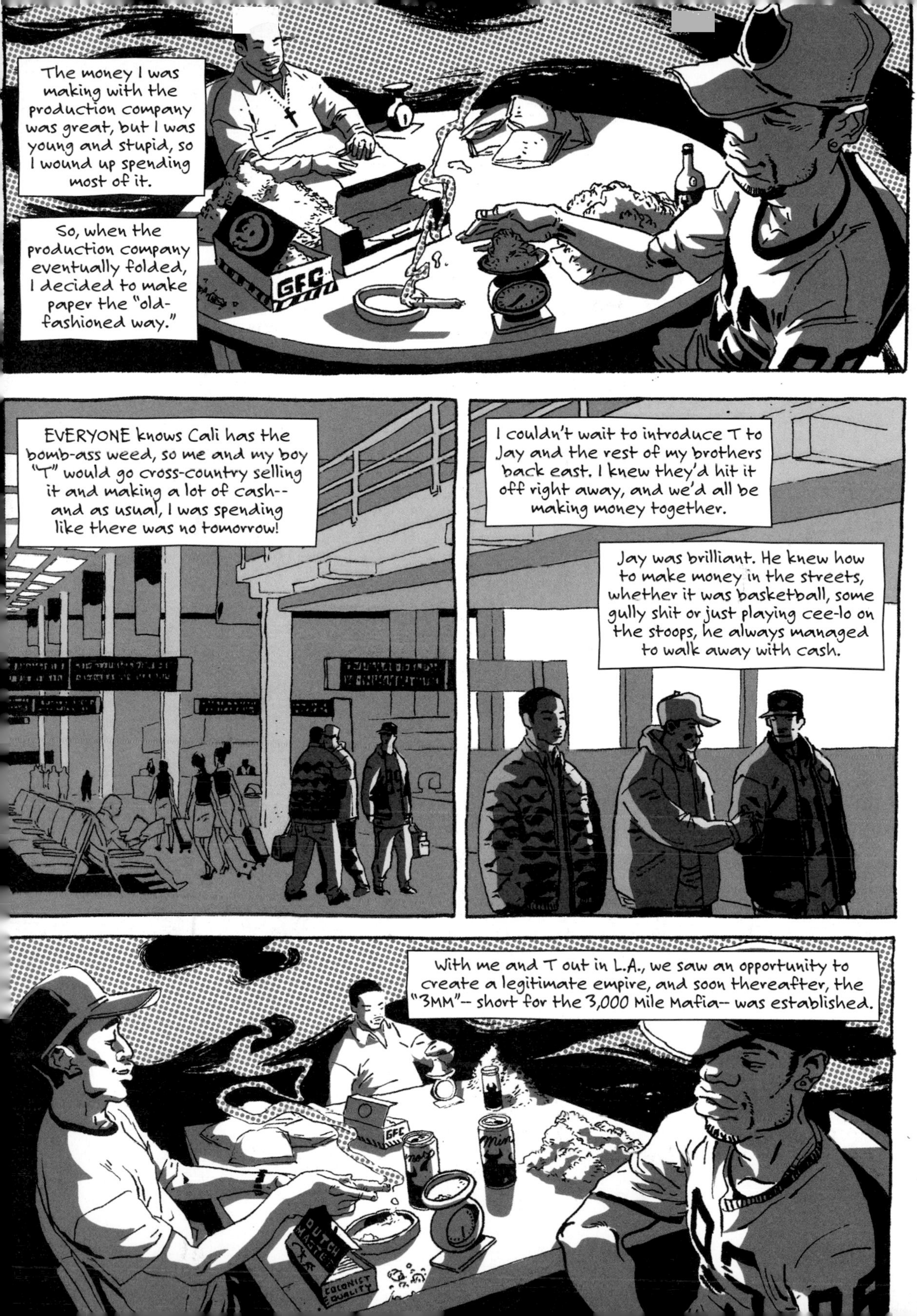
The money I was making with the production company was great, but I was young and stupid, so I wound up spending most of it.
So, when the production company eventually folded, I decided to make paper the "old-fashioned way."
GFC
EVERYONE knows Cali has the bomb-ass weed, so me and my boy "T" would go cross-country selling it and making a lot of cash-- and as usual, I was spending like there was no tomorrow!
I couldn't wait to introduce T to Jay and the rest of my brothers back east. I knew they'd hit it off right away, and we'd all be making money together.
Jay was brilliant. He knew how to make money in the streets, whether it was basketball, some gully shit or just playing cee-lo on the stoops, he always managed to walk away with cash.
With me and T out in L.A., we saw an opportunity to create a legitimate empire, and soon thereafter, the "3MM"-- short for the 3,000 Mile Mafia-- was established.

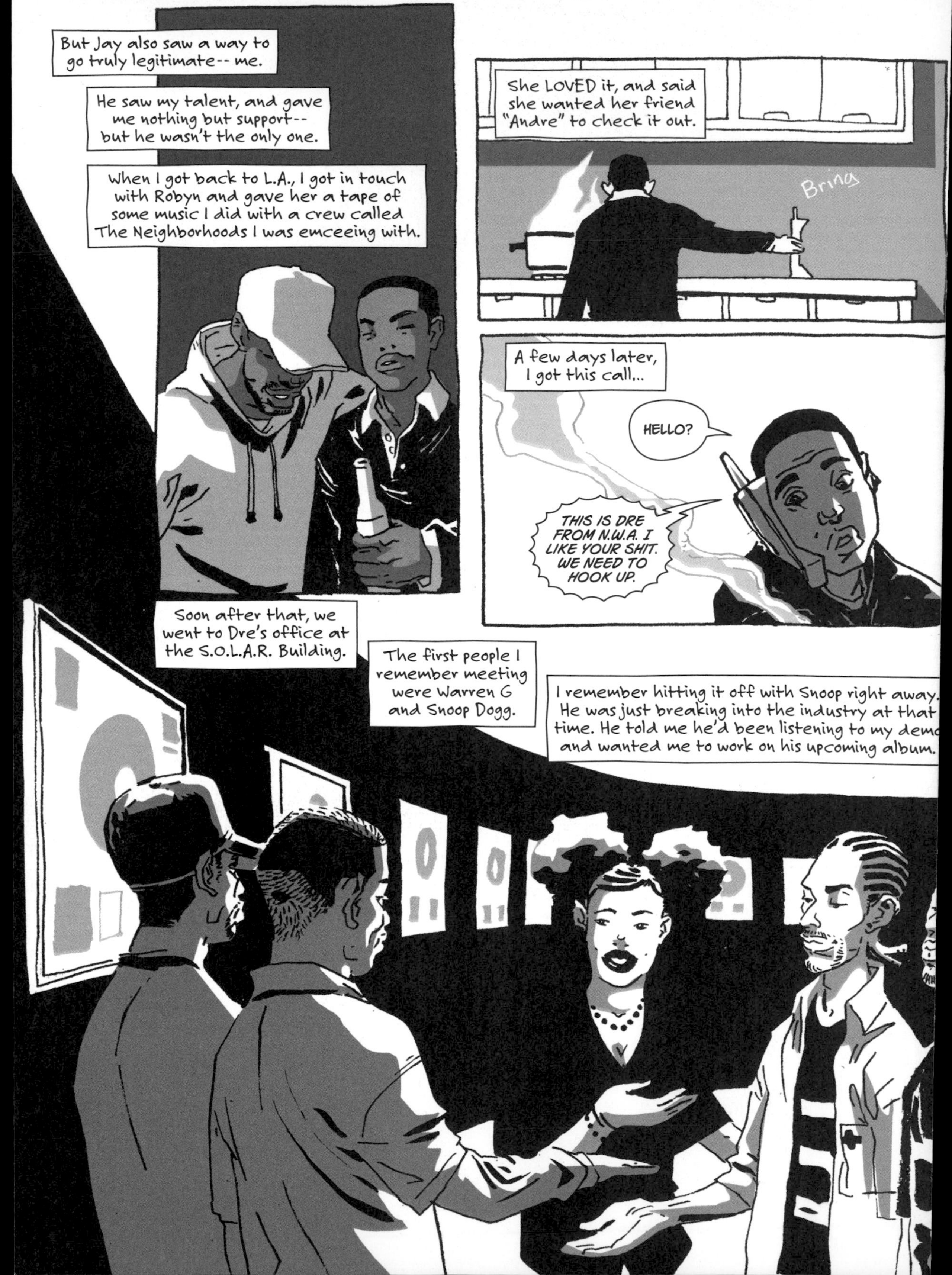
But Jay also saw a way to go truly legitimate-- me.
He saw my talent, and gave me nothing but support-- but he wasn't the only one.
When I got back to L.A., I got in touch with Robyn and gave her a tape of some music I did with a crew called The Neighborhoods I was emceeing with.
She LOVED it, and said she wanted her friend "Andre" to check it out.
Bring
A few days later, I got this call...
HELLO?
THIS IS DRE FROM N.W.A. I LIKE YOUR SHIT. WE NEED TO HOOK UP.
Soon after that, we went to Dre's office at the S.O.L.A.R. Building.
The first people I remember meeting were Warren G and Snoop Dogg.
I remember hitting it off with Snoop right away. He was just breaking into the industry at that time. He told me he'd been listening to my demo and wanted me to work on his upcoming album.

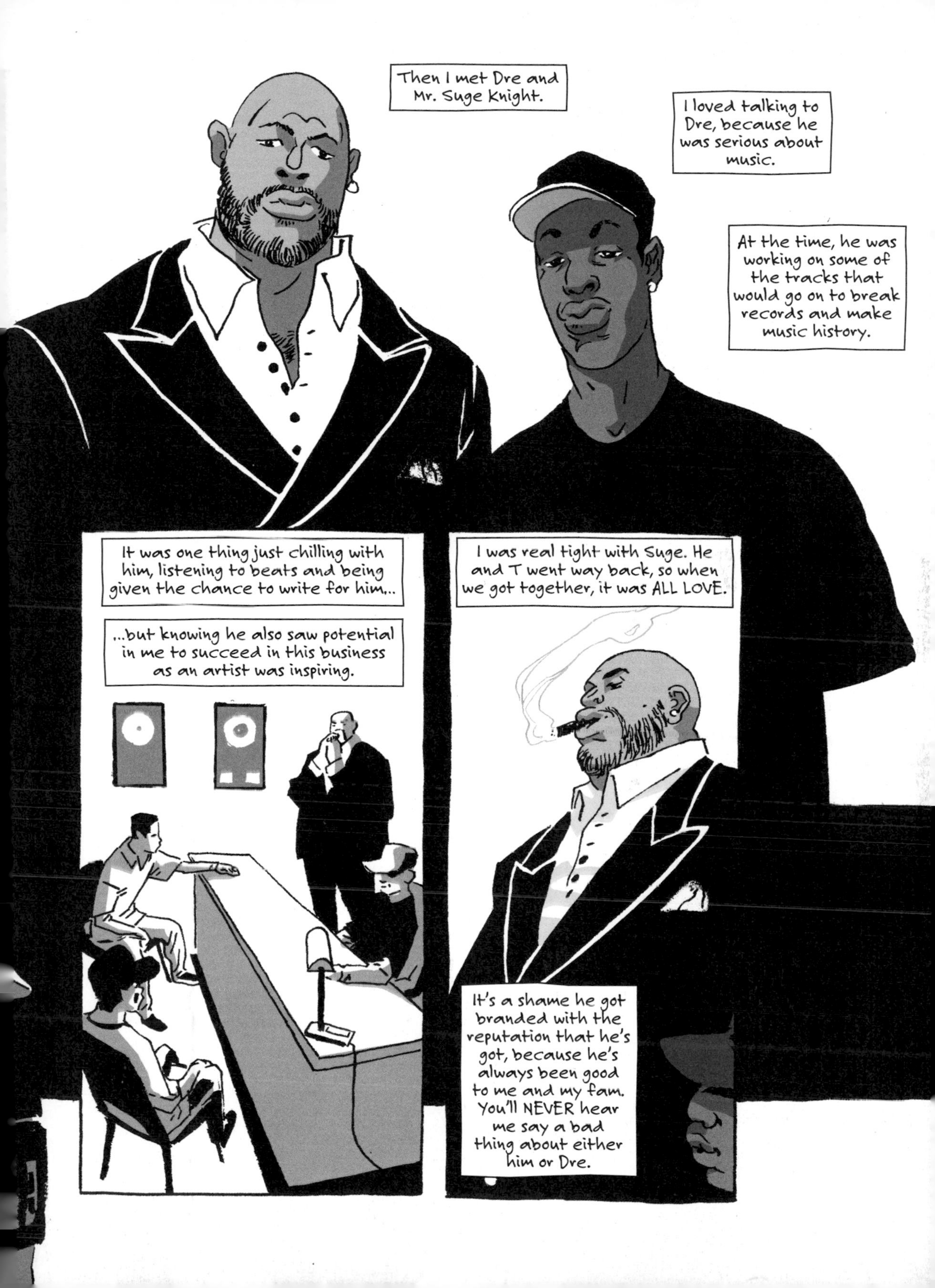
Then I met Dre and Mr. Suge Knight.
I loved talking to Dre, because he was serious about music.
At the time, he was working on some of the tracks that would go on to break records and make music history.
It was one thing just chilling with him, listening to beats and being given the chance to write for him...
...but knowing he also saw potential in me to succeed in this business as an artist was inspiring.
I was real tight with Suge. He and T went way back, so when we got together, it was ALL LOVE.
It's a shame he got branded with the reputation that he's got, because he's always been good to me and my fam. You'll NEVER hear me say a bad thing about either him or Dre.

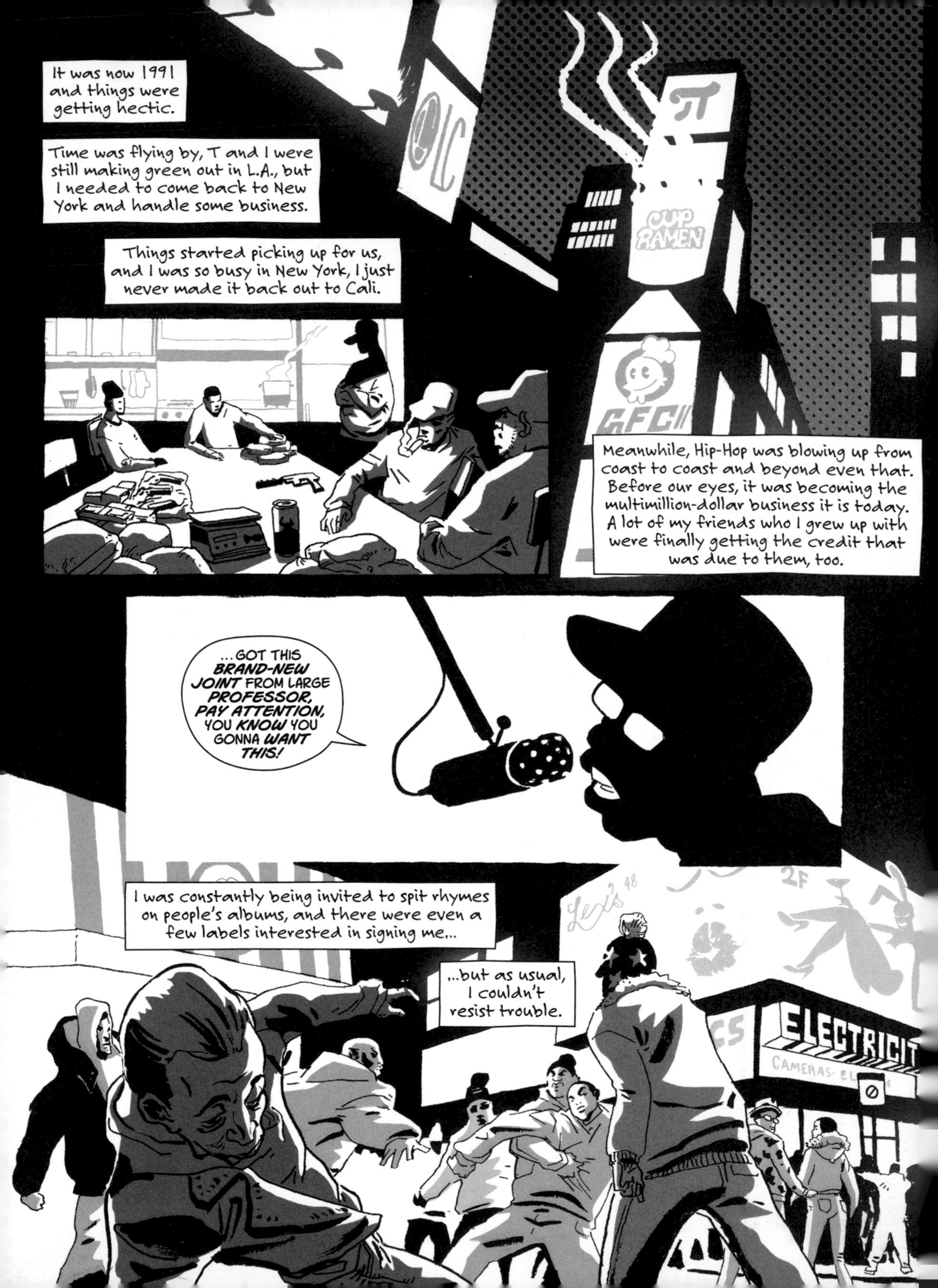
It was now 1991 and things were getting hectic.
Time was flying by, T and I were still making green out in L.A., but I needed to come back to New York and handle some business.
Things started picking up for us, and I was so busy in New York, I just never made it back out to Cali.
CUP RAMEN
Meanwhile, Hip-Hop was blowing up from coast to coast and beyond even that. Before our eyes, it was becoming the multimillion-dollar business it is today. A lot of my friends who I grew up with were finally getting the credit that was due to them, too.
...GOT THIS BRAND-NEW JOINT FROM LARGE PROFESSOR, PAY ATTENTION, YOU KNOW YOU GONNA WANT THIS!
I was constantly being invited to spit rhymes on people's albums, and there were even a few labels interested in signing me...
...but as usual, I couldn't resist trouble.
ELECTRICIT
CAMERAS

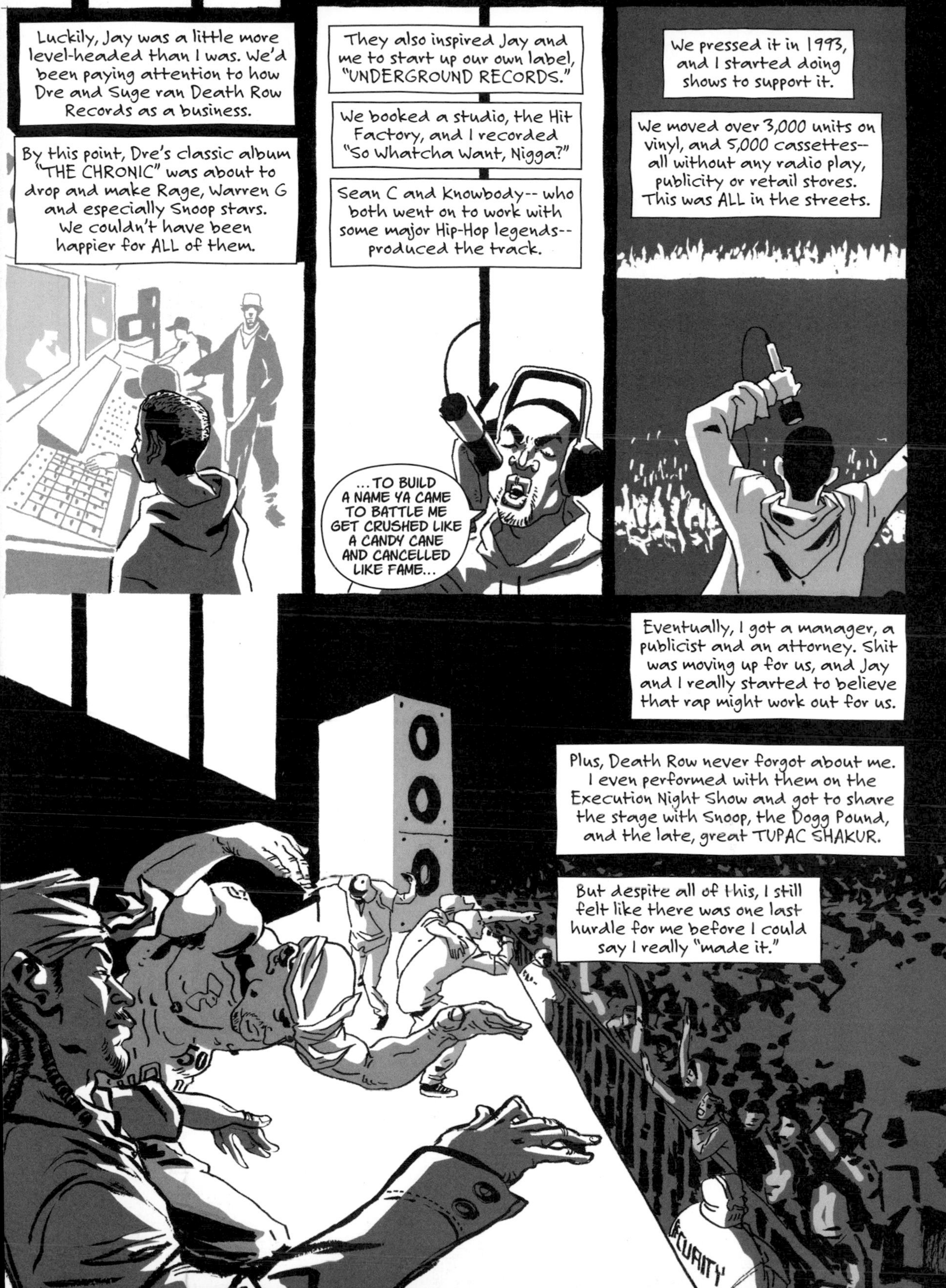
Luckily, Jay was a little more level-headed than I was. We'd been paying attention to how Dre and Suge ran Death Row Records as a business.
By this point, Dre's classic album "THE CHRONIC" was about to drop and make Rage, Warren G and especially Snoop stars. We couldn't have been happier for ALL of them.
They also inspired Jay and me to start up our own label, "UNDERGROUND RECORDS."
We booked a studio, the Hit Factory, and I recorded "So Whatcha Want, Nigga?"
Sean C and Knowbody-- who both went on to work with some major Hip-Hop legends-- produced the track.
...TO BUILD A NAME YA CAME TO BATTLE ME GET CRUSHED LIKE A CANDY CANE AND CANCELLED LIKE FAME...
We pressed it in 1993, and I started doing shows to support it.
We moved over 3,000 units on vinyl, and 5,000 cassettes-- all without any radio play, publicity or retail stores. This was ALL in the streets.
Eventually, I got a manager, a publicist and an attorney. Shit was moving up for us, and Jay and I really started to believe that rap might work out for us.
Plus, Death Row never forgot about me. I even performed with them on the Execution Night Show and got to share the stage with Snoop, the Dogg Pound, and the late, great TUPAC SHAKUR.
But despite all of this, I still felt like there was one last hurdle for me before I could say I really "made it."

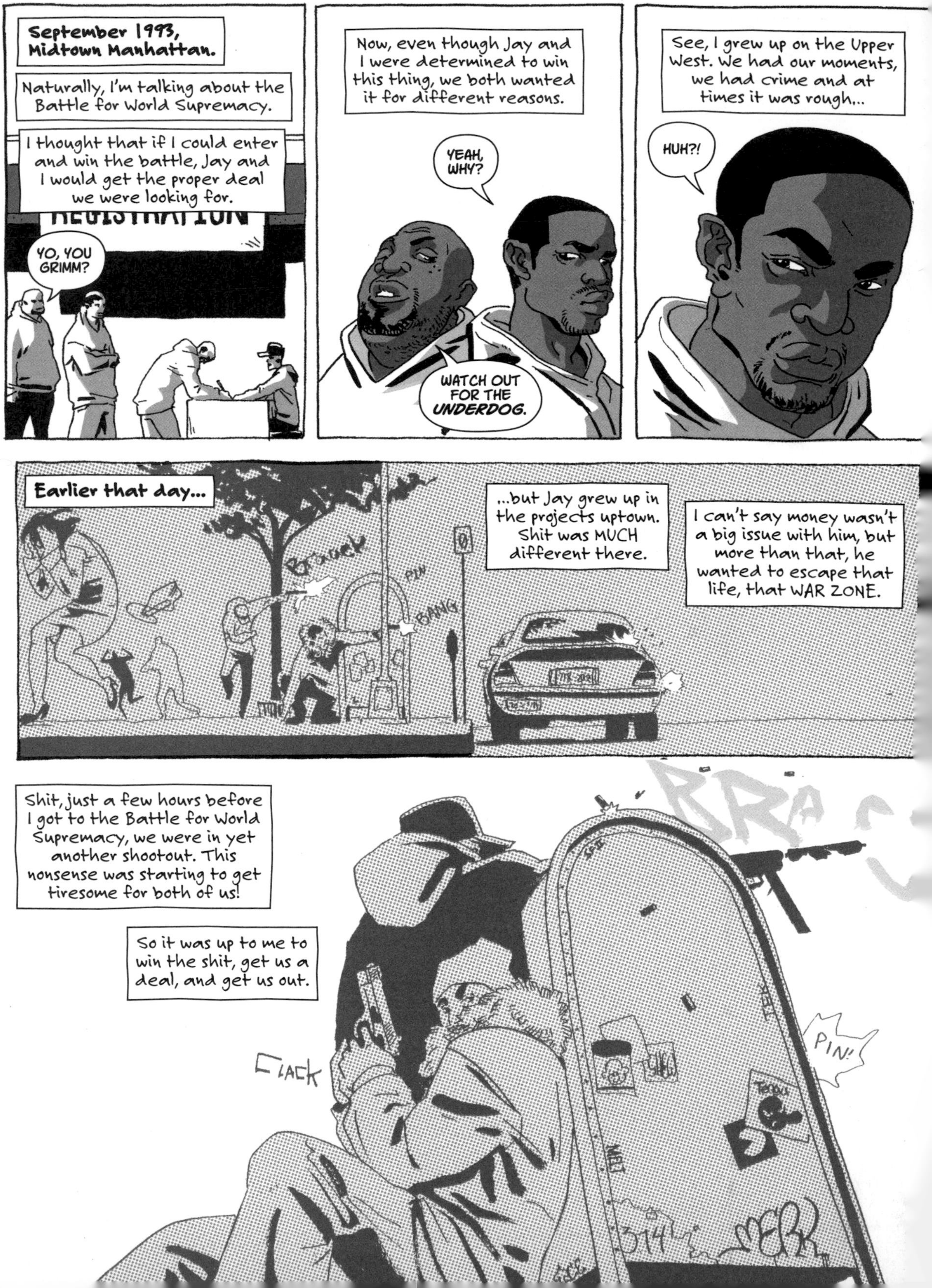
September 1993, Midtown Manhattan.
Naturally, I'm talking about the Battle for World Supremacy.
I thought that if I could enter and win the battle, Jay and I would get the proper deal we were looking for.
YO, YOU GRIMM?
Now, even though Jay and I were determined to win this thing, we both wanted it for different reasons.
YEAH, WHY?
WATCH OUT FOR THE UNDERDOG.
See, I grew up on the Upper West. We had our moments, we had crime and at times it was rough...
HUH?!
Earlier that day...
...but Jay grew up in the projects uptown. Shit was MUCH different there.
I can't say money wasn't a big issue with him, but more than that, he wanted to escape that life, that WAR ZONE.
PIN
BANG
Shit, just a few hours before I got to the Battle for World Supremacy, we were in yet another shootout. This nonsense was starting to get tiresome for both of us!
So it was up to me to win the shit, get us a deal, and get us out.
CLACK
PIN!

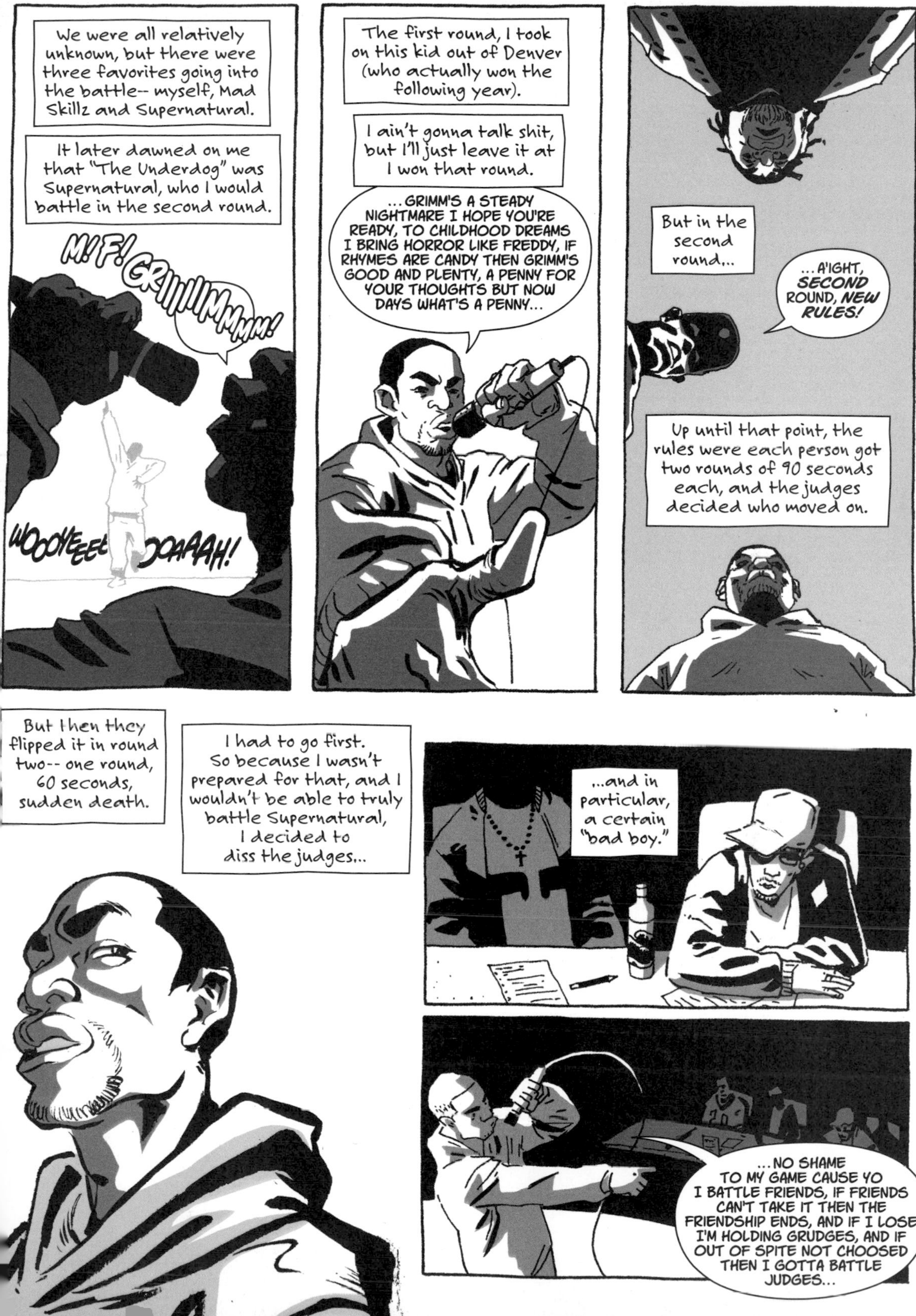
We were all relatively unknown, but there were three favorites going into the battle-- myself, Mad Skillz and Supernatural.
It later dawned on me that "The Underdog" was Supernatural, who I would battle in the second round.
M! F! GRIIIIIMMMM!
WOOOYEEE! OOAAAH!
The first round, I took on this kid out of Denver (who actually won the following year).
I ain't gonna talk shit, but I'll just leave it at I won that round.
...GRIMM'S A STEADY NIGHTMARE I HOPE YOU'RE READY, TO CHILDHOOD DREAMS I BRING HORROR LIKE FREDDY, IF RHYMES ARE CANDY THEN GRIMM'S GOOD AND PLENTY, A PENNY FOR YOUR THOUGHTS BUT NOW DAYS WHAT'S A PENNY...
But in the second round,...
...A'IGHT, SECOND ROUND, NEW RULES!
Up until that point, the rules were each person got two rounds of 90 seconds each, and the judges decided who moved on.
But then they flipped it in round two-- one round, 60 seconds, sudden death.
I had to go first. So because I wasn't prepared for that, and I wouldn't be able to truly battle Supernatural, I decided to diss the judges...
...and in particular, a certain "bad boy."
...NO SHAME TO MY GAME CAUSE YO I BATTLE FRIENDS, IF FRIENDS CAN'T TAKE IT THEN THE FRIENDSHIP ENDS, AND IF I LOSE I'M HOLDING GRUDGES, AND IF OUT OF SPITE NOT CHOOSED THEN I GOTTA BATTLE JUDGES...

Losing the Battle for World Supremacy was one of the WORST feelings I've ever felt.

Going in, I had so much hope. Like everything was gonna change for the better.

Supernatural and Mad Skillz would battle each other in the final round, and it would go down in history as one of the greatest battles ever.

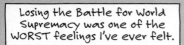

THE WINNER... SUPER! NATURAL! GIVE IT UP, YA'LL!

AAAAHYEAAAWOOOOOOO

Supernatural won that year and went on to great success. He deserves everything he got in life.

My fam tried to make me feel better about the loss and coming in third over all, but deep down, all I could think of was, "Oh well, back to shoot-outs, back to running from the cops, back to worrying about who you can trust...

"...back to the streets. Back to square one."

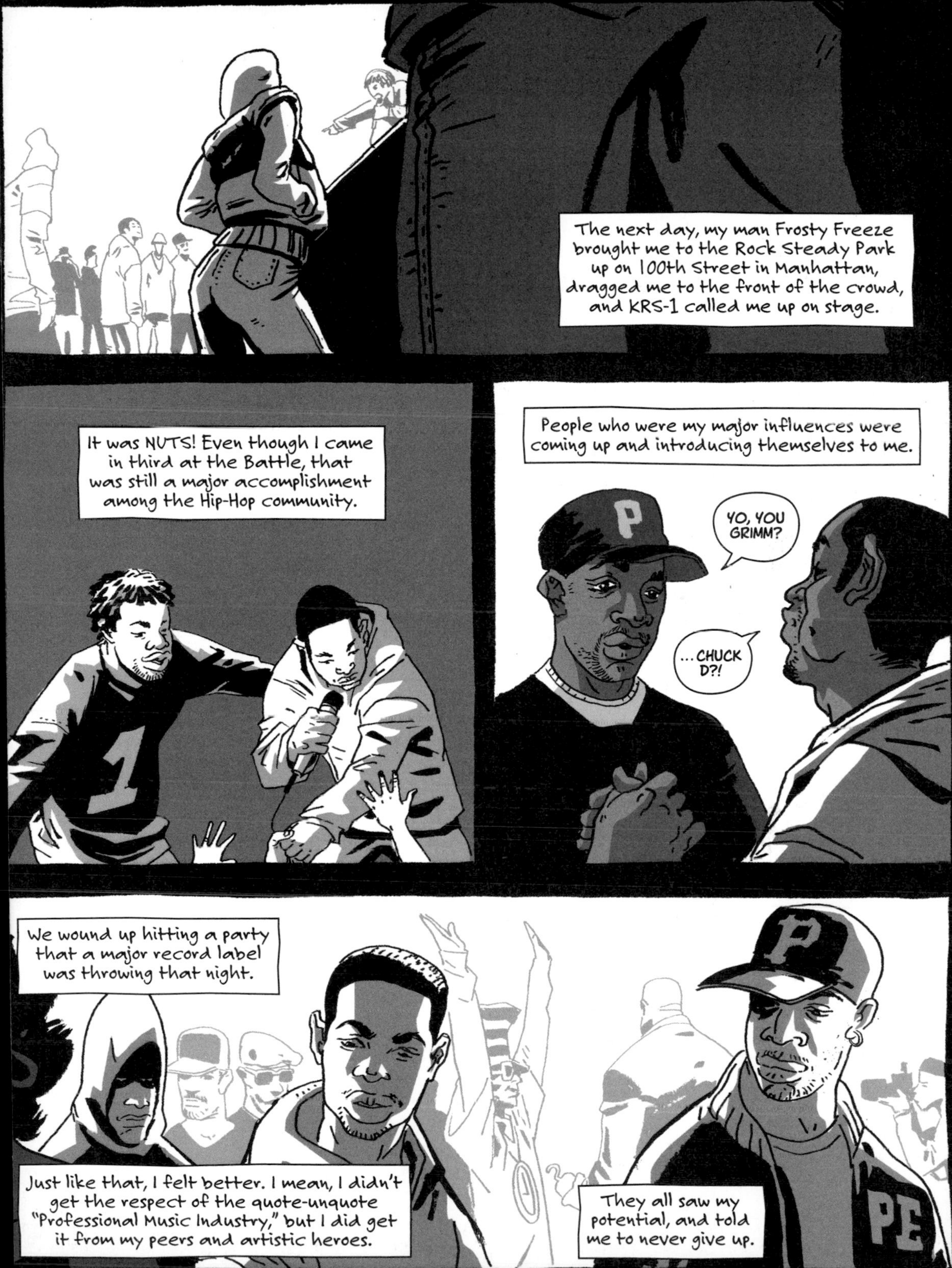

The next day, my man Frosty Freeze brought me to the Rock Steady Park up on 100th Street in Manhattan, dragged me to the front of the crowd, and KRS-1 called me up on stage.
It was NUTS! Even though I came in third at the Battle, that was still a major accomplishment among the Hip-Hop community.
1
People who were my major influences were coming up and introducing themselves to me.
P
YO, YOU GRIMM?
...CHUCK D?!
We wound up hitting a party that a major record label was throwing that night.
P
Just like that, I felt better. I mean, I didn't get the respect of the quote-unquote "Professional Music Industry," but I did get it from my peers and artistic heroes.
They all saw my potential, and told me to never give up.
PE

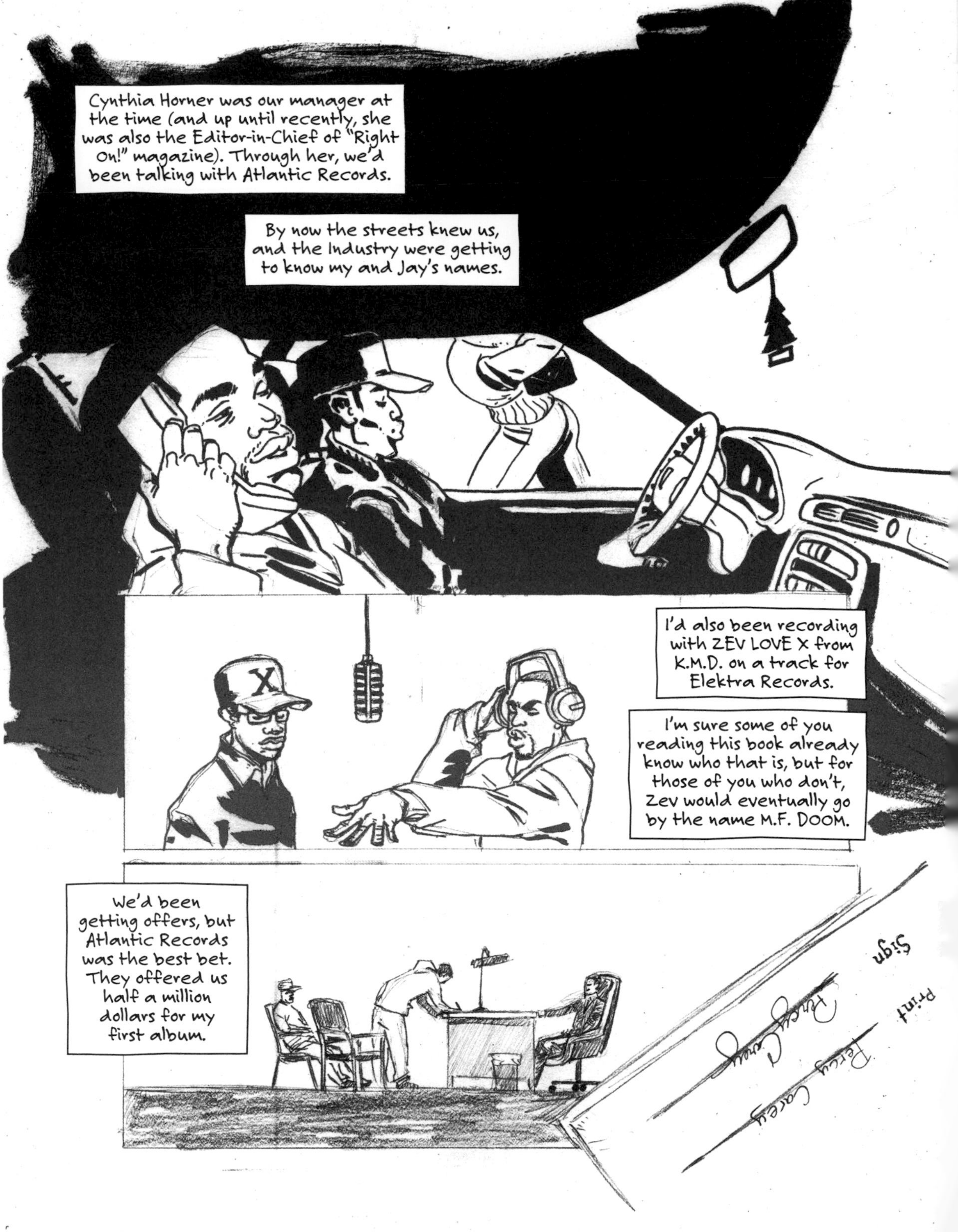
Cynthia Horner was our manager at the time (and up until recently, she was also the Editor-in-Chief of "Right On!" magazine). Through her, we'd been talking with Atlantic Records.
By now the streets knew us, and the Industry were getting to know my and Jay's names.
I'd also been recording with ZEV LOVE X from K.M.D. on a track for Elektra Records.
I'm sure some of you reading this book already know who that is, but for those of you who don't, Zev would eventually go by the name M.F. DOOM.
We'd been getting offers, but Atlantic Records was the best bet. They offered us half a million dollars for my first album.
Sign
Print
Percy Carey

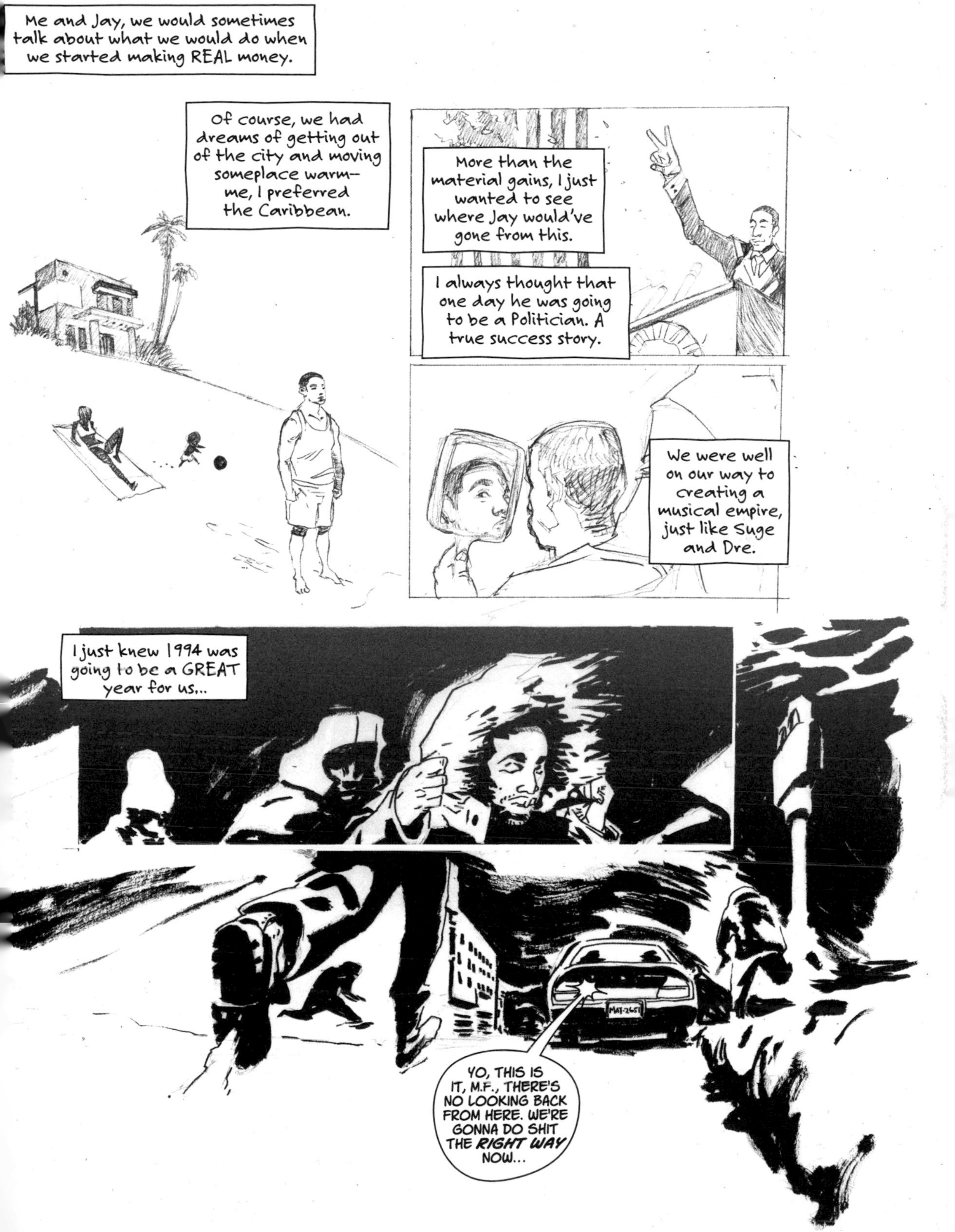
Me and Jay, we would sometimes talk about what we would do when we started making REAL money.
Of course, we had dreams of getting out of the city and moving someplace warm-- me, I preferred the Caribbean.
More than the material gains, I just wanted to see where Jay would've gone from this.
I always thought that one day he was going to be a Politician. A true success story.
We were well on our way to creating a musical empire, just like Suge and Dre.
I just knew 1994 was going to be a GREAT year for us...
MAT-265
YO, THIS IS IT, M.F., THERE'S NO LOOKING BACK FROM HERE. WE'RE GONNA DO SHIT THE *RIGHT WAY* NOW...

INTERMISSION

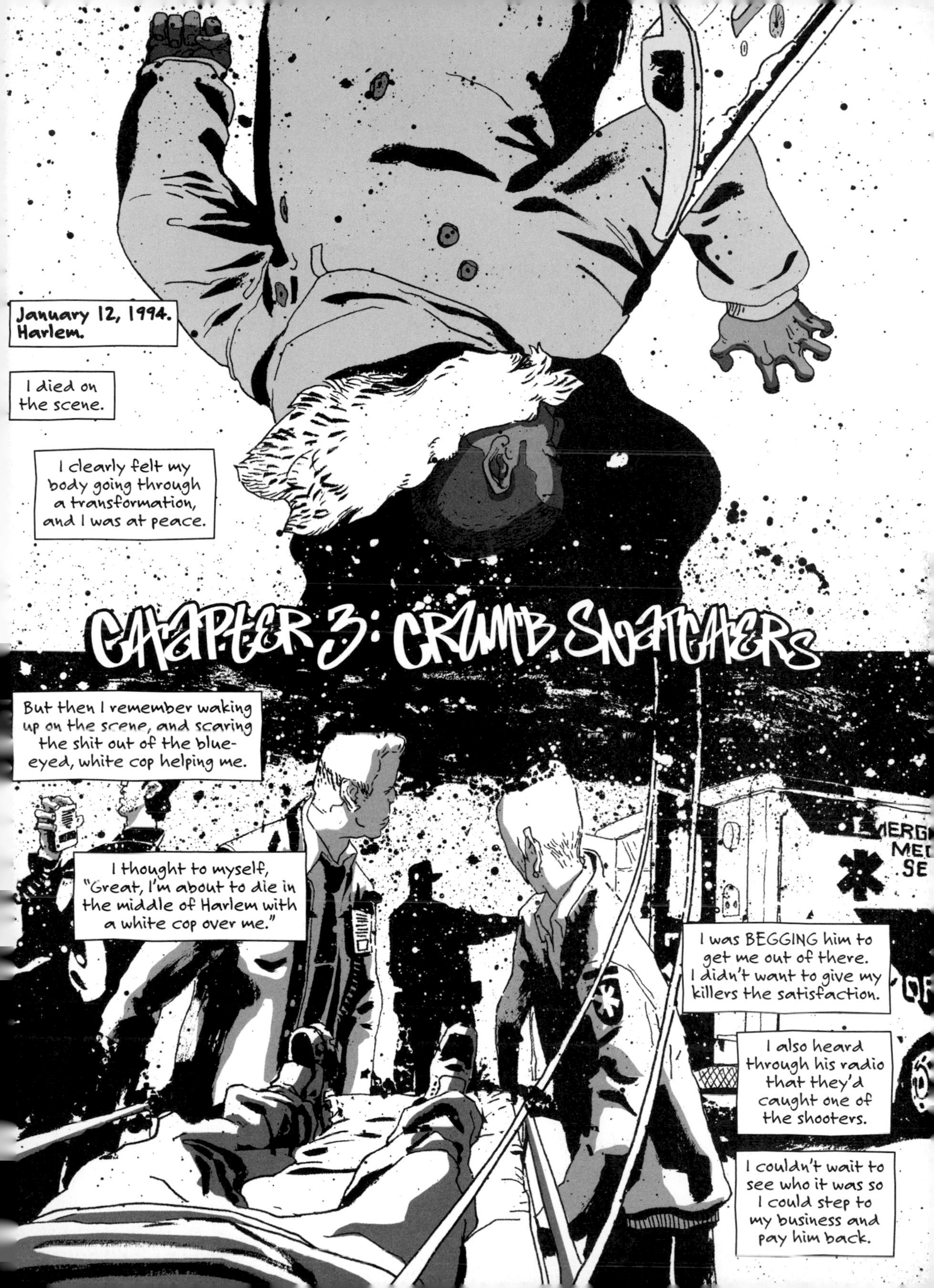
January 12, 1994. Harlem.
I died on the scene.
I clearly felt my body going through a transformation, and I was at peace.
CHAPTER 3: CRUMB SNATCHERS
But then I remember waking up on the scene, and scaring the shit out of the blue-eyed, white cop helping me.
I thought to myself, "Great, I'm about to die in the middle of Harlem with a white cop over me."
I was BEGGING him to get me out of there. I didn't want to give my killers the satisfaction.
I also heard through his radio that they'd caught one of the shooters.
I couldn't wait to see who it was so I could step to my business and pay him back.

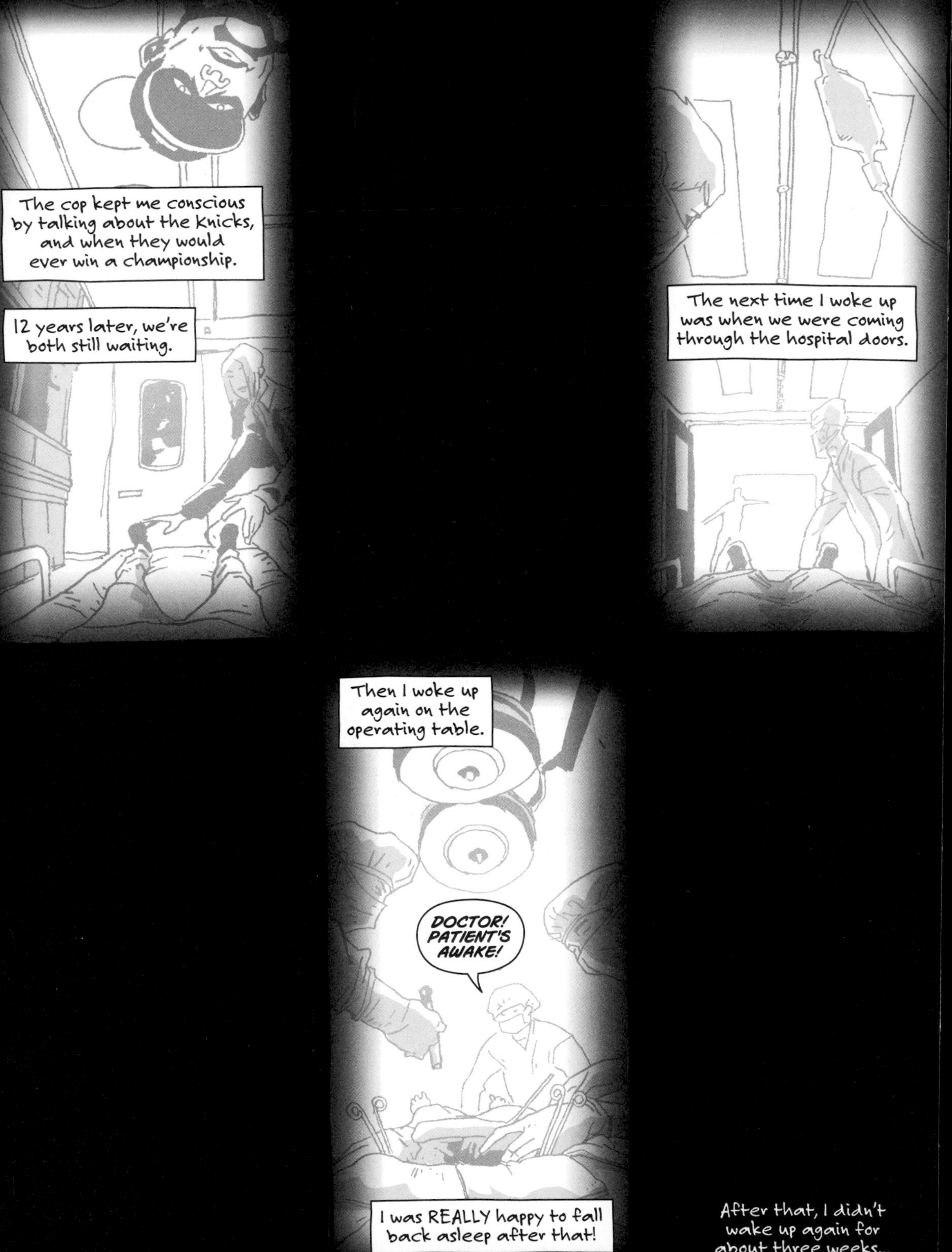
The cop kept me conscious by talking about the Knicks, and when they would ever win a championship.
12 years later, we're both still waiting.
The next time I woke up was when we were coming through the hospital doors.
Then I woke up again on the operating table.
DOCTOR! PATIENT'S AWAKE!
I was REALLY happy to fall back asleep after that!
After that, I didn't wake up again for

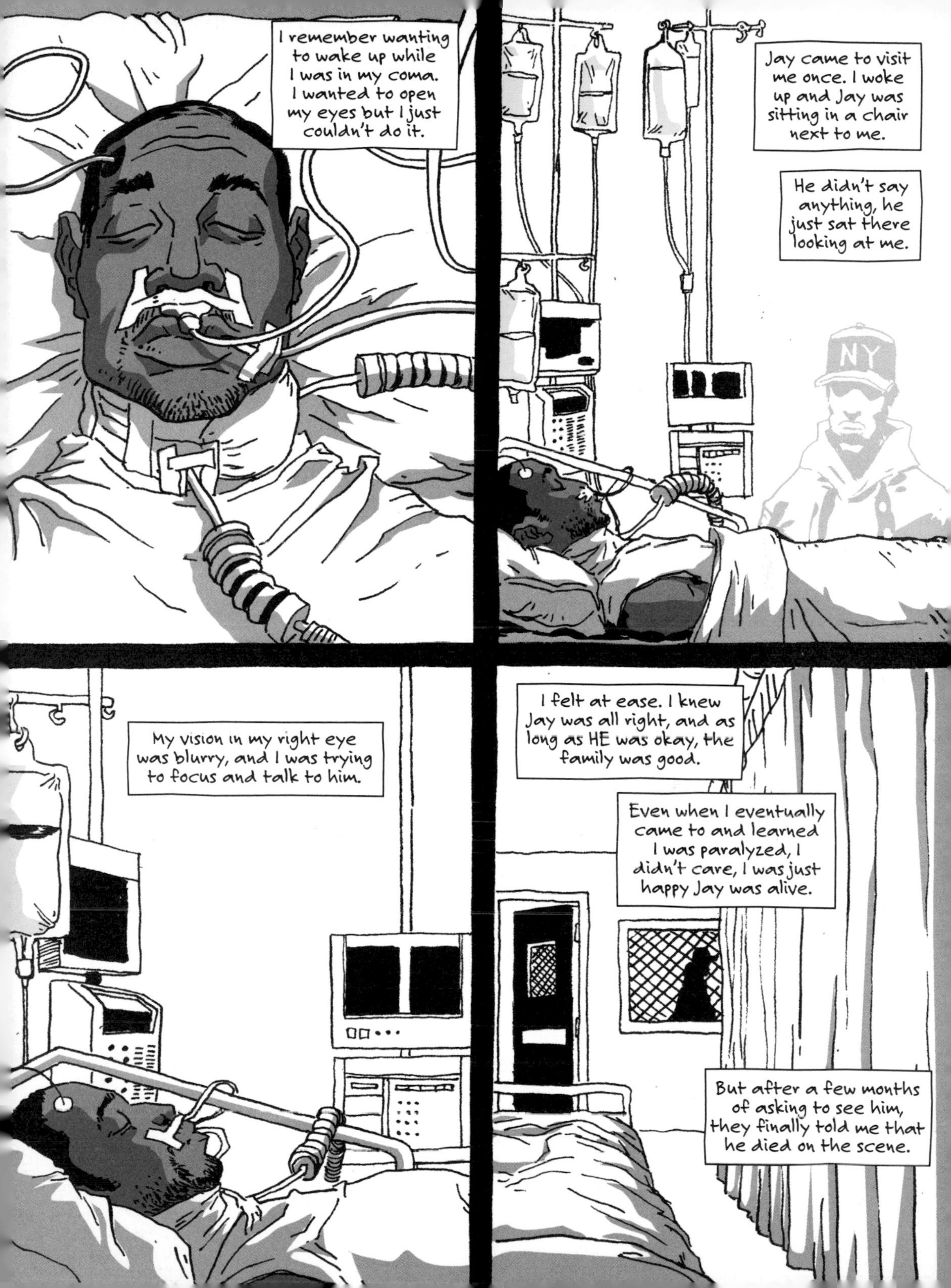
I remember wanting to wake up while I was in my coma. I wanted to open my eyes but I just couldn't do it.
Jay came to visit me once. I woke up and Jay was sitting in a chair next to me.
He didn't say anything, he just sat there looking at me.
NY
My vision in my right eye was blurry, and I was trying to focus and talk to him.
I felt at ease. I knew Jay was all right, and as long as HE was okay, the family was good.
Even when I eventually came to and learned I was paralyzed, I didn't care, I was just happy Jay was alive.
But after a few months of asking to see him, they finally told me that he died on the scene.

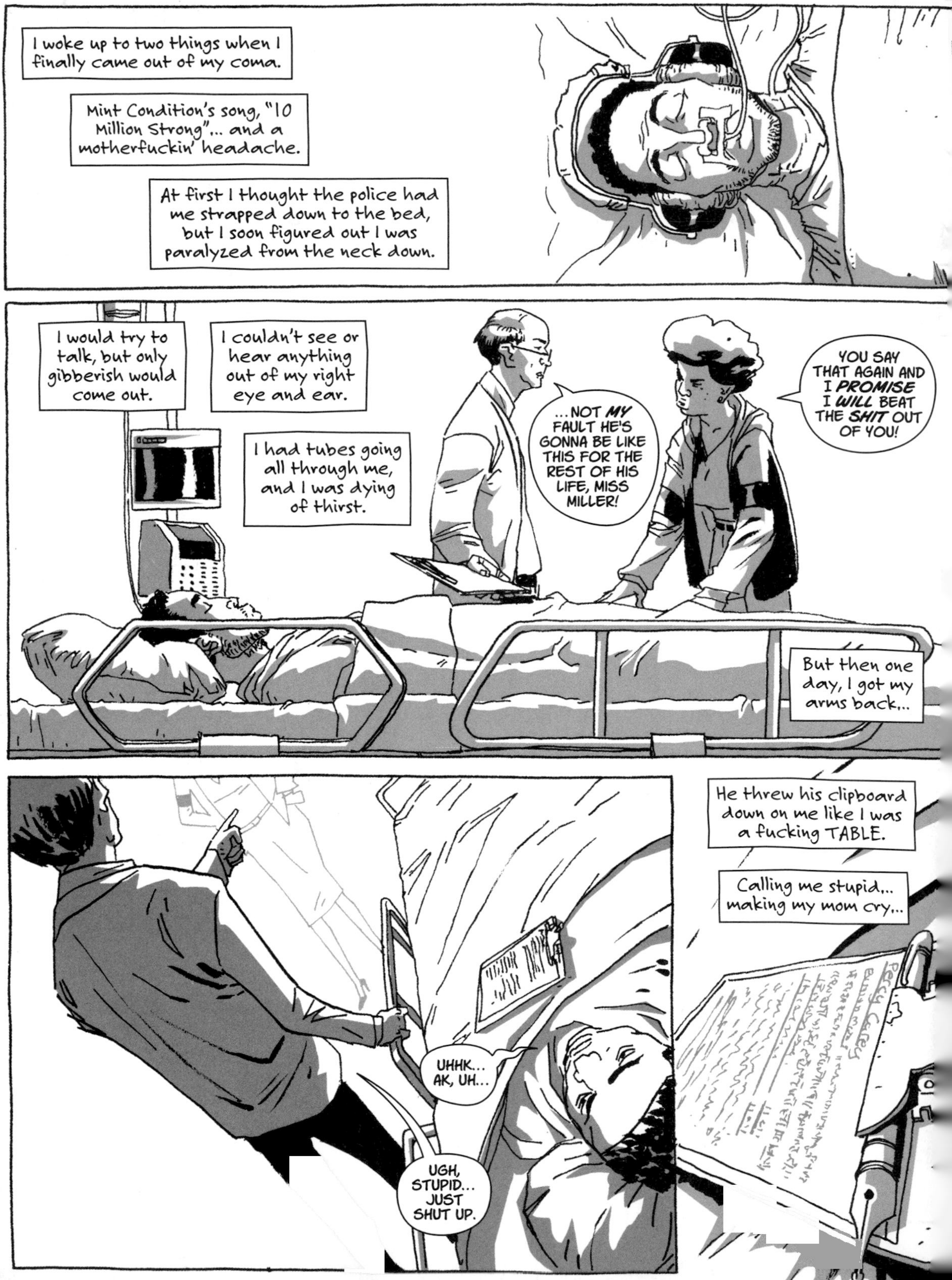
I woke up to two things when I finally came out of my coma.
Mint Condition's song, "10 Million Strong"... and a motherfuckin' headache.
At first I thought the police had me strapped down to the bed, but I soon figured out I was paralyzed from the neck down.
I would try to talk, but only gibberish would come out.
I couldn't see or hear anything out of my right eye and ear.
I had tubes going all through me, and I was dying of thirst.
...NOT MY FAULT HE'S GONNA BE LIKE THIS FOR THE REST OF HIS LIFE, MISS MILLER!
YOU SAY THAT AGAIN AND I PROMISE I WILL BEAT THE SHIT OUT OF YOU!
But then one day, I got my arms back...
He threw his clipboard down on me like I was a fucking TABLE.
Calling me stupid... making my mom cry...
UHHK... AK, UH...
UGH, STUPID... JUST SHUT UP.

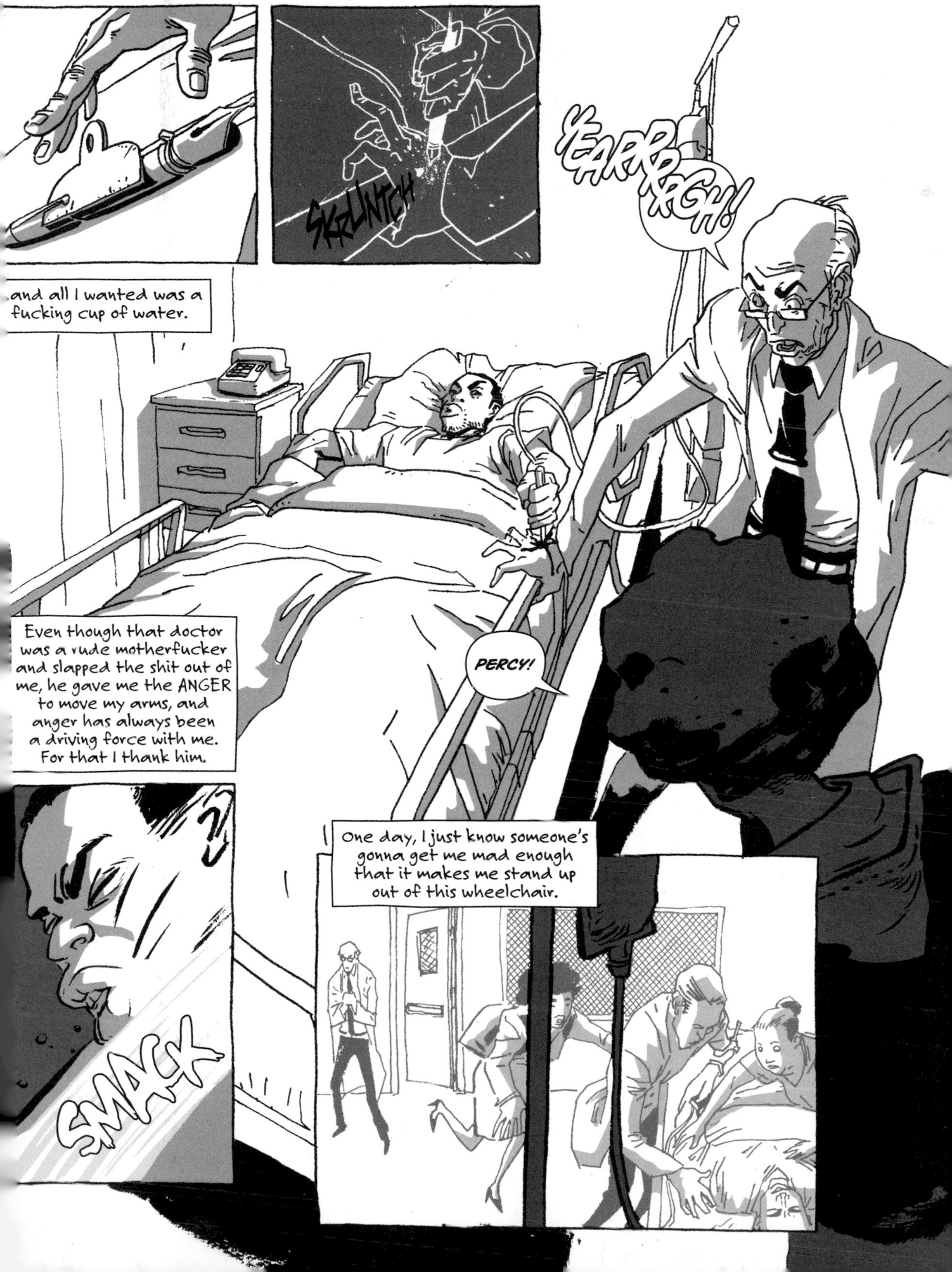

SKRUNTCH
YEARRRRGH!
...and all I wanted was a fucking cup of water.
Even though that doctor was a rude motherfucker and slapped the shit out of me, he gave me the ANGER to move my arms, and anger has always been a driving force with me. For that I thank him.
PERCY!
SMACK
One day, I just know someone's gonna get me mad enough that it makes me stand up out of this wheelchair.

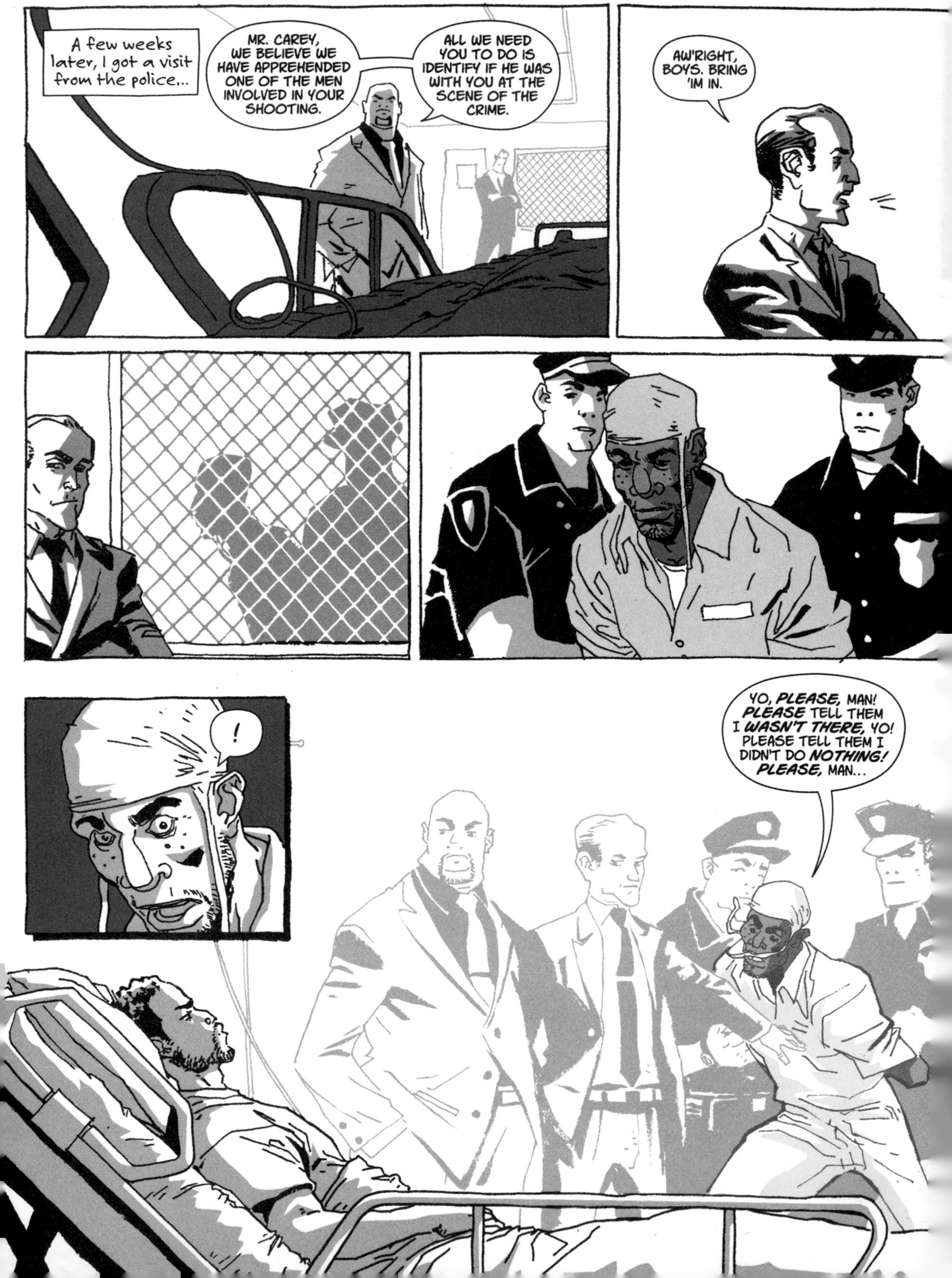
A few weeks later, I got a visit from the police...
MR. CAREY, WE BELIEVE WE HAVE APPREHENDED ONE OF THE MEN INVOLVED IN YOUR SHOOTING.
ALL WE NEED YOU TO DO IS IDENTIFY IF HE WAS WITH YOU AT THE SCENE OF THE CRIME.
AW'RIGHT, BOYS. BRING 'IM IN.
!
YO, *PLEASE,* MAN! *PLEASE* TELL THEM I *WASN'T THERE,* YO! PLEASE TELL THEM I DIDN'T DO *NOTHING! PLEASE,* MAN...

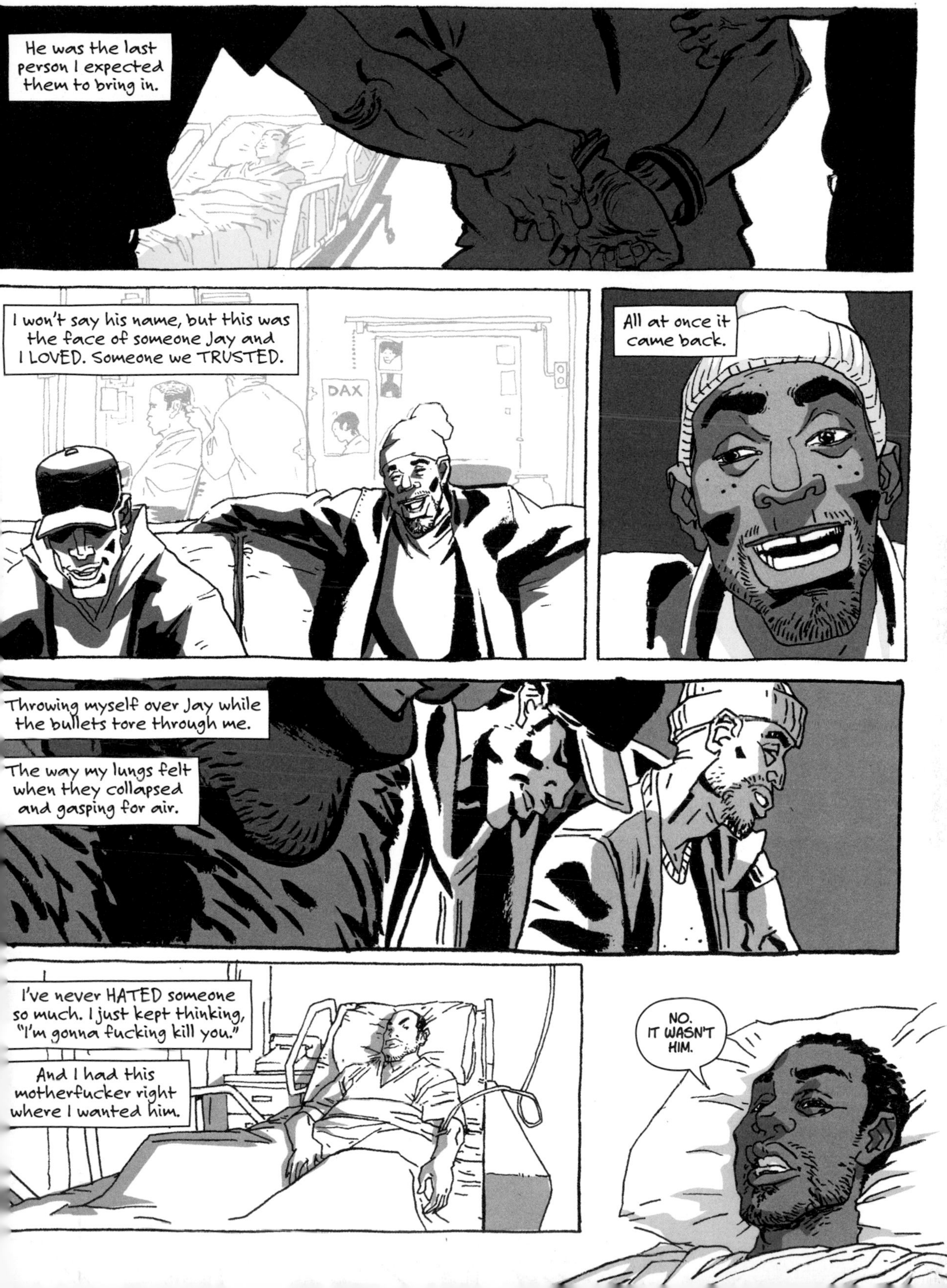
He was the last person I expected them to bring in.
I won't say his name, but this was the face of someone Jay and I LOVED. Someone we TRUSTED.
DAX
All at once it came back.
Throwing myself over Jay while the bullets tore through me.
The way my lungs felt when they collapsed and gasping for air.
I've never HATED someone so much. I just kept thinking, "I'm gonna fucking kill you."
And I had this motherfucker right where I wanted him.
NO. IT WASN'T HIM.

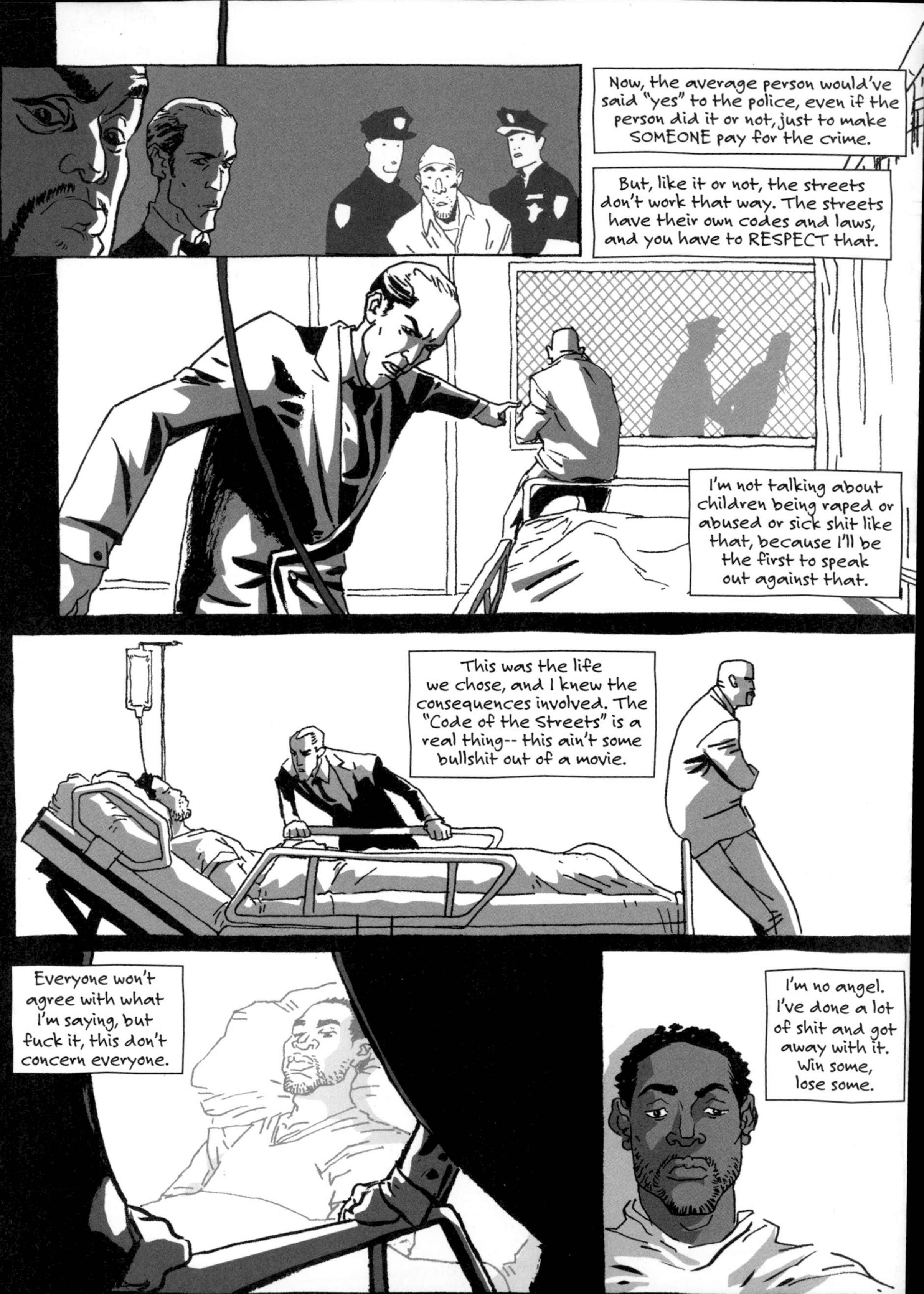
Now, the average person would've said "yes" to the police, even if the person did it or not, just to make SOMEONE pay for the crime.
But, like it or not, the streets don't work that way. The streets have their own codes and laws, and you have to RESPECT that.
I'm not talking about children being raped or abused or sick shit like that, because I'll be the first to speak out against that.
This was the life we chose, and I knew the consequences involved. The "Code of the Streets" is a real thing-- this ain't some bullshit out of a movie.
Everyone won't agree with what I'm saying, but fuck it, this don't concern everyone.
I'm no angel. I've done a lot of shit and got away with it. Win some, lose some.

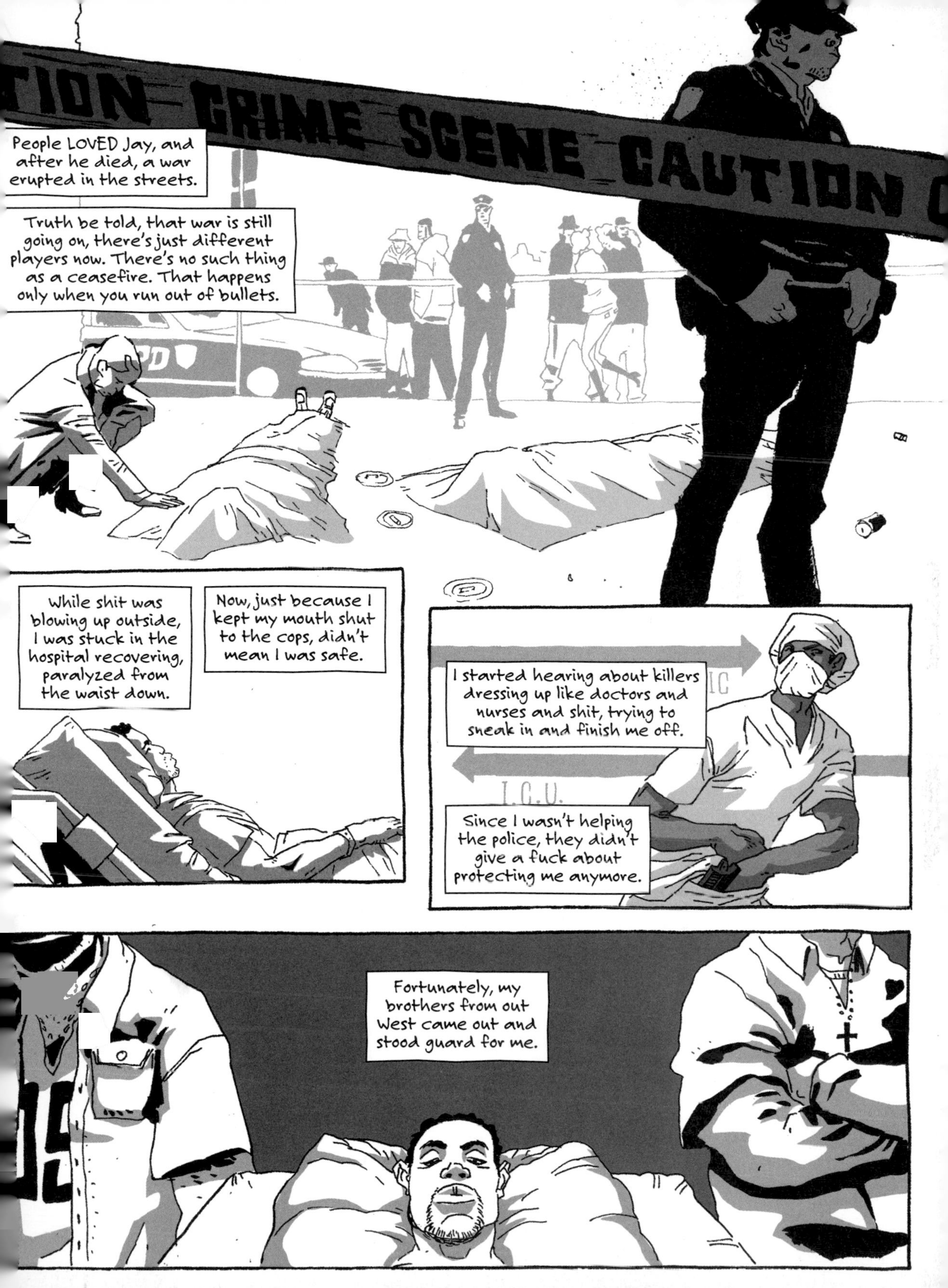
CRIME SCENE CAUTION
People LOVED Jay, and after he died, a war erupted in the streets.
Truth be told, that war is still going on, there's just different players now. There's no such thing as a ceasefire. That happens only when you run out of bullets.
While shit was blowing up outside, I was stuck in the hospital recovering, paralyzed from the waist down.
Now, just because I kept my mouth shut to the cops, didn't mean I was safe.
I started hearing about killers dressing up like doctors and nurses and shit, trying to sneak in and finish me off.
I.C.U.
Since I wasn't helping the police, they didn't give a fuck about protecting me anymore.
Fortunately, my brothers from out West came out and stood guard for me.

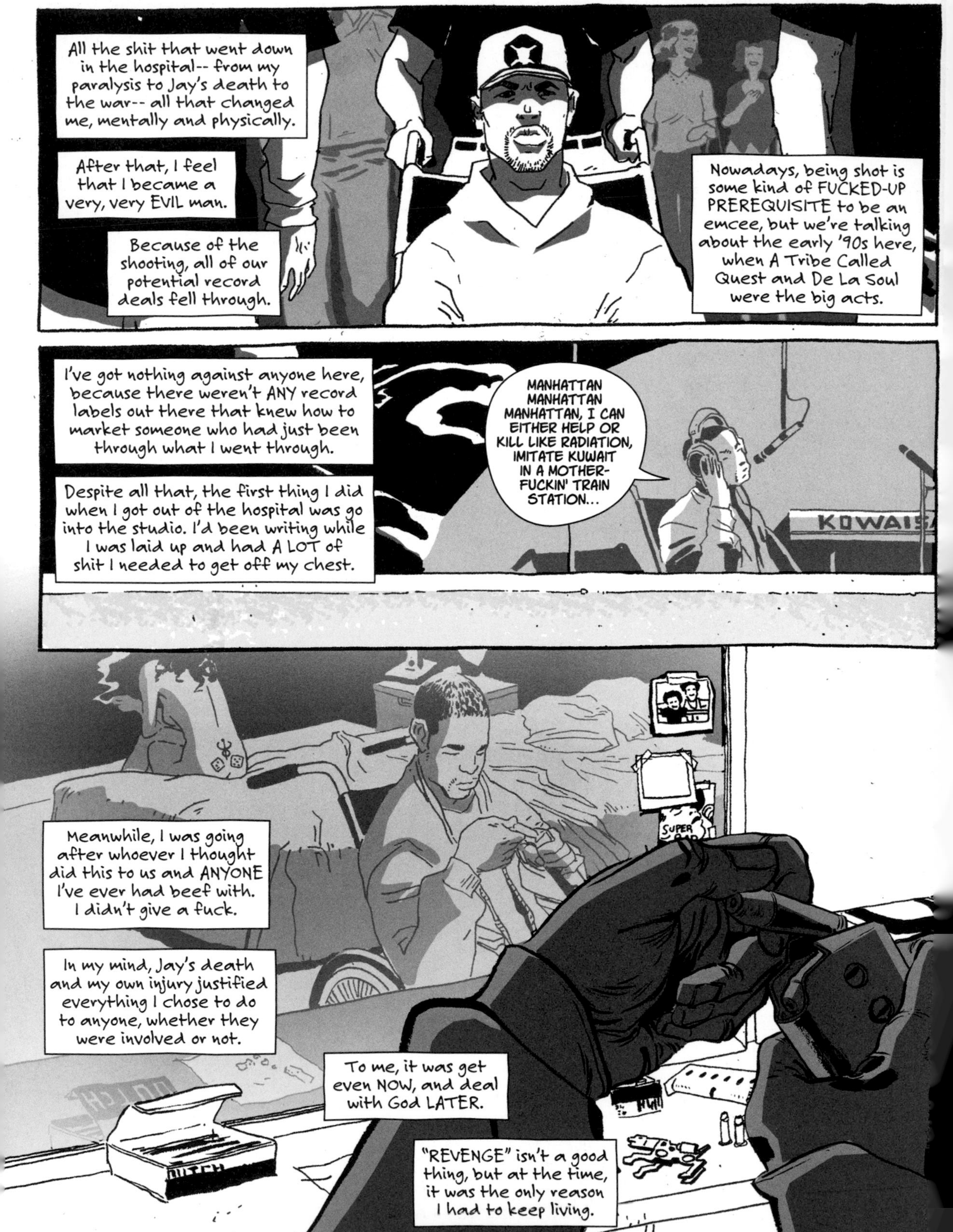

All the shit that went down in the hospital-- from my paralysis to Jay's death to the war-- all that changed me, mentally and physically.
After that, I feel that I became a very, very EVIL man.
Because of the shooting, all of our potential record deals fell through.
Nowadays, being shot is some kind of FUCKED-UP PREREQUISITE to be an emcee, but we're talking about the early '90s here, when A Tribe Called Quest and De La Soul were the big acts.
I've got nothing against anyone here, because there weren't ANY record labels out there that knew how to market someone who had just been through what I went through.
Despite all that, the first thing I did when I got out of the hospital was go into the studio. I'd been writing while I was laid up and had A LOT of shit I needed to get off my chest.
MANHATTAN MANHATTAN MANHATTAN, I CAN EITHER HELP OR KILL LIKE RADIATION, IMITATE KUWAIT IN A MOTHER-FUCKIN' TRAIN STATION...
KOWAI
Meanwhile, I was going after whoever I thought did this to us and ANYONE I've ever had beef with. I didn't give a fuck.
In my mind, Jay's death and my own injury justified everything I chose to do to anyone, whether they were involved or not.
To me, it was get even NOW, and deal with God LATER.
"REVENGE" isn't a good thing, but at the time, it was the only reason I had to keep living.
SUPER
DUTCH

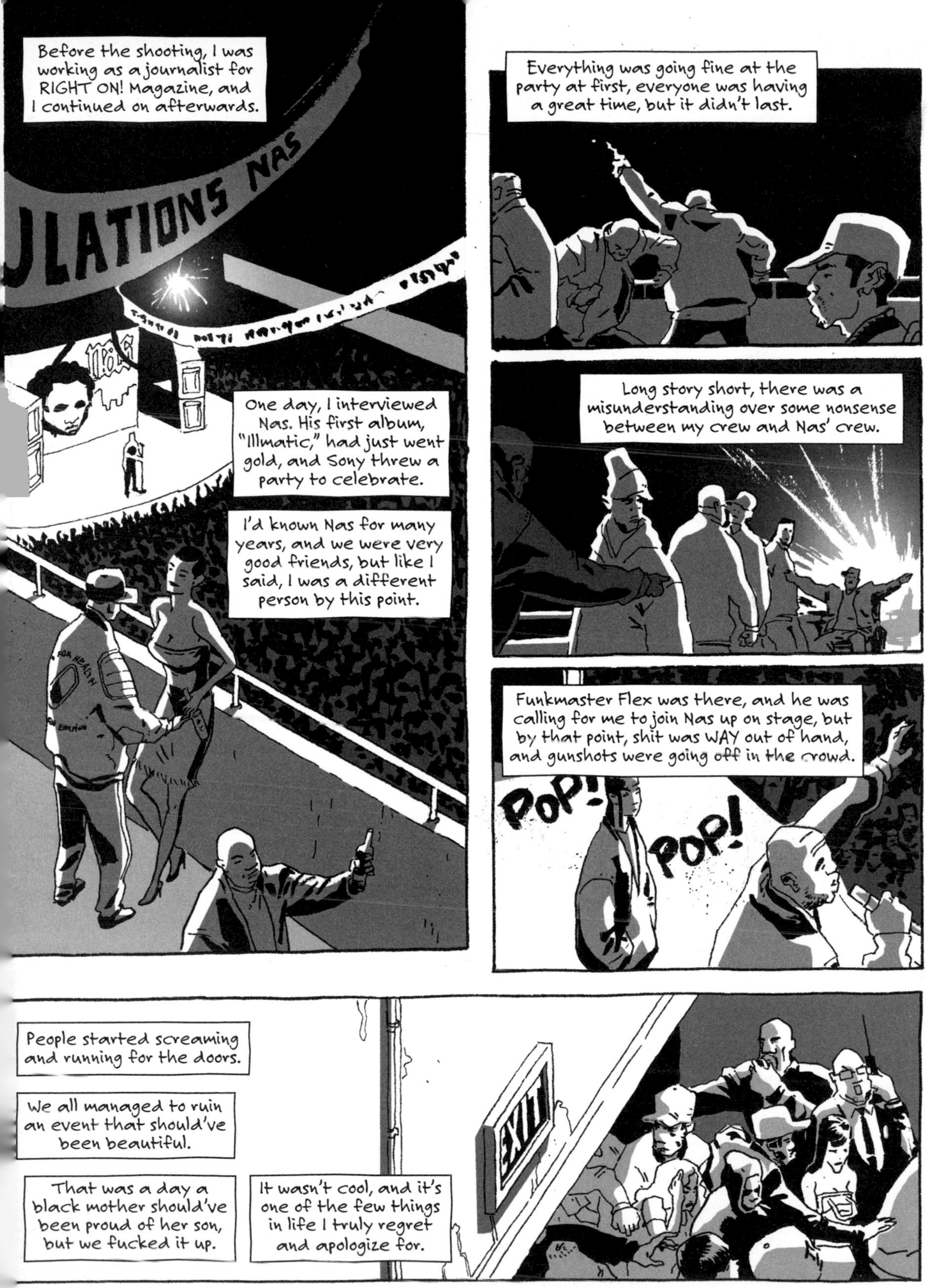

Before the shooting, I was working as a journalist for RIGHT ON! Magazine, and I continued on afterwards.
ULATIONS NAS
One day, I interviewed Nas. His first album, "Illmatic," had just went gold, and Sony threw a party to celebrate.
I'd known Nas for many years, and we were very good friends, but like I said, I was a different person by this point.
Everything was going fine at the party at first, everyone was having a great time, but it didn't last.
Long story short, there was a misunderstanding over some nonsense between my crew and Nas' crew.
Funkmaster Flex was there, and he was calling for me to join Nas up on stage, but by that point, shit was WAY out of hand, and gunshots were going off in the crowd.
POP!
POP!
People started screaming and running for the doors.
We all managed to ruin an event that should've been beautiful.
That was a day a black mother should've been proud of her son, but we fucked it up.
It wasn't cool, and it's one of the few things in life I truly regret and apologize for.
EXIT

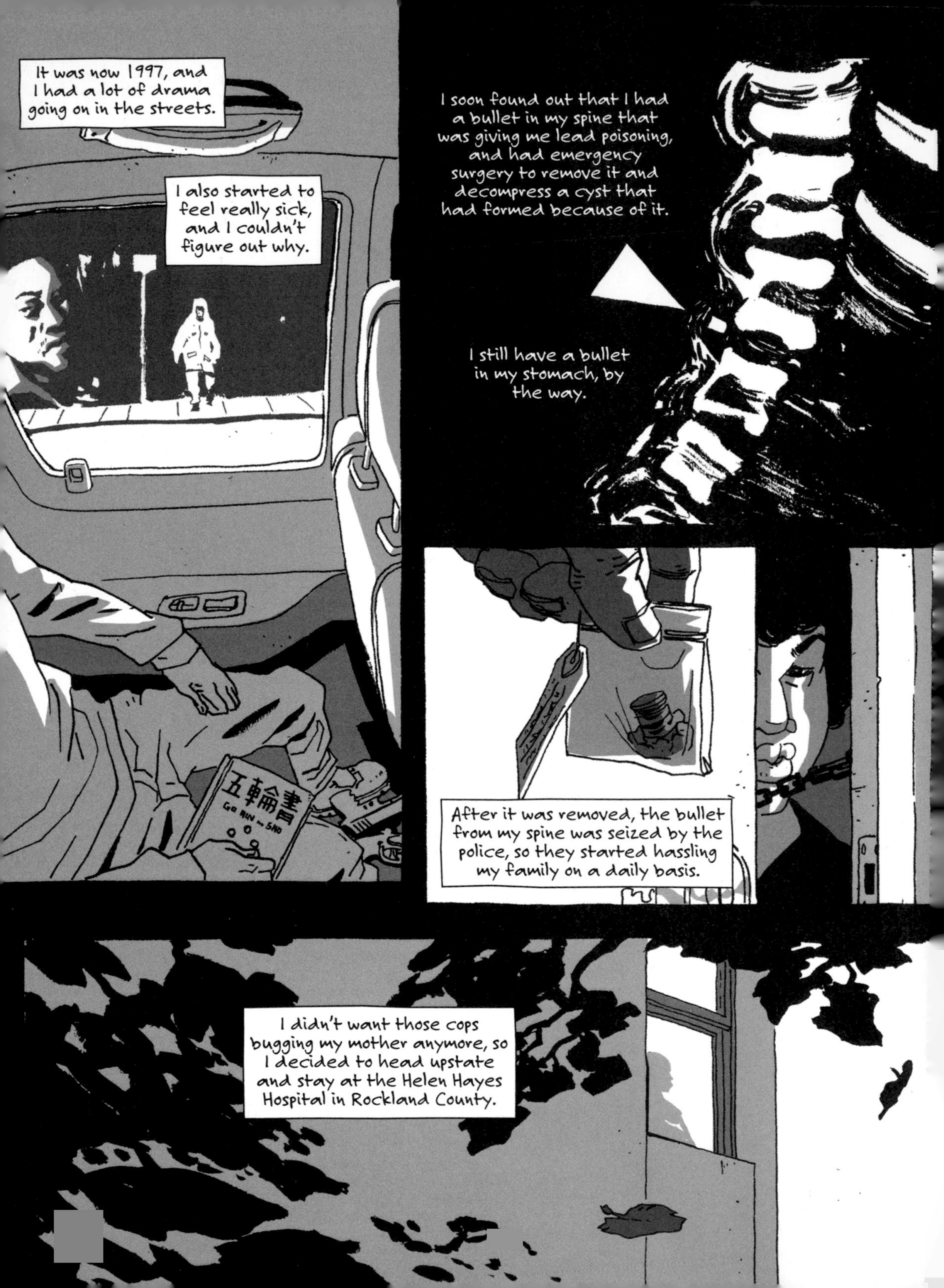
It was now 1997, and I had a lot of drama going on in the streets.
I also started to feel really sick, and I couldn't figure out why.
I soon found out that I had a bullet in my spine that was giving me lead poisoning, and had emergency surgery to remove it and decompress a cyst that had formed because of it.
I still have a bullet in my stomach, by the way.
After it was removed, the bullet from my spine was seized by the police, so they started hassling my family on a daily basis.
I didn't want those cops bugging my mother anymore, so I decided to head upstate and stay at the Helen Hayes Hospital in Rockland County.

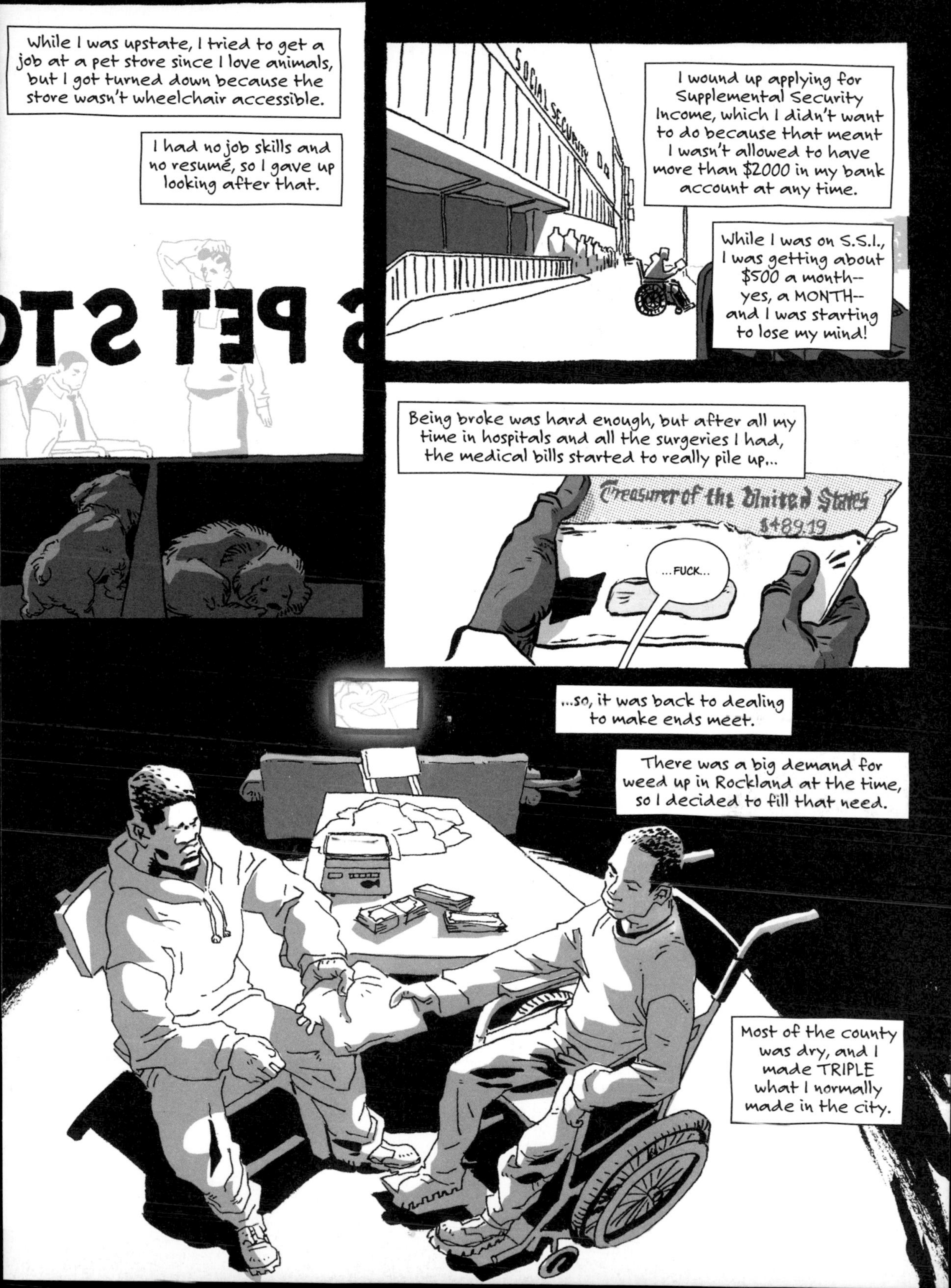

While I was upstate, I tried to get a job at a pet store since I love animals, but I got turned down because the store wasn't wheelchair accessible.
I had no job skills and no resumé, so I gave up looking after that.
PET STO
SOCIAL SECURITY
I wound up applying for Supplemental Security Income, which I didn't want to do because that meant I wasn't allowed to have more than $2000 in my bank account at any time.
While I was on S.S.I., I was getting about $500 a month-- yes, a MONTH-- and I was starting to lose my mind!
Being broke was hard enough, but after all my time in hospitals and all the surgeries I had, the medical bills started to really pile up...
Treasurer of the United States
$489.19
...FUCK...
...so, it was back to dealing to make ends meet.
There was a big demand for weed up in Rockland at the time, so I decided to fill that need.
Most of the county was dry, and I made TRIPLE what I normally made in the city.

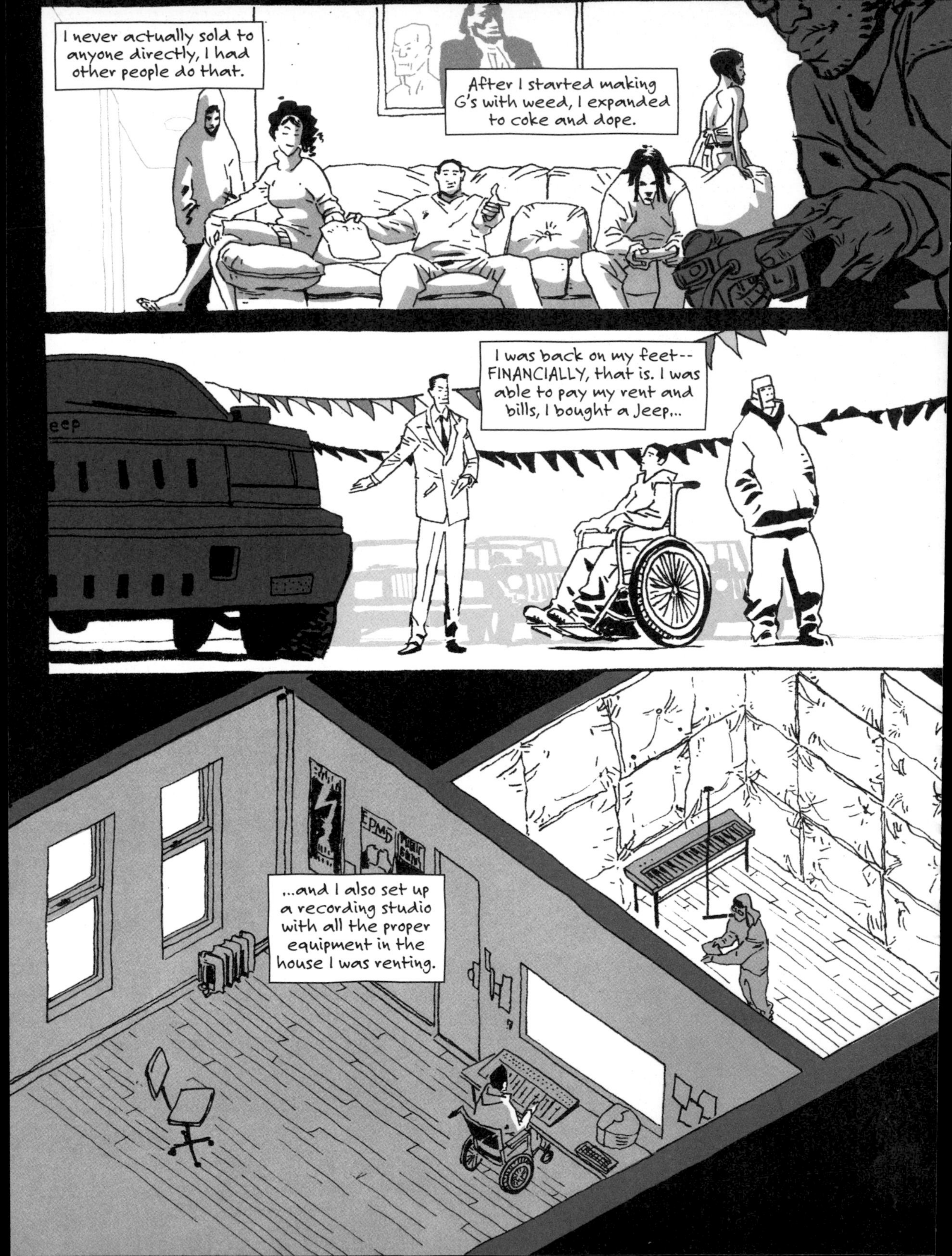
I never actually sold to anyone directly, I had other people do that.
After I started making G's with weed, I expanded to coke and dope.
I was back on my feet-- FINANCIALLY, that is. I was able to pay my rent and bills, I bought a Jeep...
EPMD
...and I also set up a recording studio with all the proper equipment in the house I was renting.

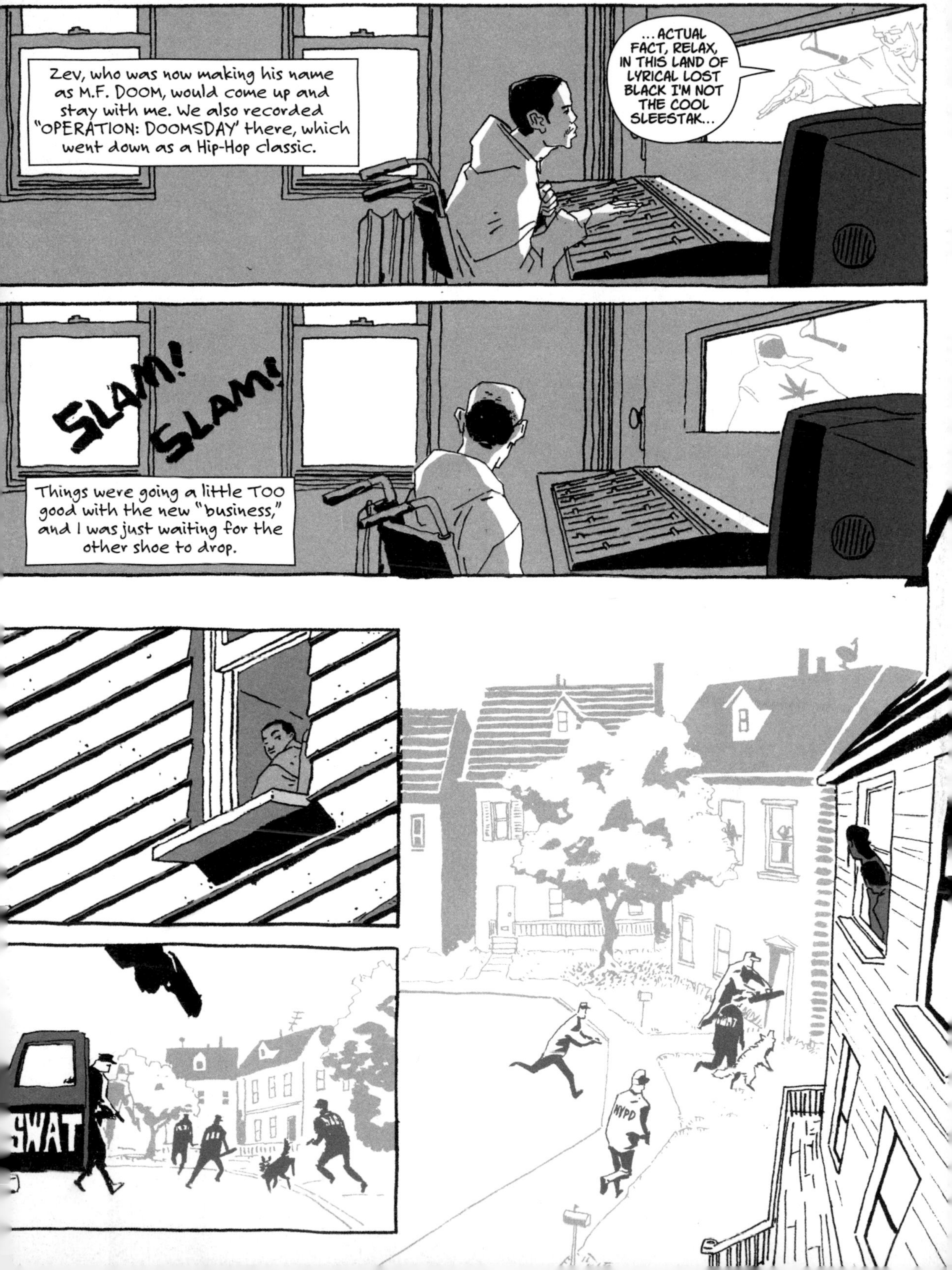
Zev, who was now making his name as M.F. DOOM, would come up and stay with me. We also recorded "OPERATION: DOOMSDAY' there, which went down as a Hip-Hop classic.
...ACTUAL FACT, RELAX, IN THIS LAND OF LYRICAL LOST BLACK I'M NOT THE COOL SLEESTAK...
SLAM! SLAM!
Things were going a little TOO good with the new "business," and I was just waiting for the other shoe to drop.
SWAT
NYPD

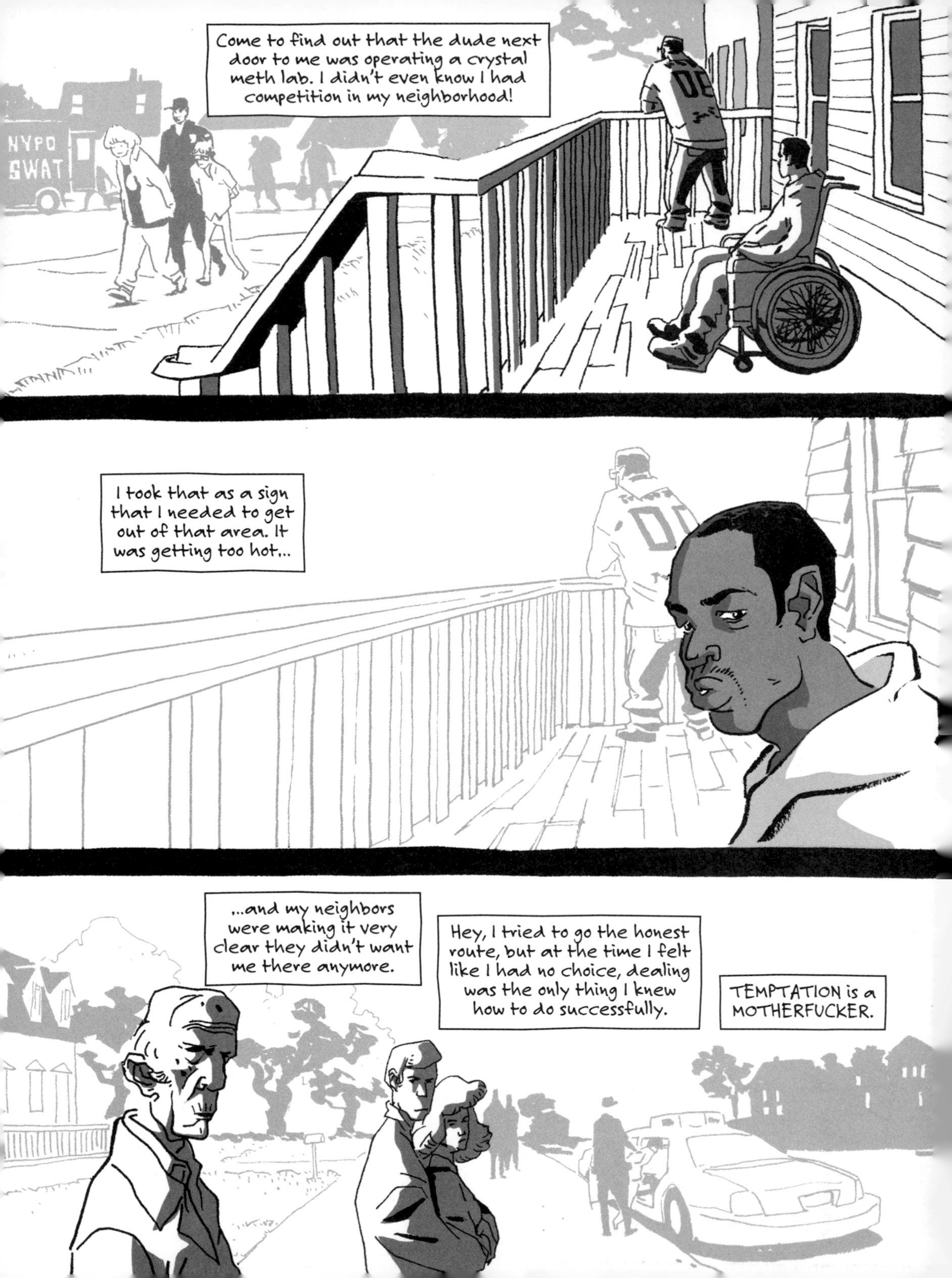

Come to find out that the dude next door to me was operating a crystal meth lab. I didn't even know I had competition in my neighborhood!
NYPD SWAT
I took that as a sign that I needed to get out of that area. It was getting too hot...
...and my neighbors were making it very clear they didn't want me there anymore.
Hey, I tried to go the honest route, but at the time I felt like I had no choice, dealing was the only thing I knew how to do successfully.
TEMPTATION is a MOTHERFUCKER.

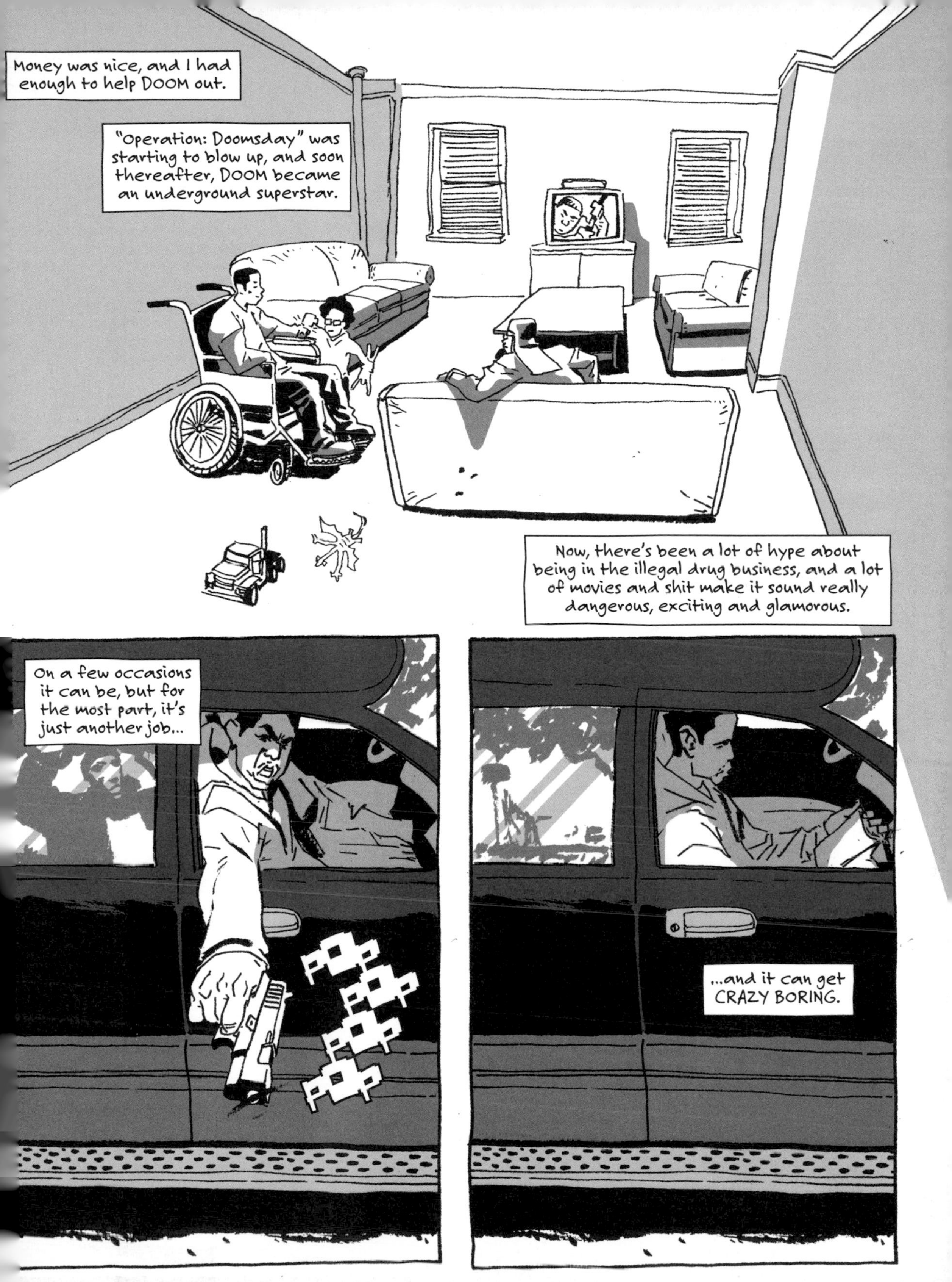
Money was nice, and I had enough to help DOOM out.
"Operation: Doomsday" was starting to blow up, and soon thereafter, DOOM became an underground superstar.
Now, there's been a lot of hype about being in the illegal drug business, and a lot of movies and shit make it sound really dangerous, exciting and glamorous.
On a few occasions it can be, but for the most part, it's just another job...
POP
POP
POP
POP
...and it can get CRAZY BORING.

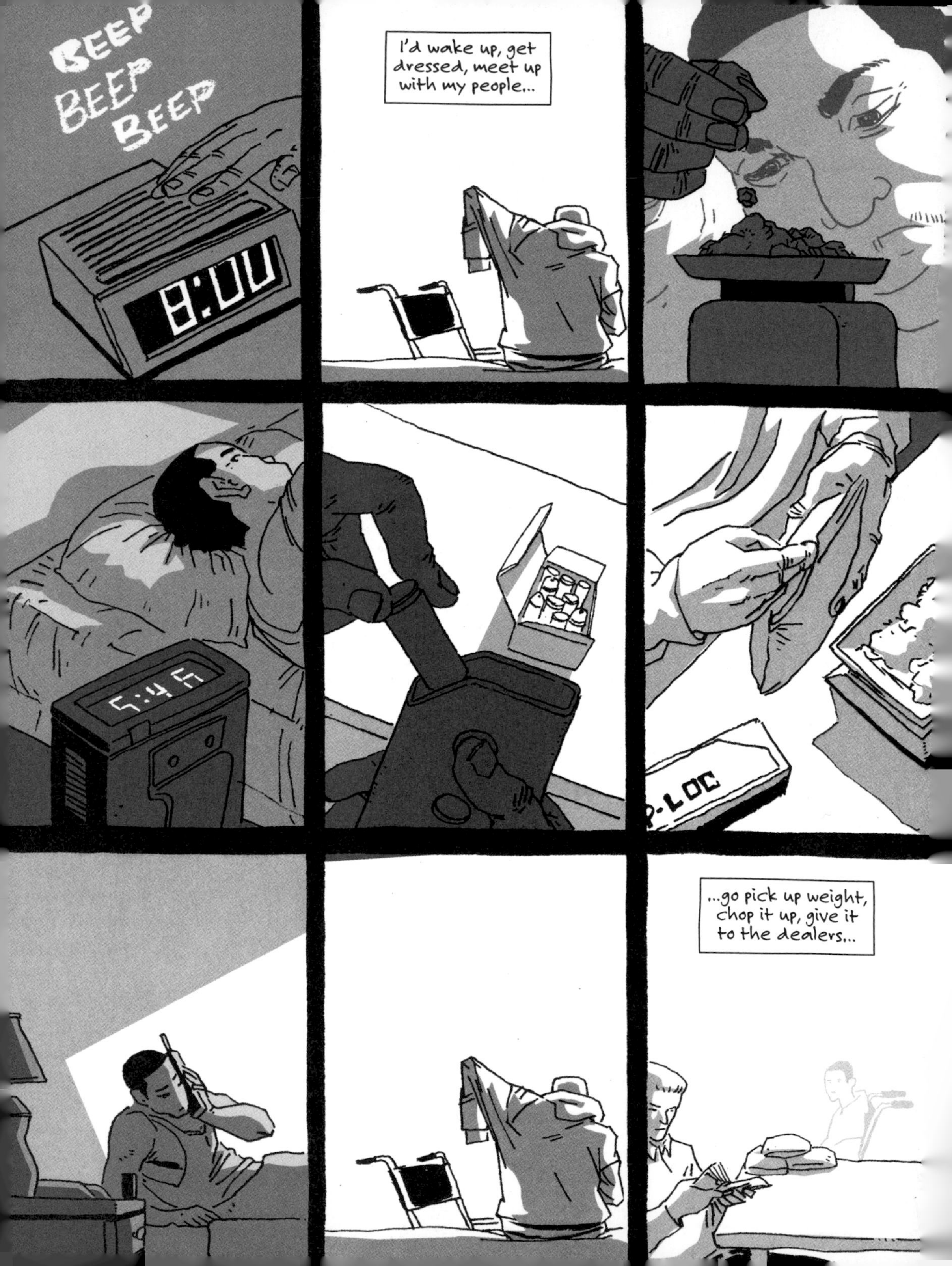
BEEP
BEEP
BEEP
8:00
I'd wake up, get dressed, meet up with my people...
5:45
-LOC
...go pick up weight, chop it up, give it to the dealers...

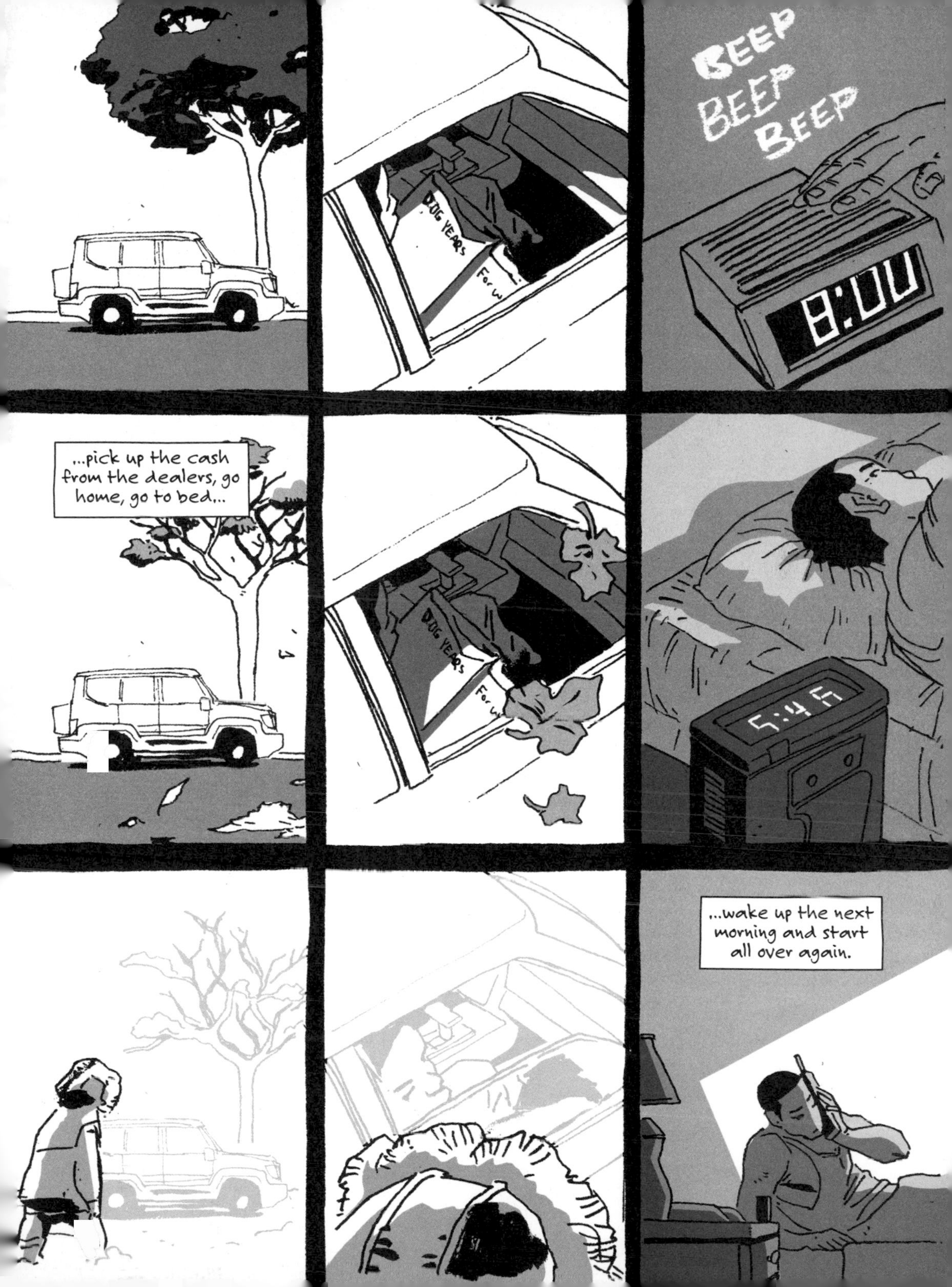
DUG YEARS
For W
BEEP
BEEP
BEEP
8:00
...pick up the cash from the dealers, go home, go to bed...
DUG YEARS
For W
5:45
...wake up the next morning and start all over again.

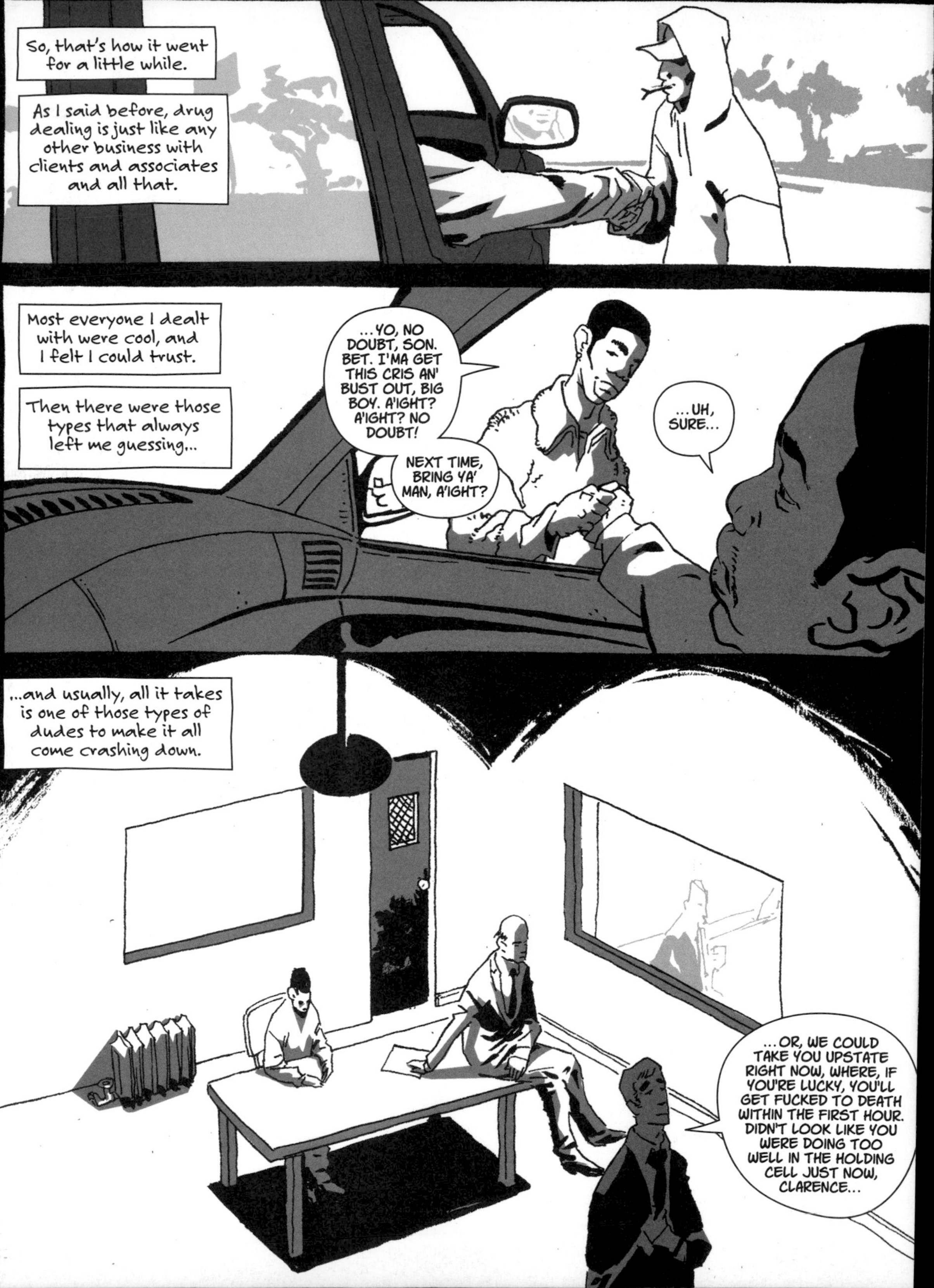
So, that's how it went for a little while.
As I said before, drug dealing is just like any other business with clients and associates and all that.
Most everyone I dealt with were cool, and I felt I could trust.
Then there were those types that always left me guessing...
...YO, NO DOUBT, SON. BET. I'MA GET THIS CRIS AN' BUST OUT, BIG BOY. A'IGHT? A'IGHT? NO DOUBT!
NEXT TIME, BRING YA' MAN, A'IGHT?
...UH, SURE...
...and usually, all it takes is one of those types of dudes to make it all come crashing down.
...OR, WE COULD TAKE YOU UPSTATE RIGHT NOW, WHERE, IF YOU'RE LUCKY, YOU'LL GET FUCKED TO DEATH WITHIN THE FIRST HOUR. DIDN'T LOOK LIKE YOU WERE DOING TOO WELL IN THE HOLDING CELL JUST NOW, CLARENCE...

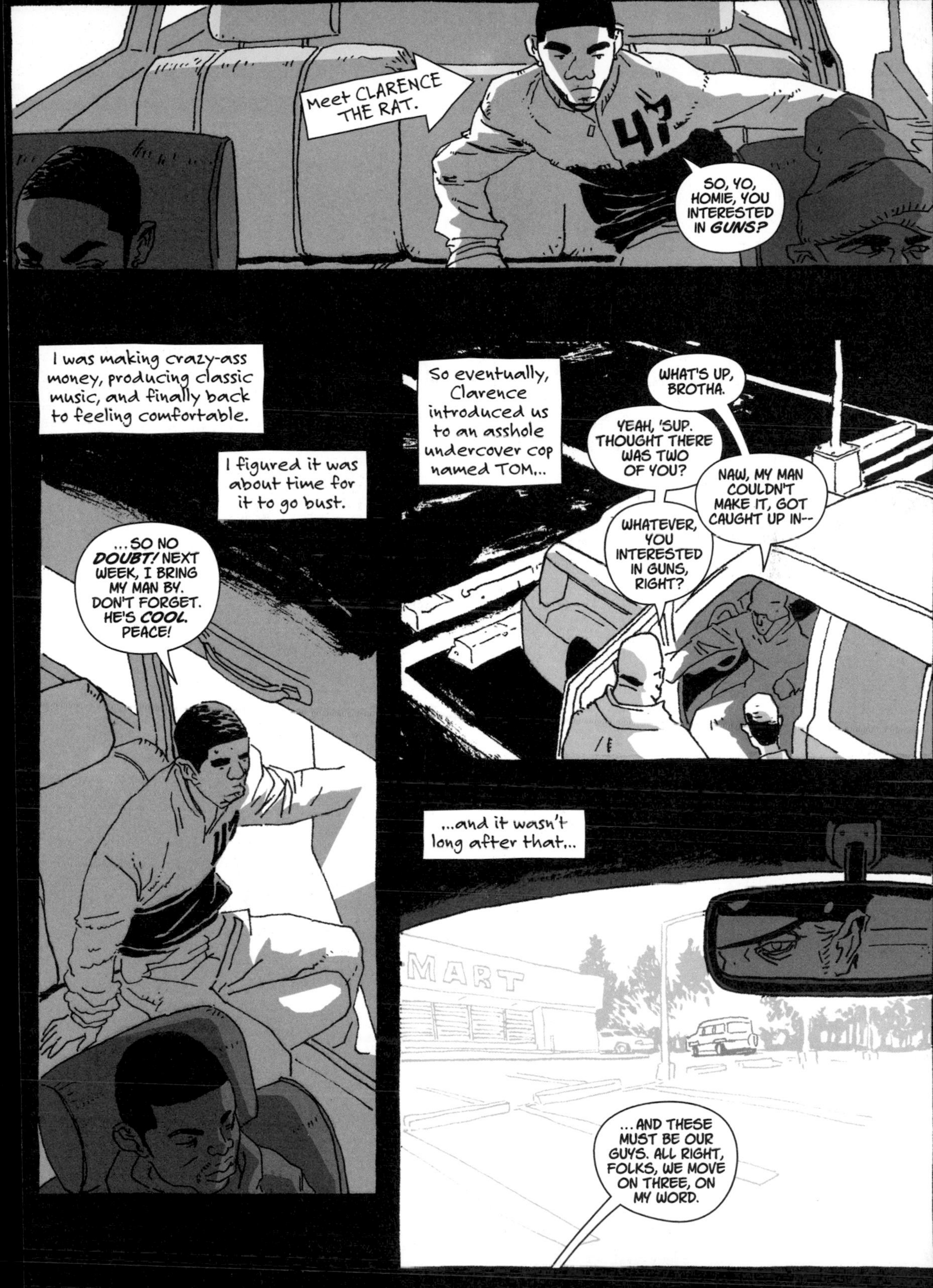
Meet CLARENCE THE RAT.
SO, YO, HOMIE, YOU INTERESTED IN GUNS?
I was making crazy-ass money, producing classic music, and finally back to feeling comfortable.
I figured it was about time for it to go bust.
...SO NO DOUBT! NEXT WEEK, I BRING MY MAN BY. DON'T FORGET. HE'S COOL. PEACE!
So eventually, Clarence introduced us to an asshole undercover cop named TOM...
WHAT'S UP, BROTHA.
YEAH, 'SUP. THOUGHT THERE WAS TWO OF YOU?
NAW, MY MAN COULDN'T MAKE IT, GOT CAUGHT UP IN--
WHATEVER, YOU INTERESTED IN GUNS, RIGHT?
...and it wasn't long after that...
MART
...AND THESE MUST BE OUR GUYS. ALL RIGHT, FOLKS, WE MOVE ON THREE, ON MY WORD.

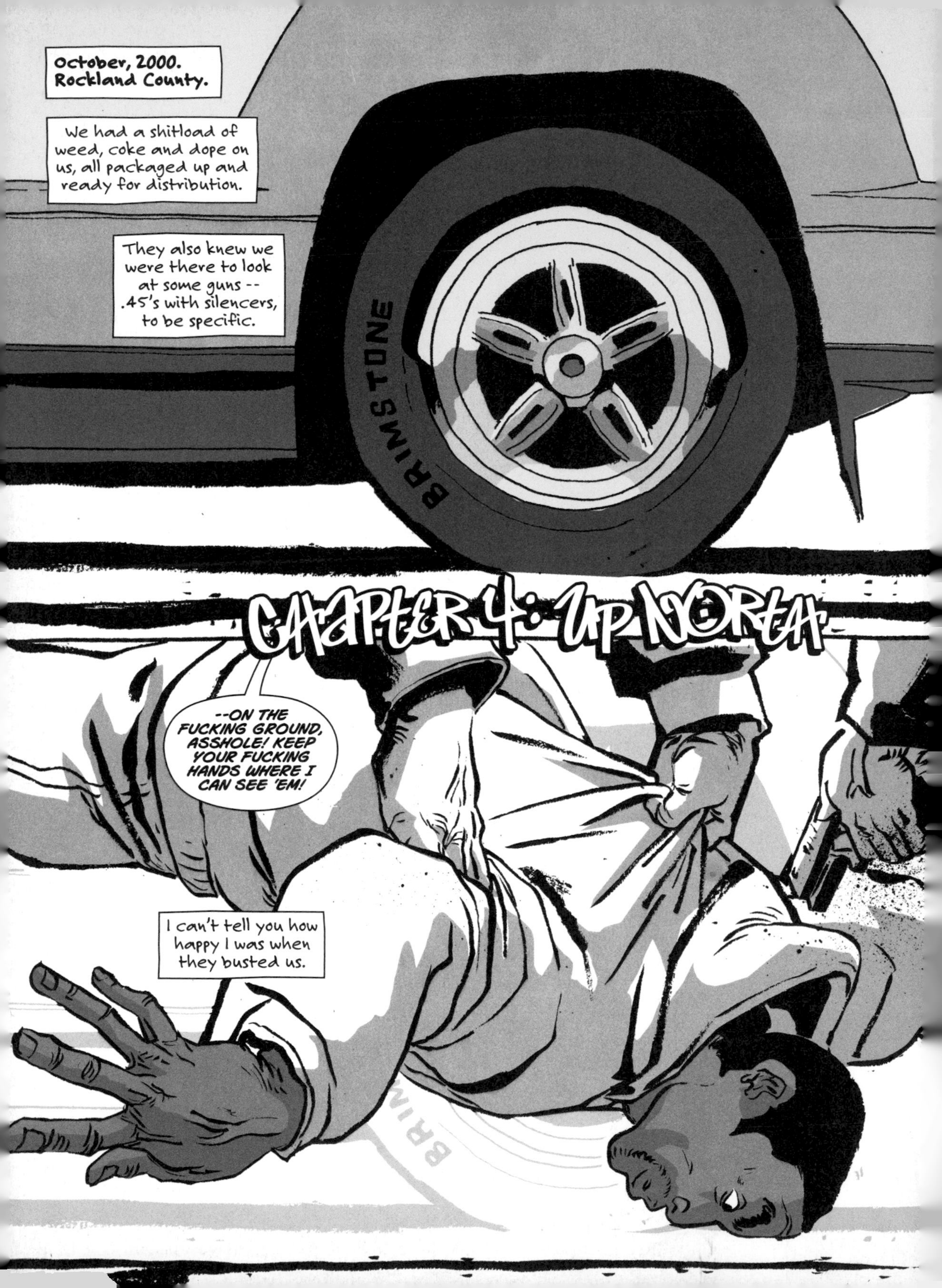
October, 2000. Rockland County.
We had a shitload of weed, coke and dope on us, all packaged up and ready for distribution.
They also knew we were there to look at some guns -- .45's with silencers, to be specific.
BRIMSTONE
CHAPTER 4: UP NORTH
--ON THE FUCKING GROUND, ASSHOLE! KEEP YOUR FUCKING HANDS WHERE I CAN SEE 'EM!
I can't tell you how happy I was when they busted us.

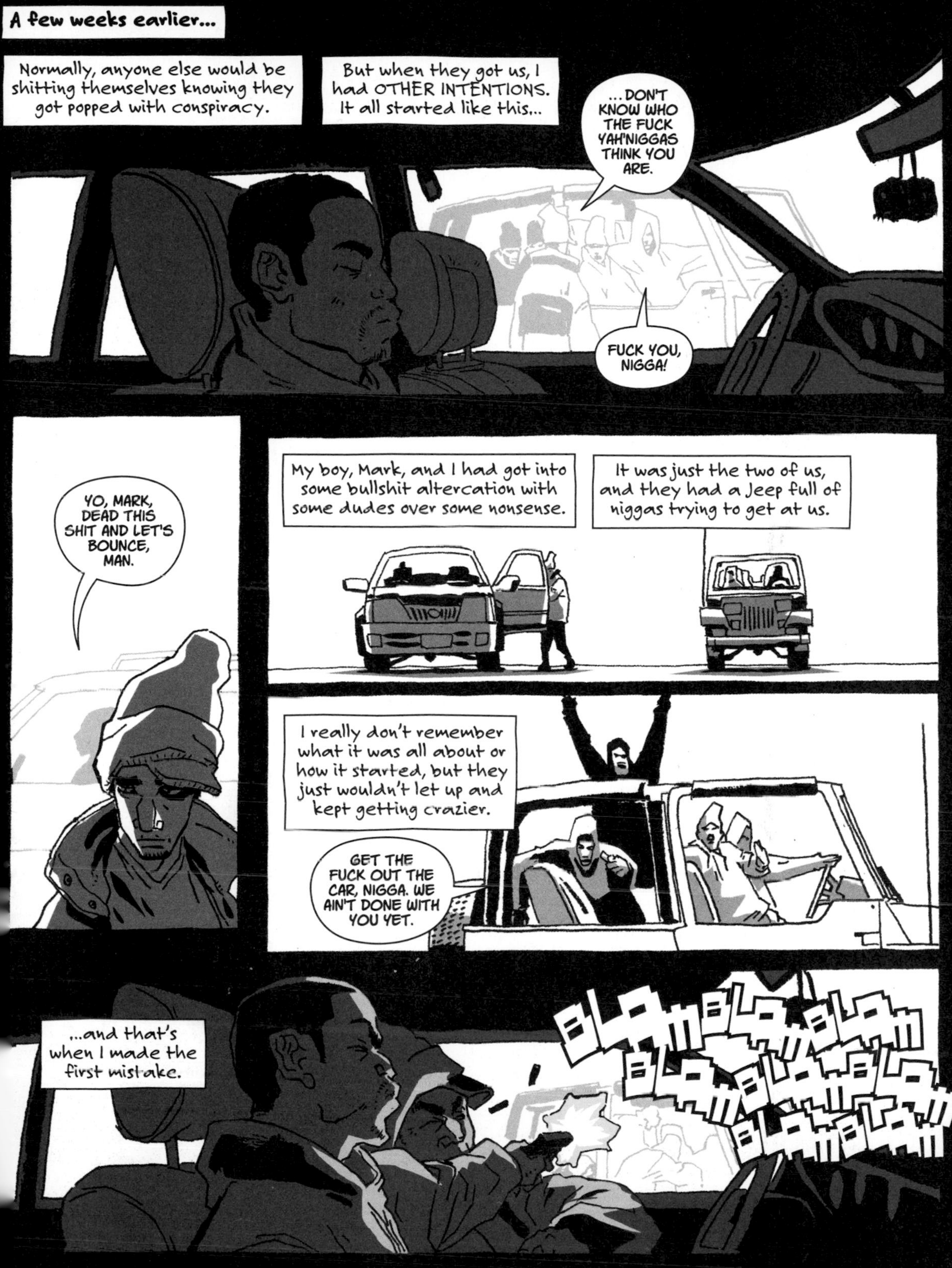
A few weeks earlier...
Normally, anyone else would be shitting themselves knowing they got popped with conspiracy.
But when they got us, I had OTHER INTENTIONS. It all started like this...
...DON'T KNOW WHO THE FUCK YAH'NIGGAS THINK YOU ARE.
FUCK YOU, NIGGA!
YO, MARK, DEAD THIS SHIT AND LET'S BOUNCE, MAN.
My boy, Mark, and I had got into some bullshit altercation with some dudes over some nonsense.
It was just the two of us, and they had a Jeep full of niggas trying to get at us.
I really don't remember what it was all about or how it started, but they just wouldn't let up and kept getting crazier.
GET THE FUCK OUT THE CAR, NIGGA. WE AIN'T DONE WITH YOU YET.
...and that's when I made the first mistake.
BLAM BLAM BLAM
BLAM BLAM BLAM
BLAM BLAM

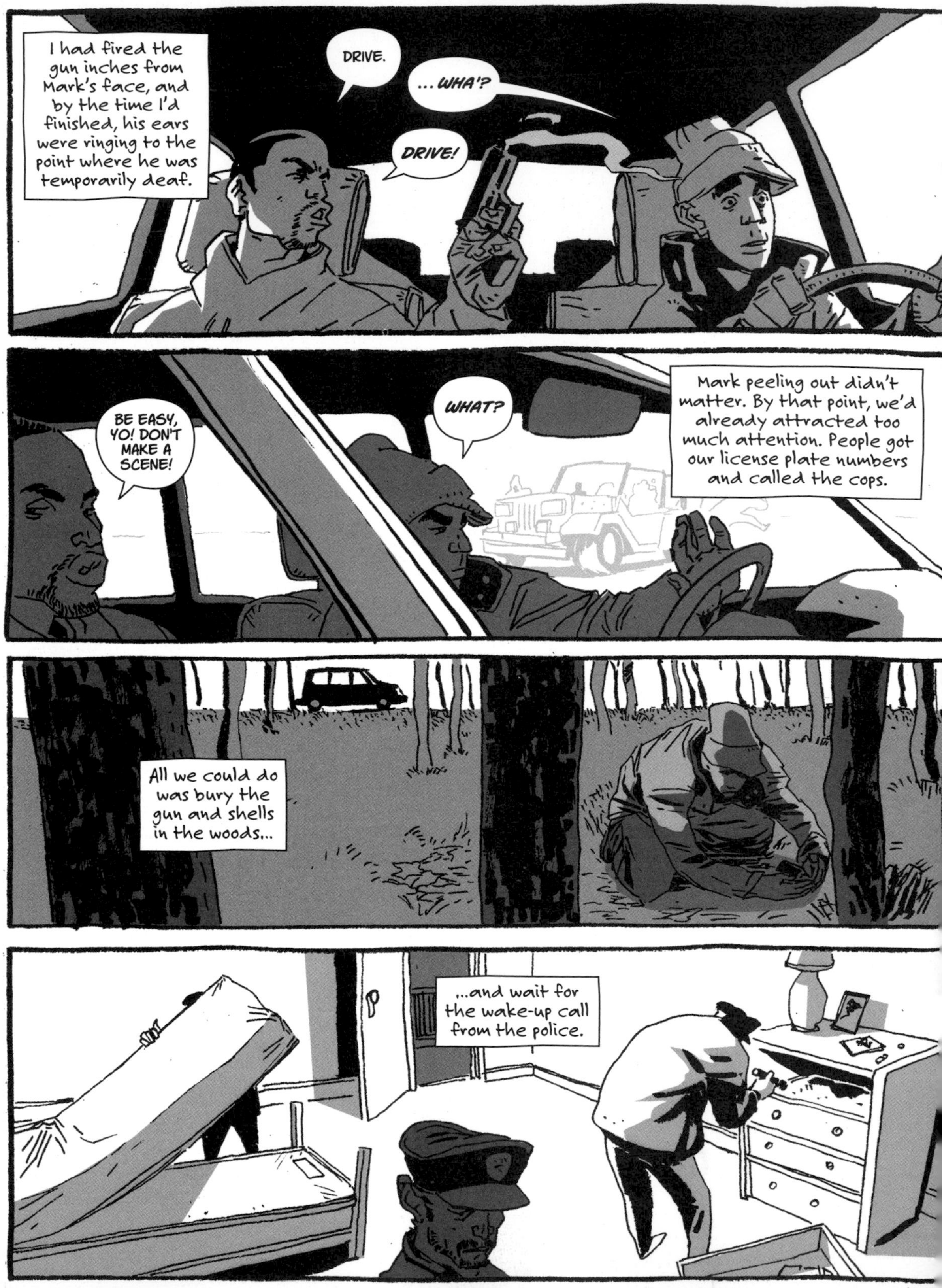
I had fired the gun inches from Mark's face, and by the time I'd finished, his ears were ringing to the point where he was temporarily deaf.
DRIVE.
...WHA'?
DRIVE!
BE EASY, YO! DON'T MAKE A SCENE!
WHAT?
Mark peeling out didn't matter. By that point, we'd already attracted too much attention. People got our license plate numbers and called the cops.
All we could do was bury the gun and shells in the woods...
...and wait for the wake-up call from the police.

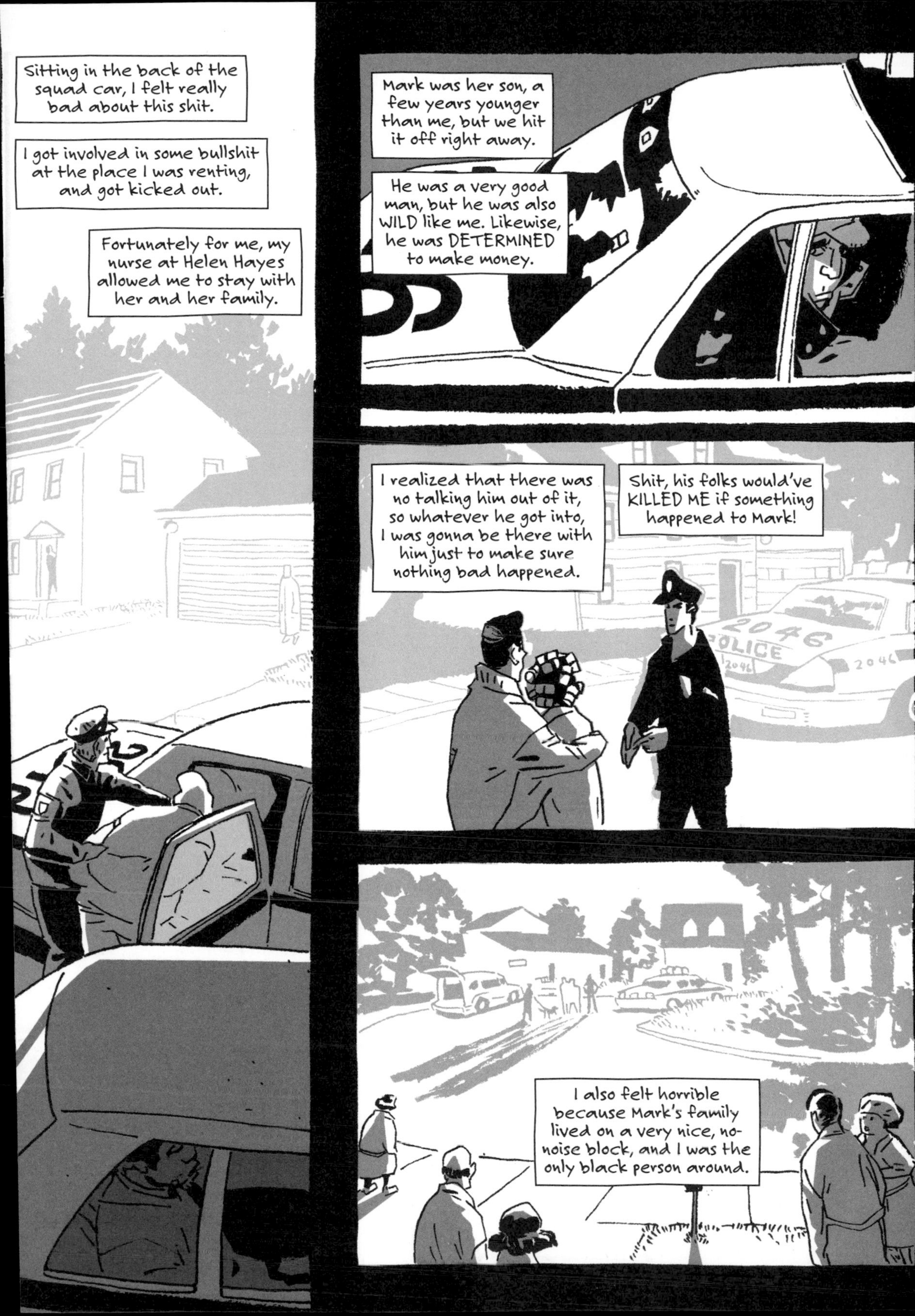
Sitting in the back of the squad car, I felt really bad about this shit.
I got involved in some bullshit at the place I was renting, and got kicked out.
Fortunately for me, my nurse at Helen Hayes allowed me to stay with her and her family.
Mark was her son, a few years younger than me, but we hit it off right away.
He was a very good man, but he was also WILD like me. Likewise, he was DETERMINED to make money.
I realized that there was no talking him out of it, so whatever he got into, I was gonna be there with him just to make sure nothing bad happened.
Shit, his folks would've KILLED ME if something happened to Mark!
2046
POLICE
I also felt horrible because Mark's family lived on a very nice, no-noise block, and I was the only black person around.

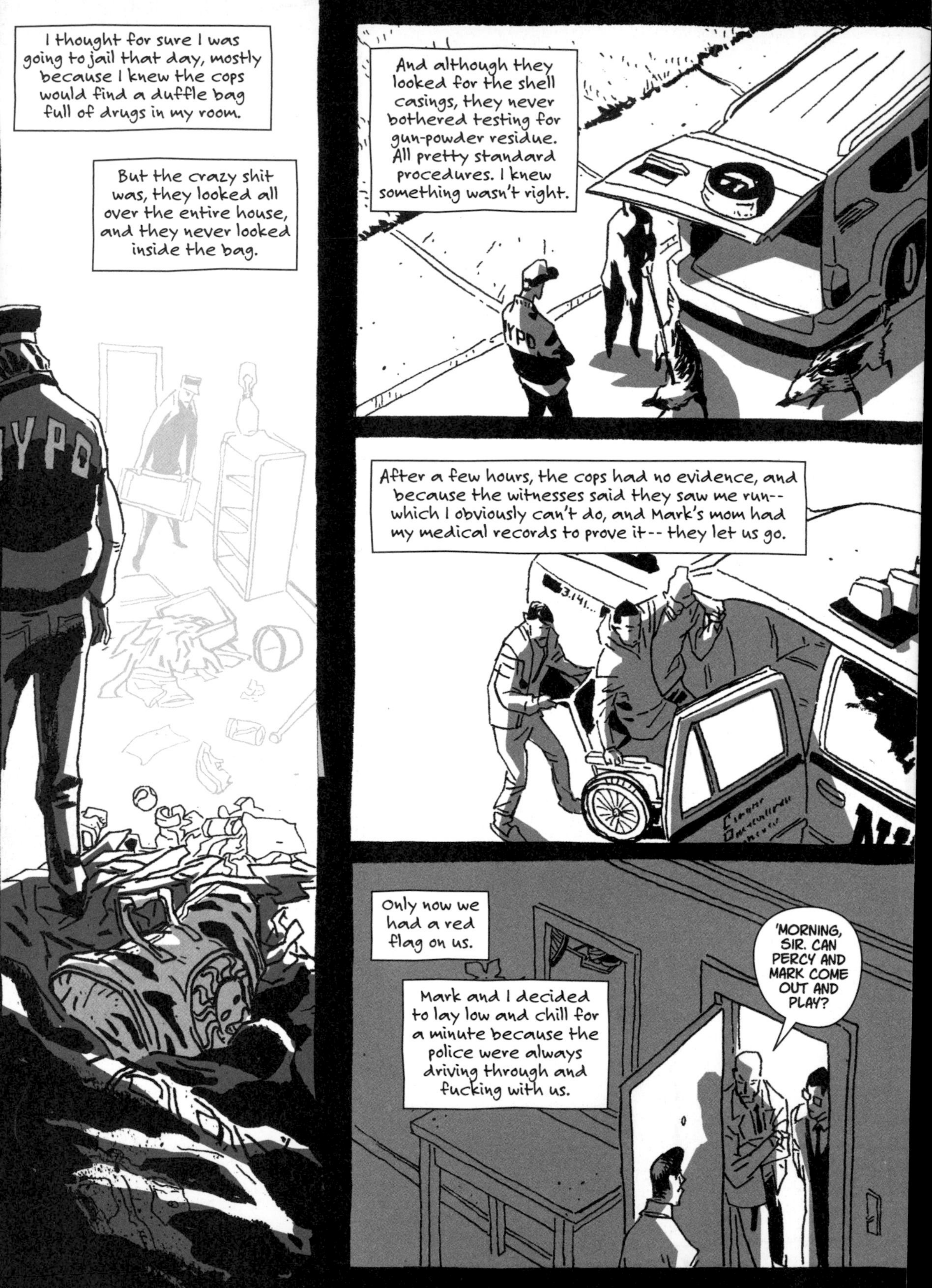
I thought for sure I was going to jail that day, mostly because I knew the cops would find a duffle bag full of drugs in my room.
But the crazy shit was, they looked all over the entire house, and they never looked inside the bag.
And although they looked for the shell casings, they never bothered testing for gun-powder residue. All pretty standard procedures. I knew something wasn't right.
After a few hours, the cops had no evidence, and because the witnesses said they saw me run-- which I obviously can't do, and Mark's mom had my medical records to prove it-- they let us go.
Only now we had a red flag on us.
Mark and I decided to lay low and chill for a minute because the police were always driving through and fucking with us.
'MORNING, SIR. CAN PERCY AND MARK COME OUT AND PLAY?

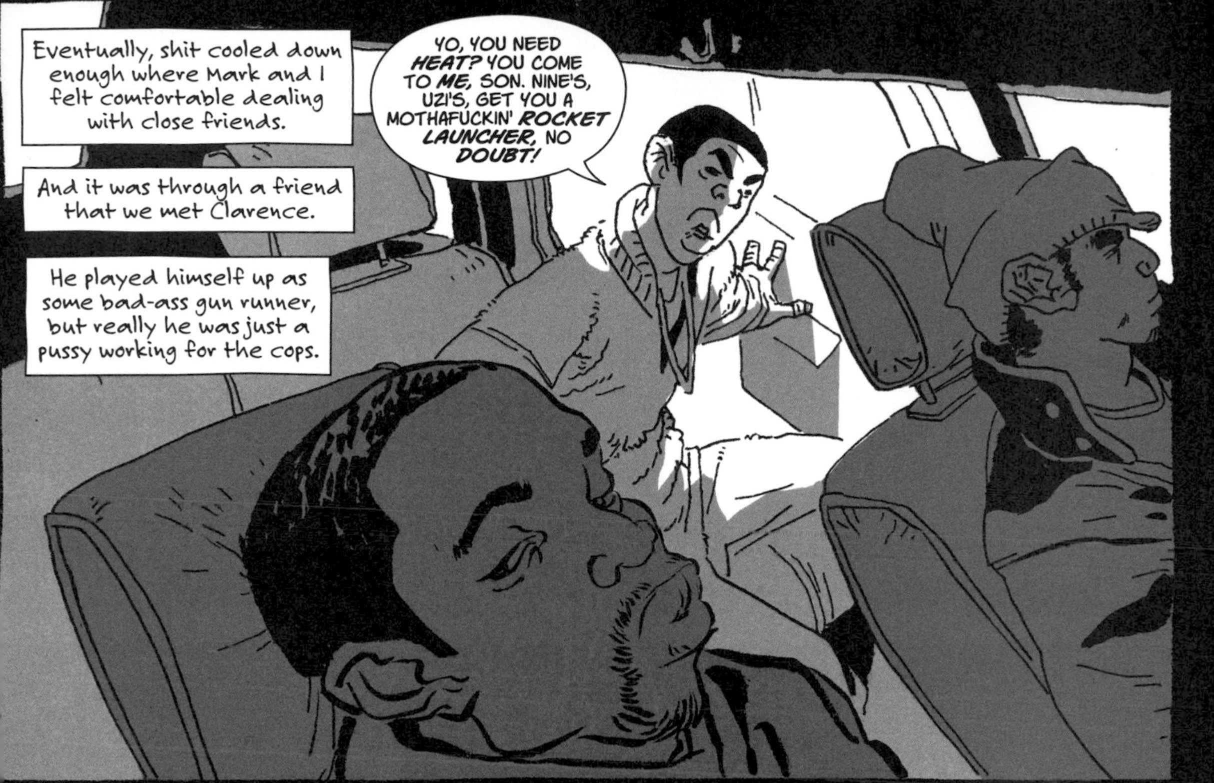
Eventually, shit cooled down enough where Mark and I felt comfortable dealing with close friends.
YO, YOU NEED HEAT? YOU COME TO ME, SON. NINE'S, UZI'S, GET YOU A MOTHAFUCKIN' ROCKET LAUNCHER, NO DOUBT!
And it was through a friend that we met Clarence.
He played himself up as some bad-ass gun runner, but really he was just a pussy working for the cops.

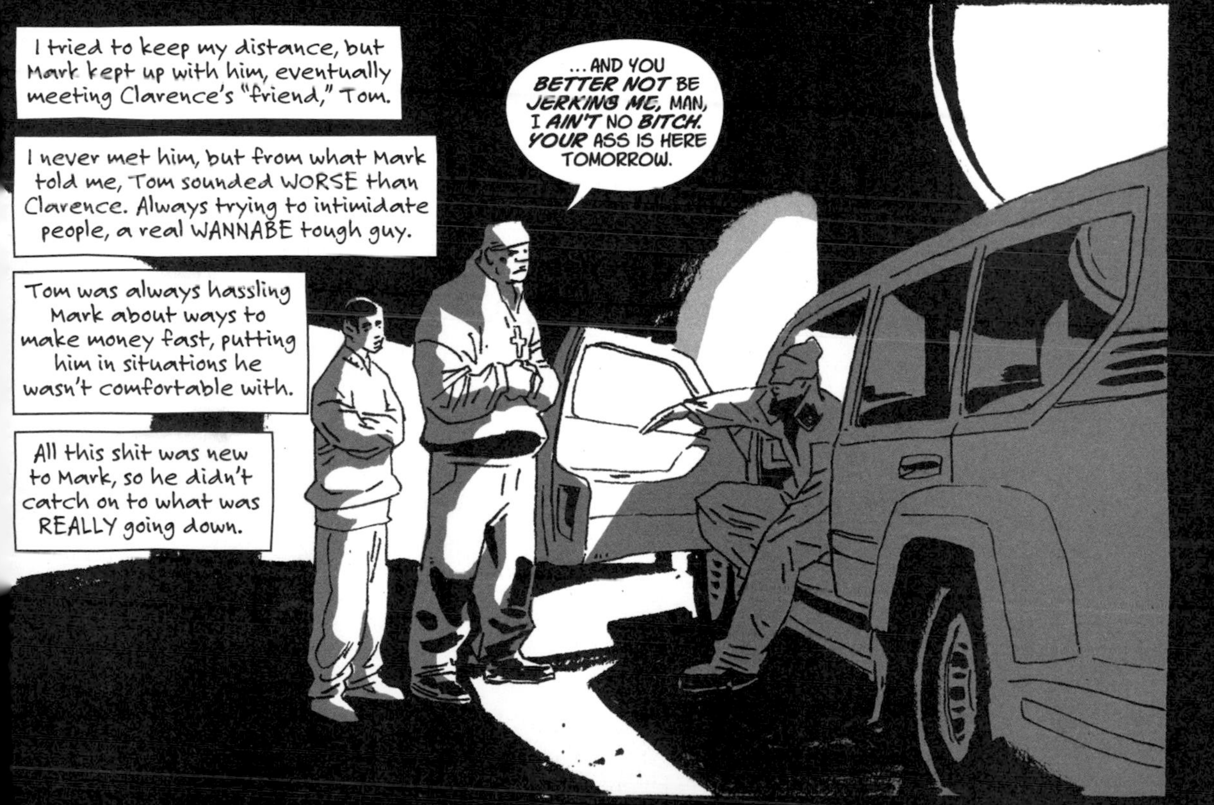
I tried to keep my distance, but Mark kept up with him, eventually meeting Clarence's "friend," Tom.
...AND YOU BETTER NOT BE JERKING ME, MAN, I AIN'T NO BITCH. YOUR ASS IS HERE TOMORROW.
I never met him, but from what Mark told me, Tom sounded WORSE than Clarence. Always trying to intimidate people, a real WANNABE tough guy.
Tom was always hassling Mark about ways to make money fast, putting him in situations he wasn't comfortable with.
All this shit was new to Mark, so he didn't catch on to what was REALLY going down.

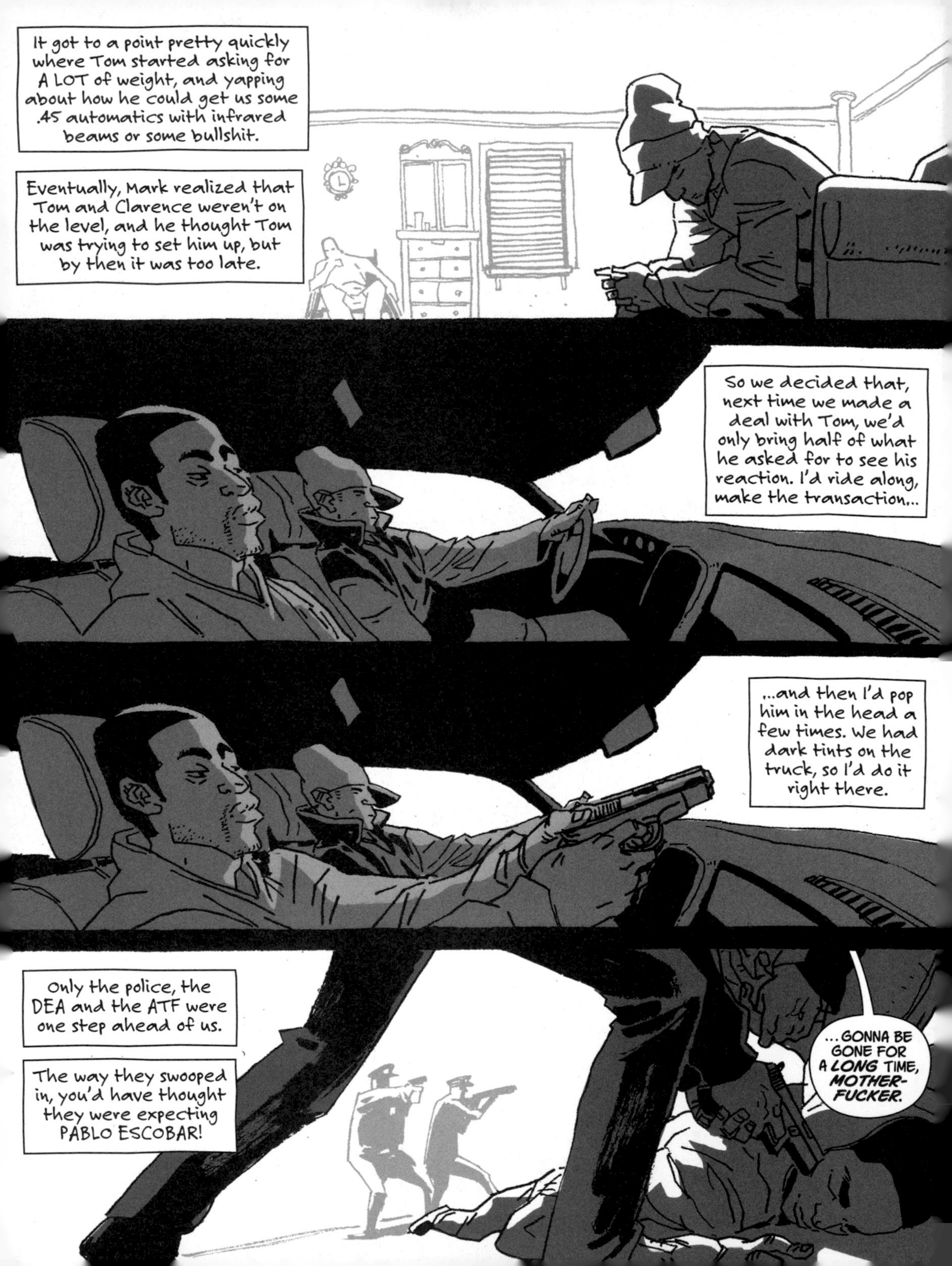
It got to a point pretty quickly where Tom started asking for A LOT of weight, and yapping about how he could get us some .45 automatics with infrared beams or some bullshit.
Eventually, Mark realized that Tom and Clarence weren't on the level, and he thought Tom was trying to set him up, but by then it was too late.
So we decided that, next time we made a deal with Tom, we'd only bring half of what he asked for to see his reaction. I'd ride along, make the transaction...
...and then I'd pop him in the head a few times. We had dark tints on the truck, so I'd do it right there.
Only the police, the DEA and the ATF were one step ahead of us.
The way they swooped in, you'd have thought they were expecting PABLO ESCOBAR!
...GONNA BE GONE FOR A LONG TIME, MOTHER-FUCKER.

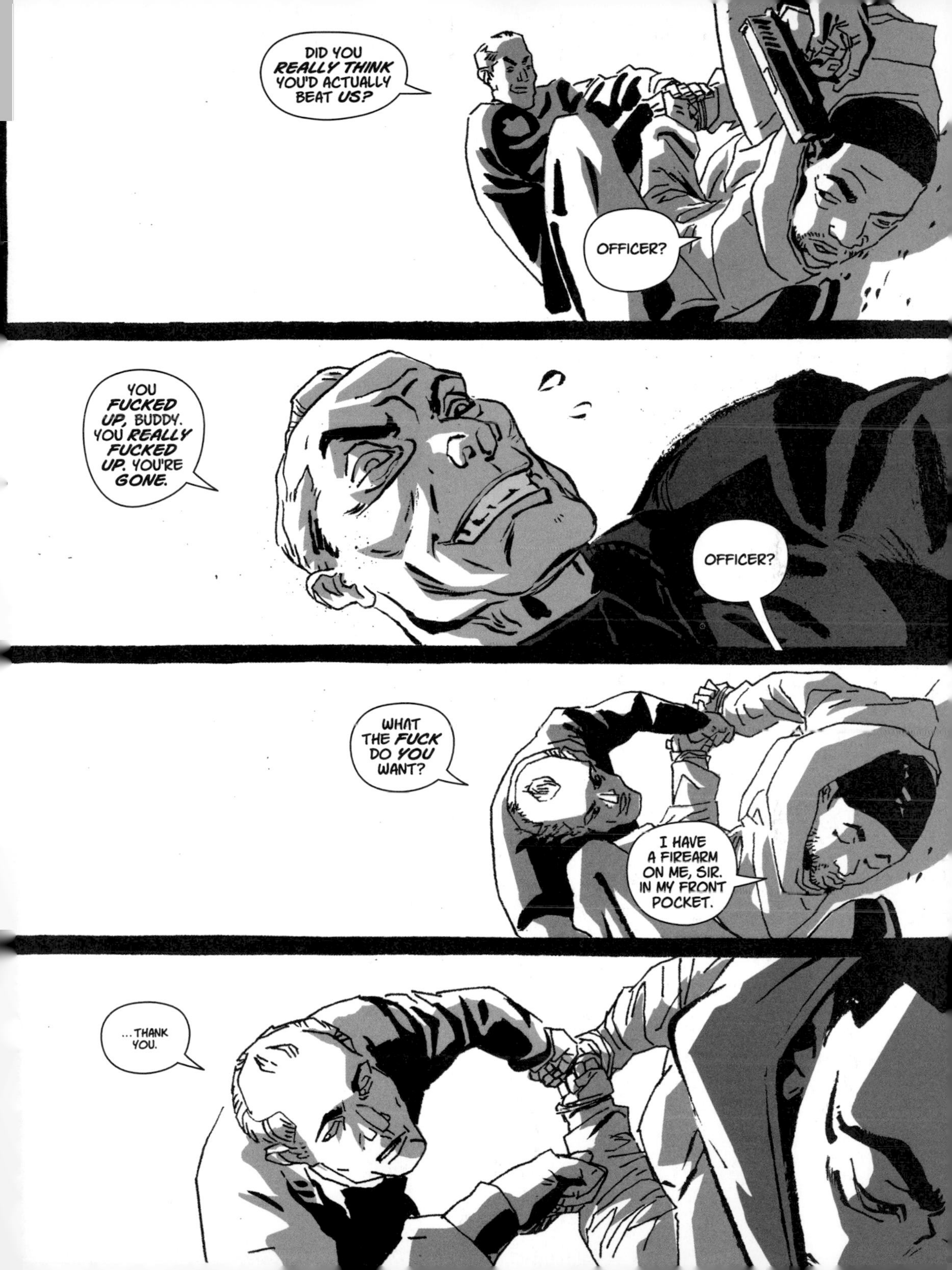
DID YOU REALLY THINK YOU'D ACTUALLY BEAT US?
OFFICER?
YOU FUCKED UP, BUDDY. YOU REALLY FUCKED UP. YOU'RE GONE.
OFFICER?
WHAT THE FUCK DO YOU WANT?
I HAVE A FIREARM ON ME, SIR. IN MY FRONT POCKET.
...THANK YOU.

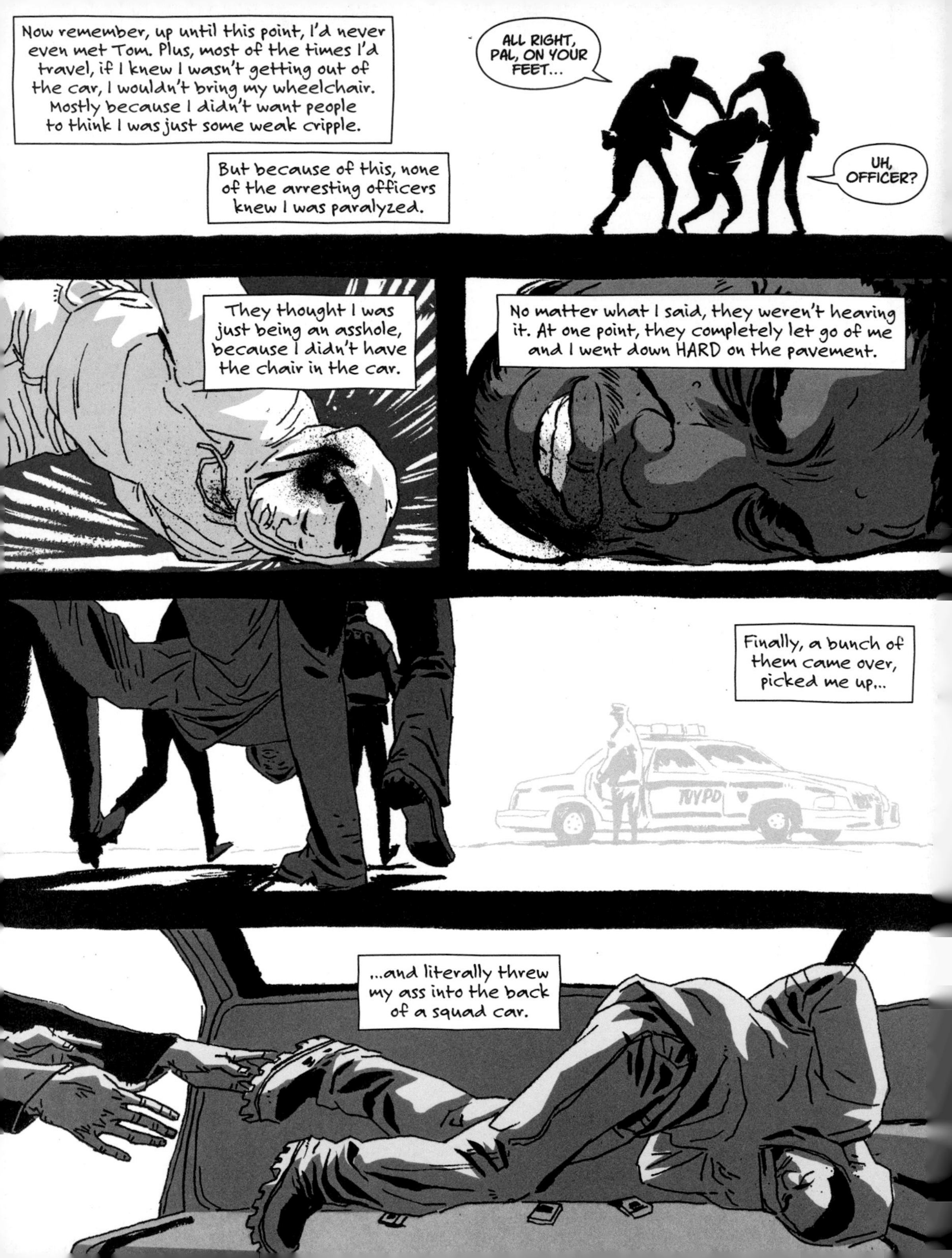
Now remember, up until this point, I'd never even met Tom. Plus, most of the times I'd travel, if I knew I wasn't getting out of the car, I wouldn't bring my wheelchair. Mostly because I didn't want people to think I was just some weak cripple.
ALL RIGHT, PAL, ON YOUR FEET...
But because of this, none of the arresting officers knew I was paralyzed.
UH, OFFICER?
They thought I was just being an asshole, because I didn't have the chair in the car.
No matter what I said, they weren't hearing it. At one point, they completely let go of me and I went down HARD on the pavement.
Finally, a bunch of them came over, picked me up...
NYPD
...and literally threw my ass into the back of a squad car.

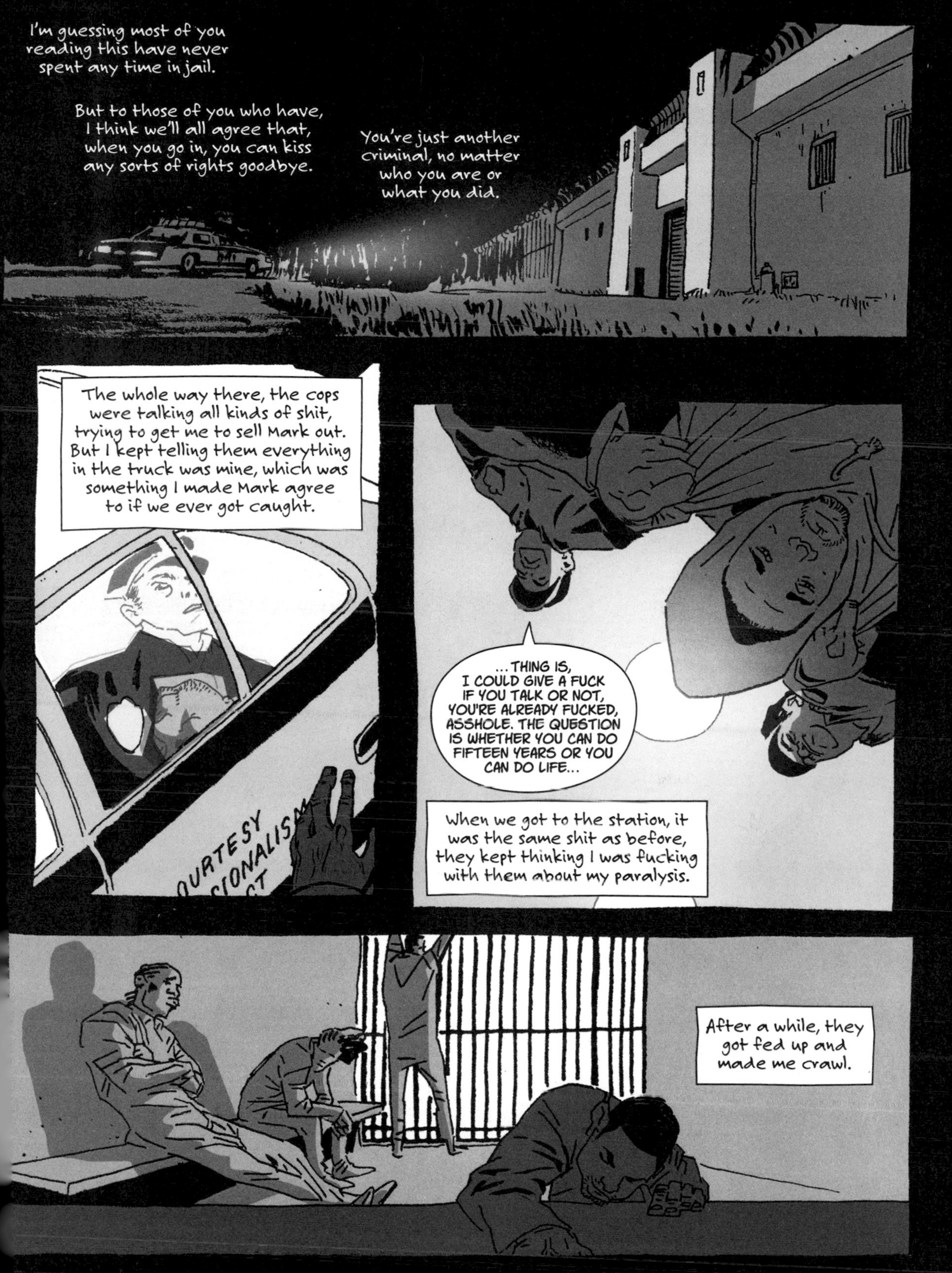
I'm guessing most of you reading this have never spent any time in jail.
But to those of you who have, I think we'll all agree that, when you go in, you can kiss any sorts of rights goodbye.
You're just another criminal, no matter who you are or what you did.
The whole way there, the cops were talking all kinds of shit, trying to get me to sell Mark out. But I kept telling them everything in the truck was mine, which was something I made Mark agree to if we ever got caught.
...THING IS, I COULD GIVE A FUCK IF YOU TALK OR NOT, YOU'RE ALREADY FUCKED, ASSHOLE. THE QUESTION IS WHETHER YOU CAN DO FIFTEEN YEARS OR YOU CAN DO LIFE...
When we got to the station, it was the same shit as before, they kept thinking I was fucking with them about my paralysis.
After a while, they got fed up and made me crawl.

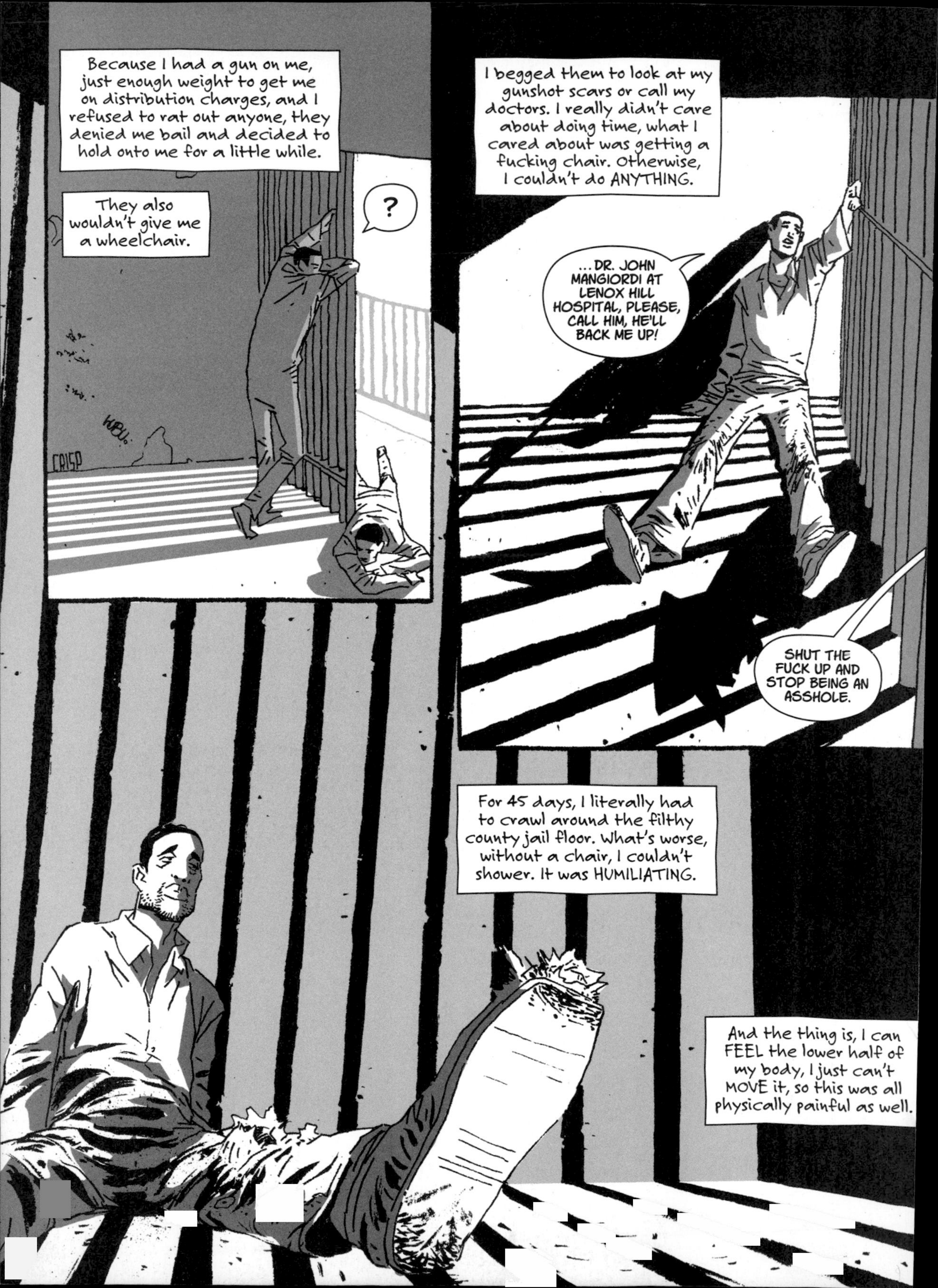
Because I had a gun on me, just enough weight to get me on distribution charges, and I refused to rat out anyone, they denied me bail and decided to hold onto me for a little while.
They also wouldn't give me a wheelchair.
?
I begged them to look at my gunshot scars or call my doctors. I really didn't care about doing time, what I cared about was getting a fucking chair. Otherwise, I couldn't do ANYTHING.
...DR. JOHN MANGIORDI AT LENOX HILL HOSPITAL, PLEASE, CALL HIM, HE'LL BACK ME UP!
SHUT THE FUCK UP AND STOP BEING AN ASSHOLE.
For 45 days, I literally had to crawl around the filthy county jail floor. What's worse, without a chair, I couldn't shower. It was HUMILIATING.
And the thing is, I can FEEL the lower half of my body, I just can't MOVE it, so this was all physically painful as well.

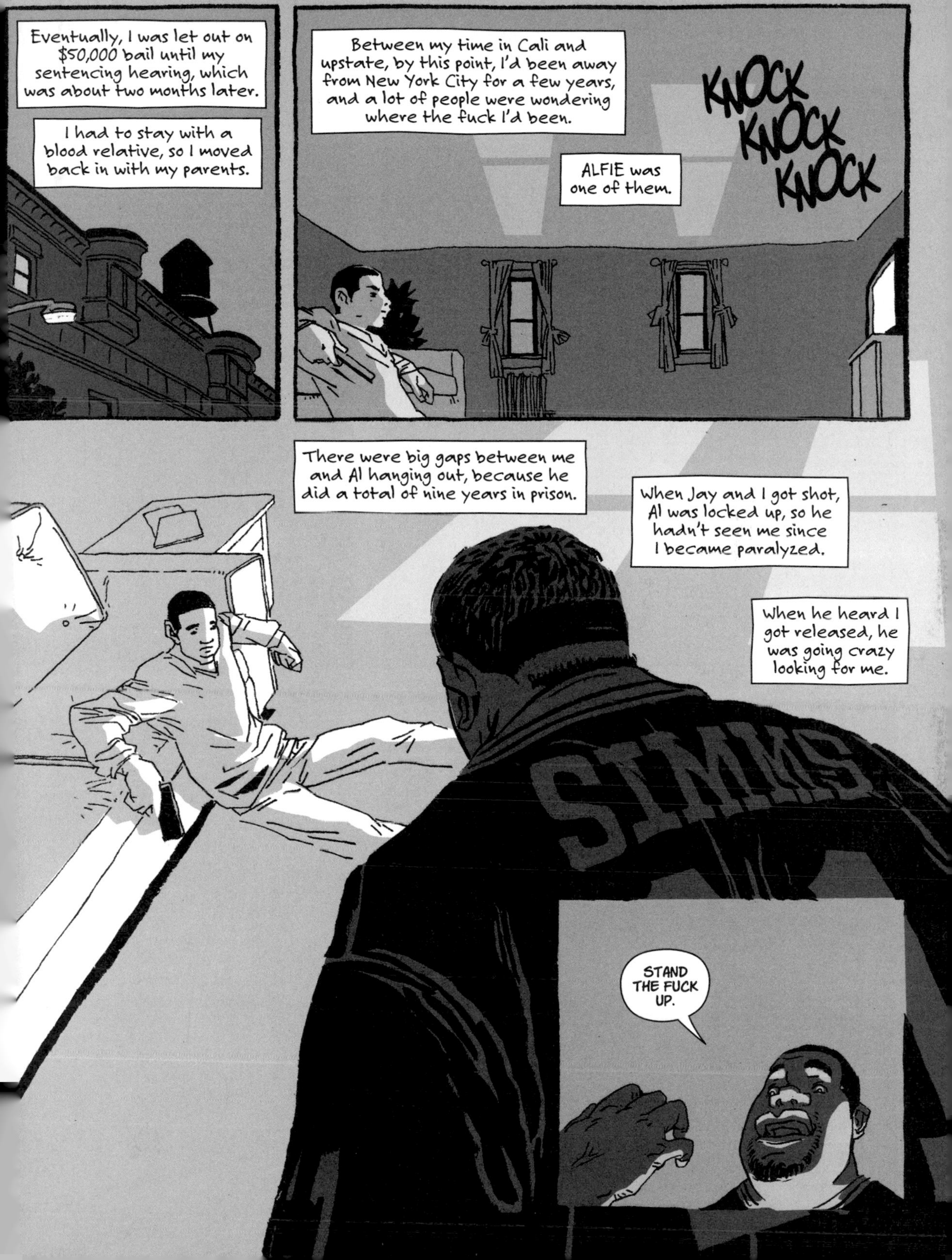
Eventually, I was let out on $50,000 bail until my sentencing hearing, which was about two months later.
I had to stay with a blood relative, so I moved back in with my parents.
Between my time in Cali and upstate, by this point, I'd been away from New York City for a few years, and a lot of people were wondering where the fuck I'd been.
KNOCK KNOCK KNOCK
ALFIE was one of them.
There were big gaps between me and Al hanging out, because he did a total of nine years in prison.
When Jay and I got shot, Al was locked up, so he hadn't seen me since I became paralyzed.
When he heard I got released, he was going crazy looking for me.
SIMMS
STAND THE FUCK UP.

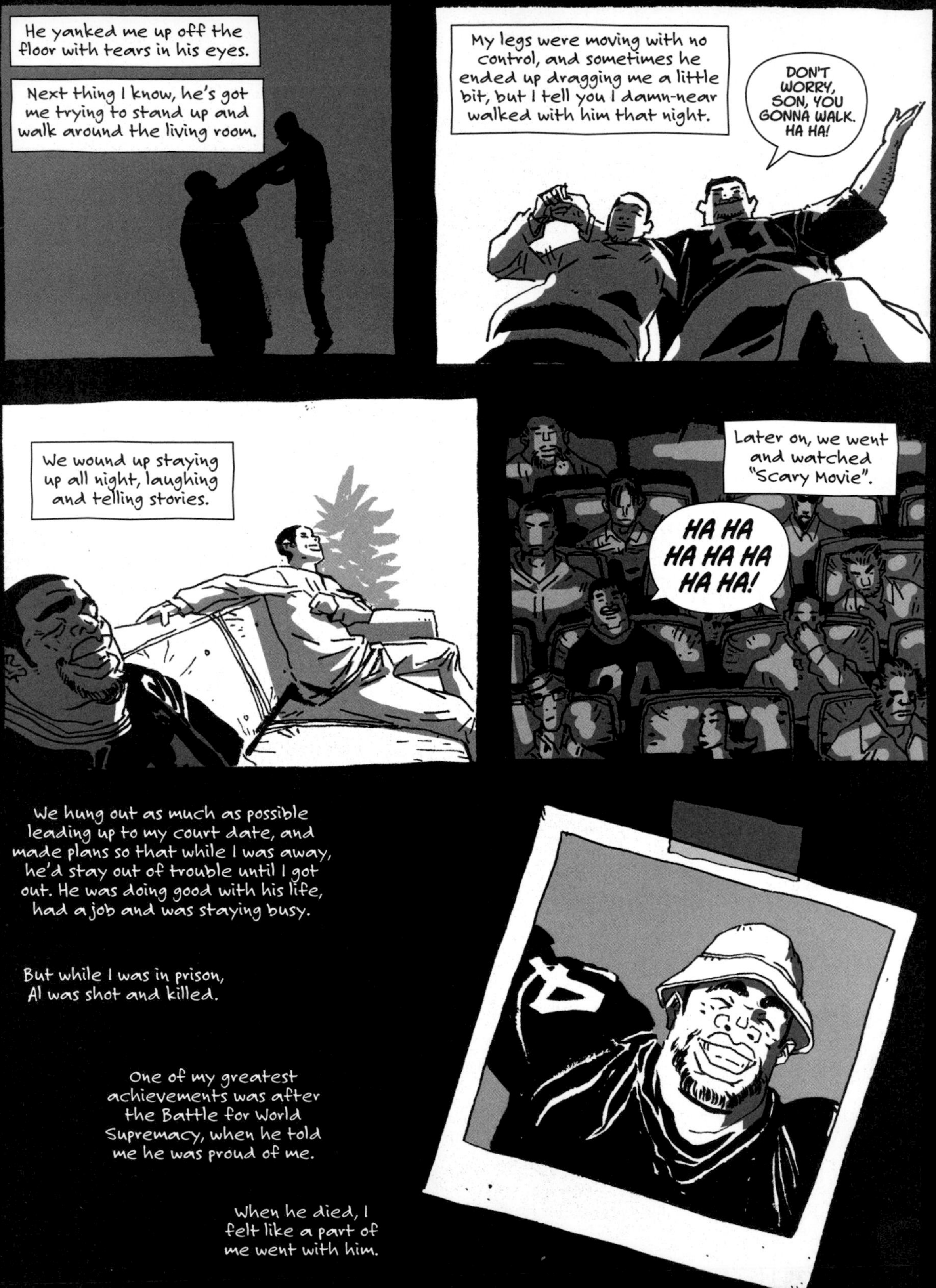

He yanked me up off the floor with tears in his eyes.
Next thing I know, he's got me trying to stand up and walk around the living room.
My legs were moving with no control, and sometimes he ended up dragging me a little bit, but I tell you I damn-near walked with him that night.
DON'T WORRY, SON, YOU GONNA WALK. HA HA!
We wound up staying up all night, laughing and telling stories.
Later on, we went and watched "Scary Movie".
HA HA HA HA HA HA HA!
We hung out as much as possible leading up to my court date, and made plans so that while I was away, he'd stay out of trouble until I got out. He was doing good with his life, had a job and was staying busy.
But while I was in prison, Al was shot and killed.
One of my greatest achievements was after the Battle for World Supremacy, when he told me he was proud of me.
When he died, I felt like a part of me went with him.

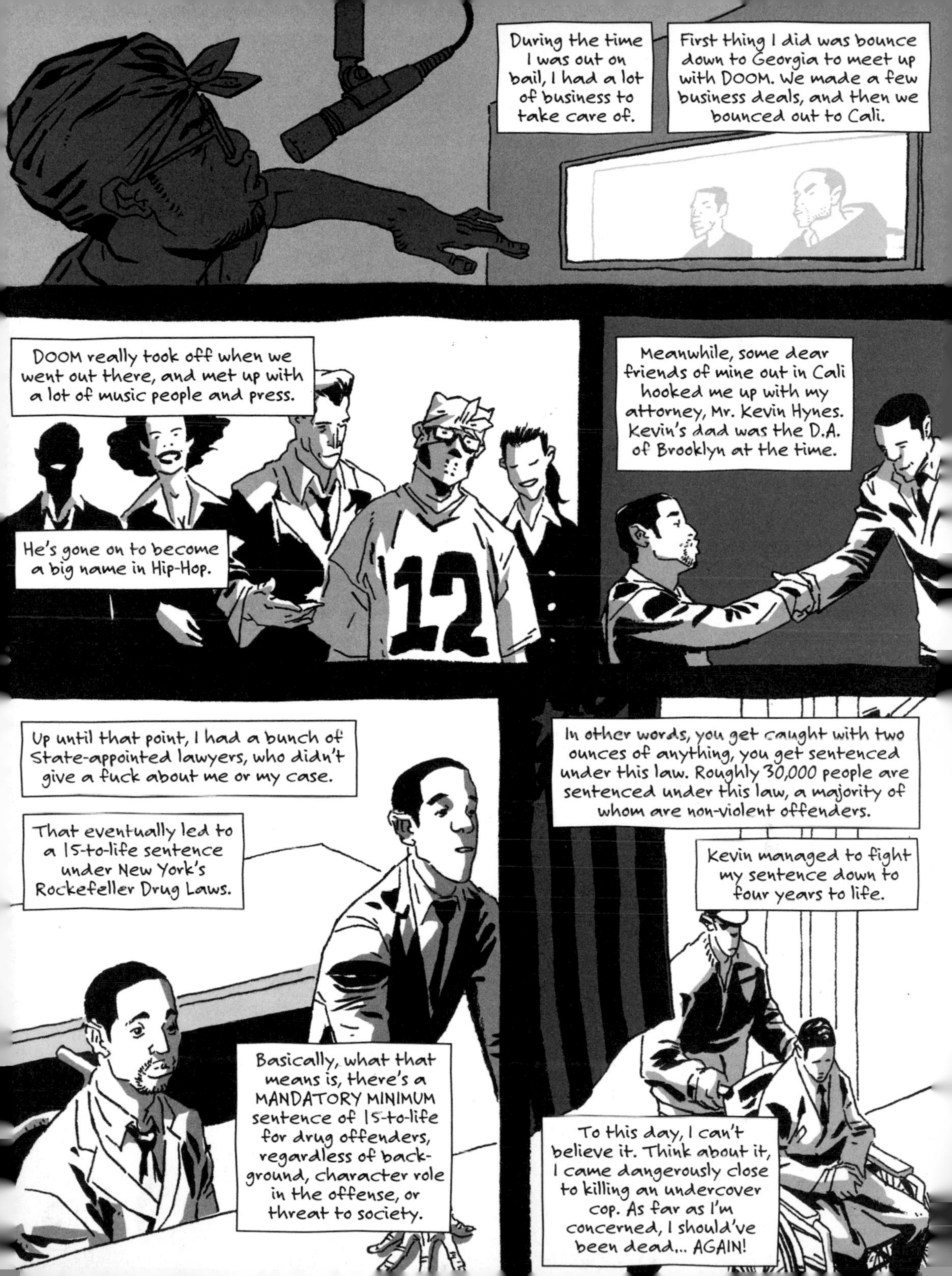
During the time I was out on bail, I had a lot of business to take care of.
First thing I did was bounce down to Georgia to meet up with DOOM. We made a few business deals, and then we bounced out to Cali.
DOOM really took off when we went out there, and met up with a lot of music people and press.
He's gone on to become a big name in Hip-Hop.
12
Meanwhile, some dear friends of mine out in Cali hooked me up with my attorney, Mr. Kevin Hynes. Kevin's dad was the D.A. of Brooklyn at the time.
Up until that point, I had a bunch of State-appointed lawyers, who didn't give a fuck about me or my case.
That eventually led to a 15-to-life sentence under New York's Rockefeller Drug Laws.
Basically, what that means is, there's a MANDATORY MINIMUM sentence of 15-to-life for drug offenders, regardless of back-ground, character role in the offense, or threat to society.
In other words, you get caught with two ounces of anything, you get sentenced under this law. Roughly 30,000 people are sentenced under this law, a majority of whom are non-violent offenders.
Kevin managed to fight my sentence down to four years to life.
To this day, I can't believe it. Think about it, I came dangerously close to killing an undercover cop. As far as I'm concerned, I should've been dead... AGAIN!

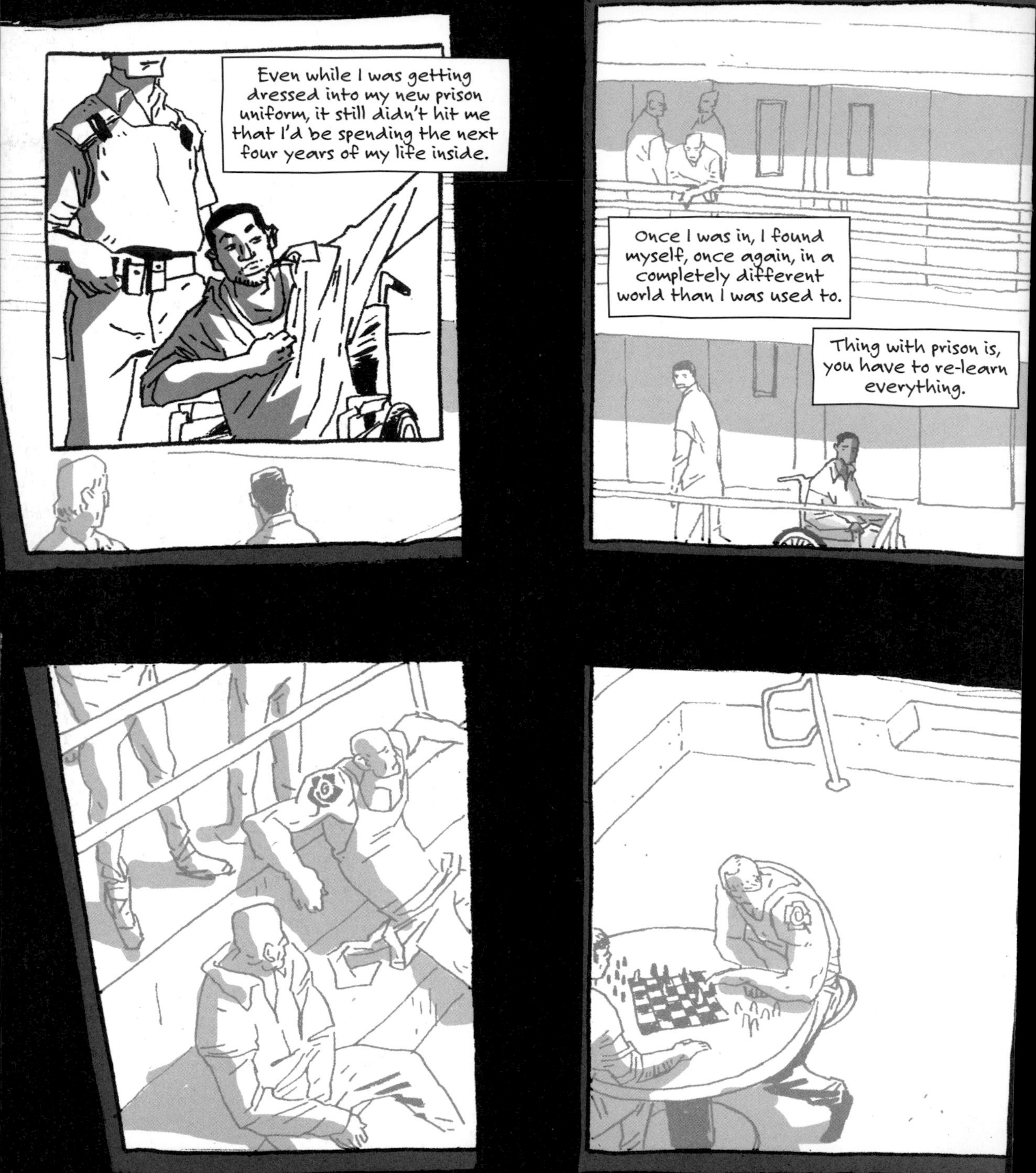
Even while I was getting dressed into my new prison uniform, it still didn't hit me that I'd be spending the next four years of my life inside.
Once I was in, I found myself, once again, in a completely different world than I was used to.
Thing with prison is, you have to re-learn everything.

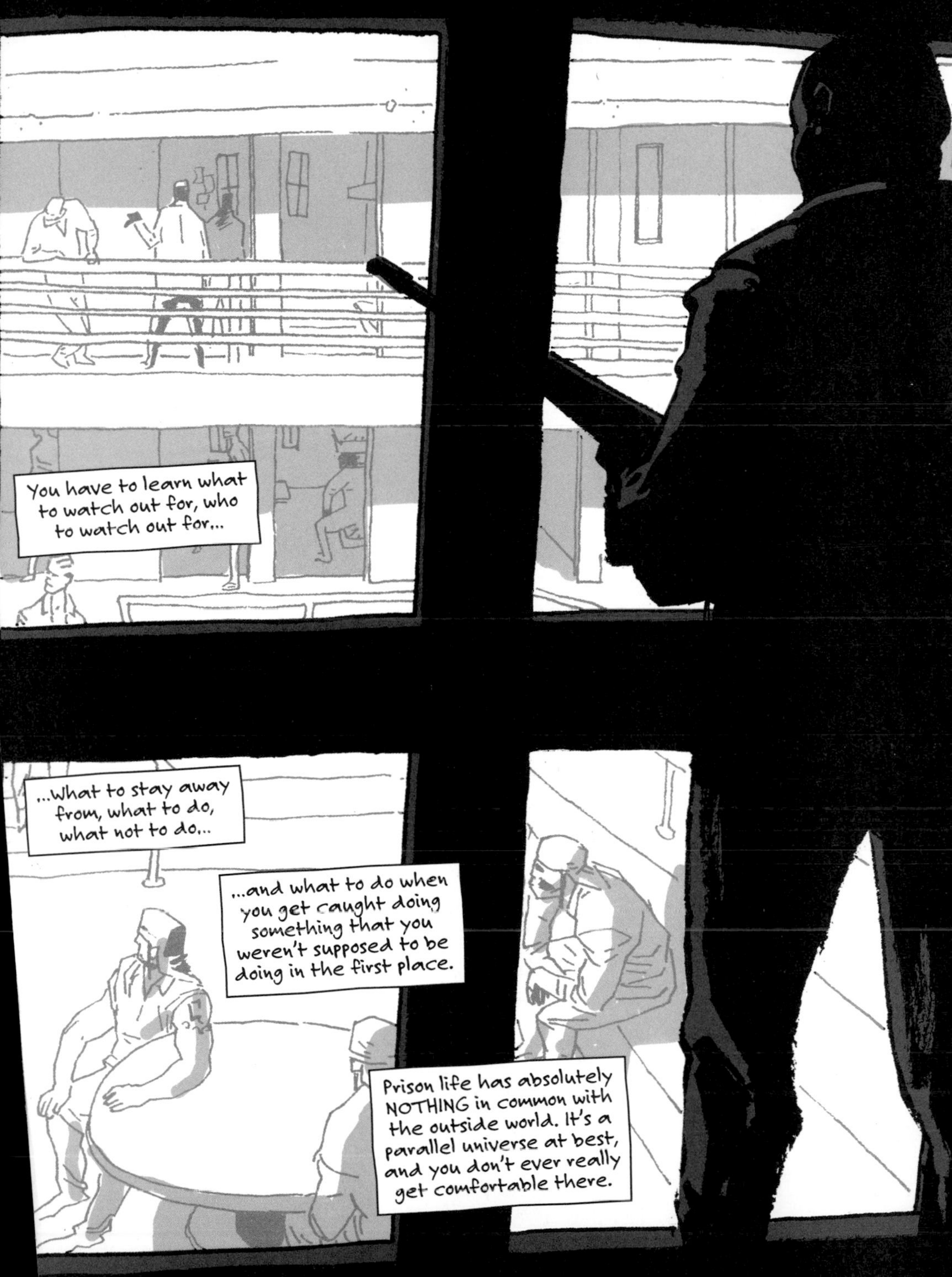
You have to learn what to watch out for, who to watch out for...
...what to stay away from, what to do, what not to do...
...and what to do when you get caught doing something that you weren't supposed to be doing in the first place.
Prison life has absolutely NOTHING in common with the outside world. It's a parallel universe at best, and you don't ever really get comfortable there.

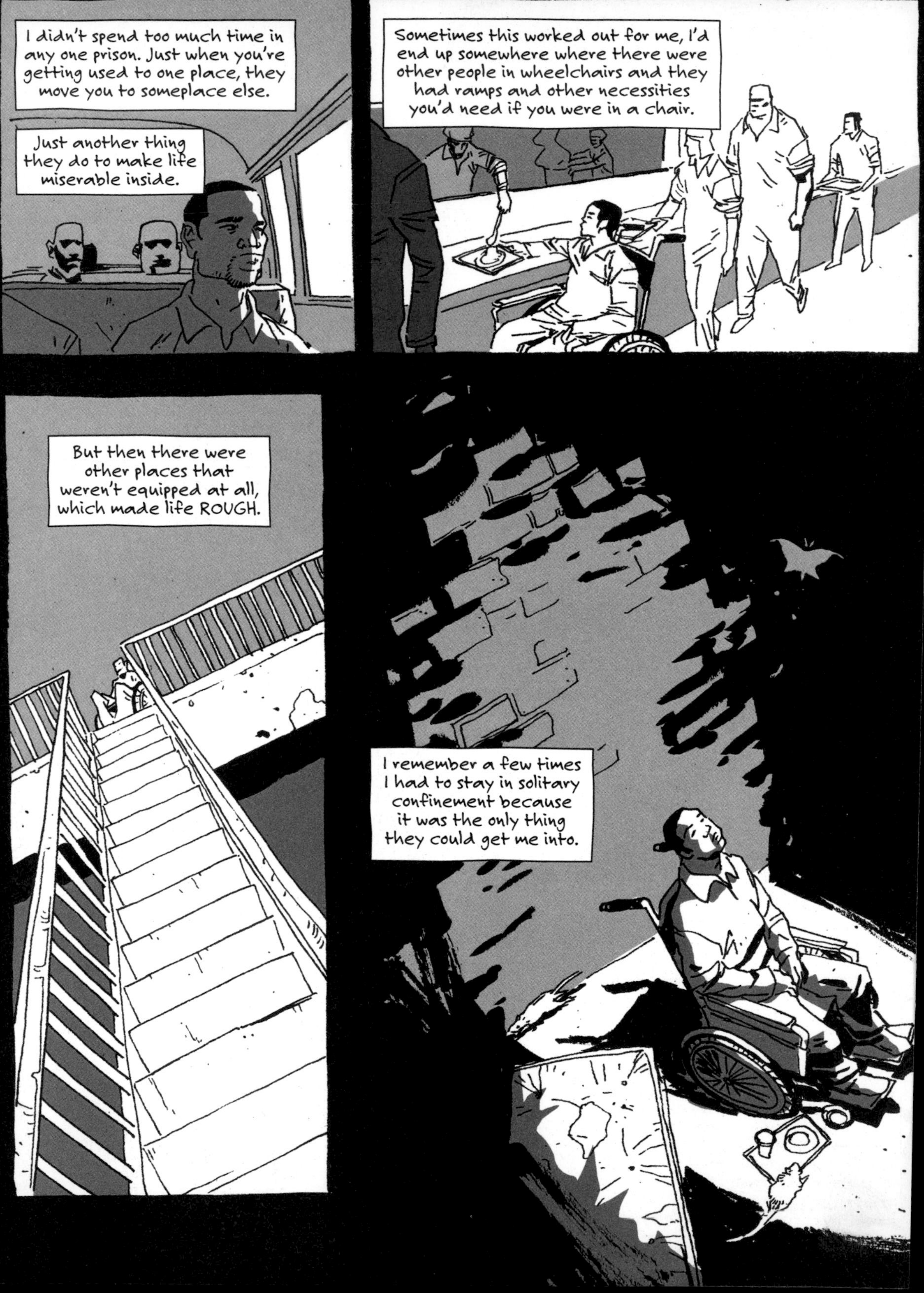
I didn't spend too much time in any one prison. Just when you're getting used to one place, they move you to someplace else.
Just another thing they do to make life miserable inside.
Sometimes this worked out for me, I'd end up somewhere where there were other people in wheelchairs and they had ramps and other necessities you'd need if you were in a chair.
But then there were other places that weren't equipped at all, which made life ROUGH.
I remember a few times I had to stay in solitary confinement because it was the only thing they could get me into.

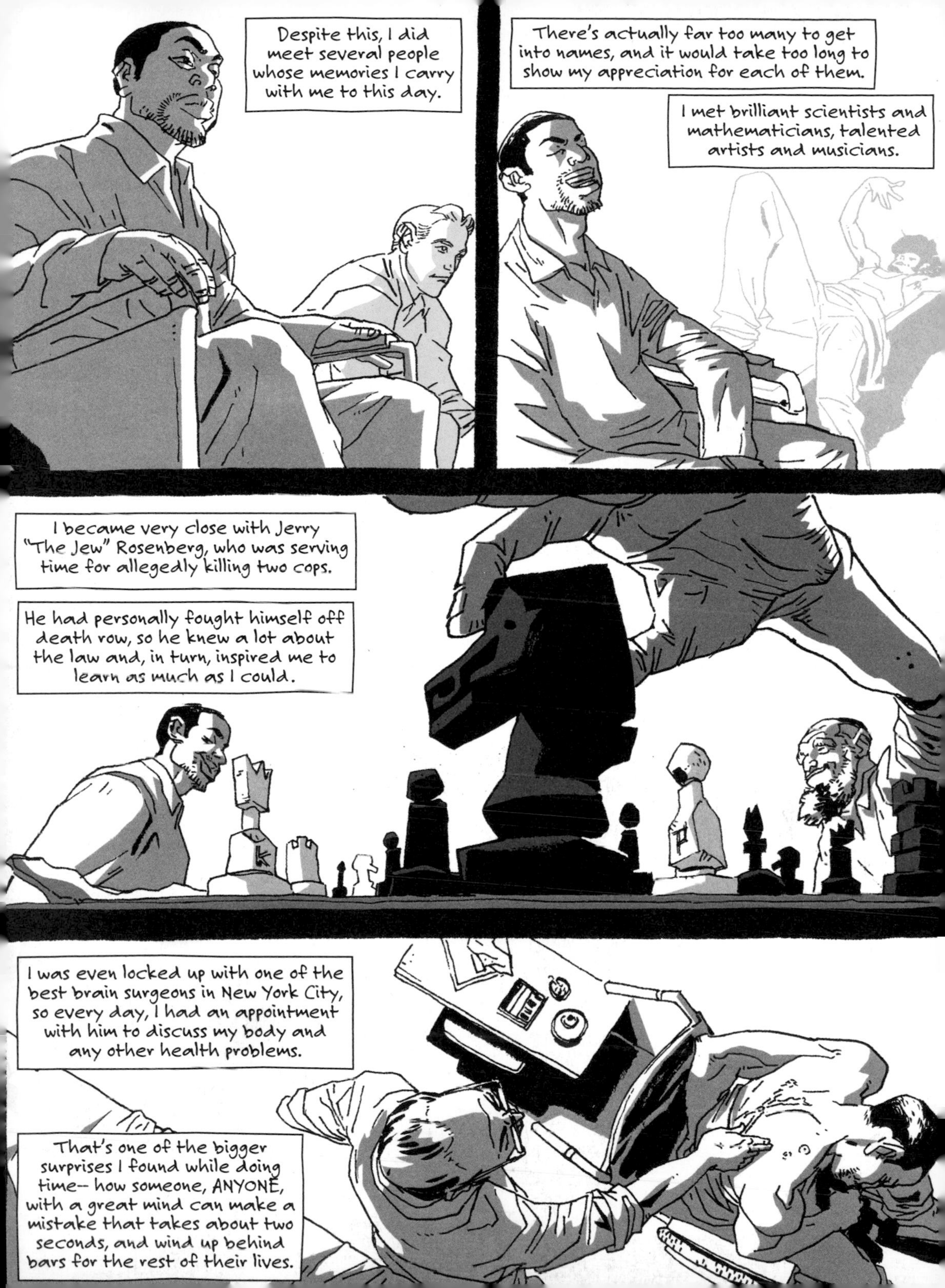
Despite this, I did meet several people whose memories I carry with me to this day.
There's actually far too many to get into names, and it would take too long to show my appreciation for each of them.
I met brilliant scientists and mathematicians, talented artists and musicians.
I became very close with Jerry "The Jew" Rosenberg, who was serving time for allegedly killing two cops.
He had personally fought himself off death row, so he knew a lot about the law and, in turn, inspired me to learn as much as I could.
I was even locked up with one of the best brain surgeons in New York City, so every day, I had an appointment with him to discuss my body and any other health problems.
That's one of the bigger surprises I found while doing time-- how someone, ANYONE, with a great mind can make a mistake that takes about two seconds, and wind up behind bars for the rest of their lives.

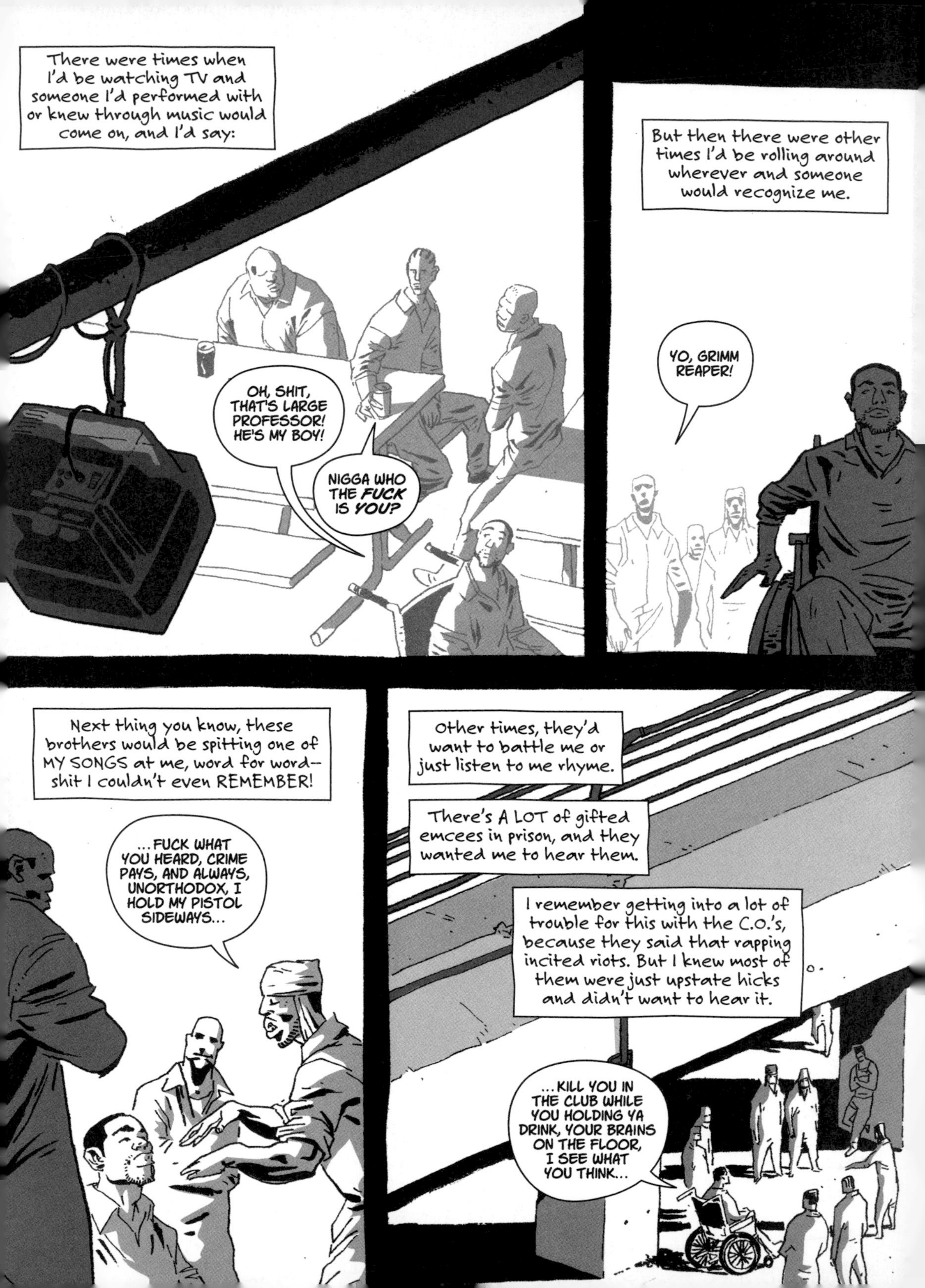
There were times when I'd be watching TV and someone I'd performed with or knew through music would come on, and I'd say:
OH, SHIT, THAT'S LARGE PROFESSOR! HE'S MY BOY!
NIGGA WHO THE *FUCK* IS *YOU?*
But then there were other times I'd be rolling around wherever and someone would recognize me.
YO, GRIMM REAPER!
Next thing you know, these brothers would be spitting one of MY SONGS at me, word for word--shit I couldn't even REMEMBER!
...FUCK WHAT YOU HEARD, CRIME PAYS, AND ALWAYS, UNORTHODOX, I HOLD MY PISTOL SIDEWAYS...
Other times, they'd want to battle me or just listen to me rhyme.
There's A LOT of gifted emcees in prison, and they wanted me to hear them.
I remember getting into a lot of trouble for this with the C.O.'s, because they said that rapping incited riots. But I knew most of them were just upstate hicks and didn't want to hear it.
...KILL YOU IN THE CLUB WHILE YOU HOLDING YA DRINK, YOUR BRAINS ON THE FLOOR, I SEE WHAT YOU THINK...

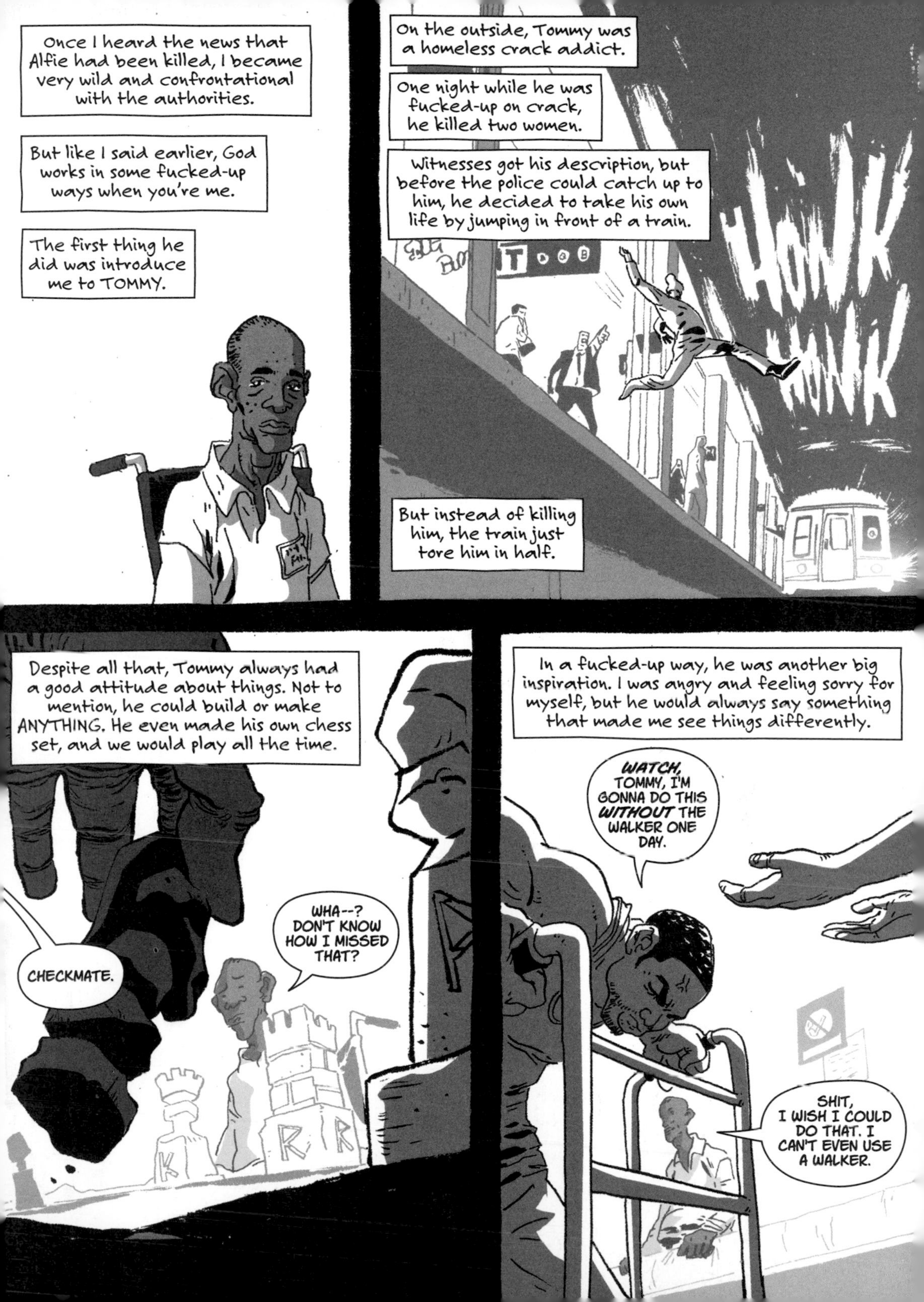
Once I heard the news that Alfie had been killed, I became very wild and confrontational with the authorities.
But like I said earlier, God works in some fucked-up ways when you're me.
The first thing he did was introduce me to TOMMY.
On the outside, Tommy was a homeless crack addict.
One night while he was fucked-up on crack, he killed two women.
Witnesses got his description, but before the police could catch up to him, he decided to take his own life by jumping in front of a train.
HONK
HONK
But instead of killing him, the train just tore him in half.
Despite all that, Tommy always had a good attitude about things. Not to mention, he could build or make ANYTHING. He even made his own chess set, and we would play all the time.
CHECKMATE.
WHA--? DON'T KNOW HOW I MISSED THAT?
In a fucked-up way, he was another big inspiration. I was angry and feeling sorry for myself, but he would always say something that made me see things differently.
WATCH, TOMMY, I'M GONNA DO THIS WITHOUT THE WALKER ONE DAY.
SHIT, I WISH I COULD DO THAT. I CAN'T EVEN USE A WALKER.

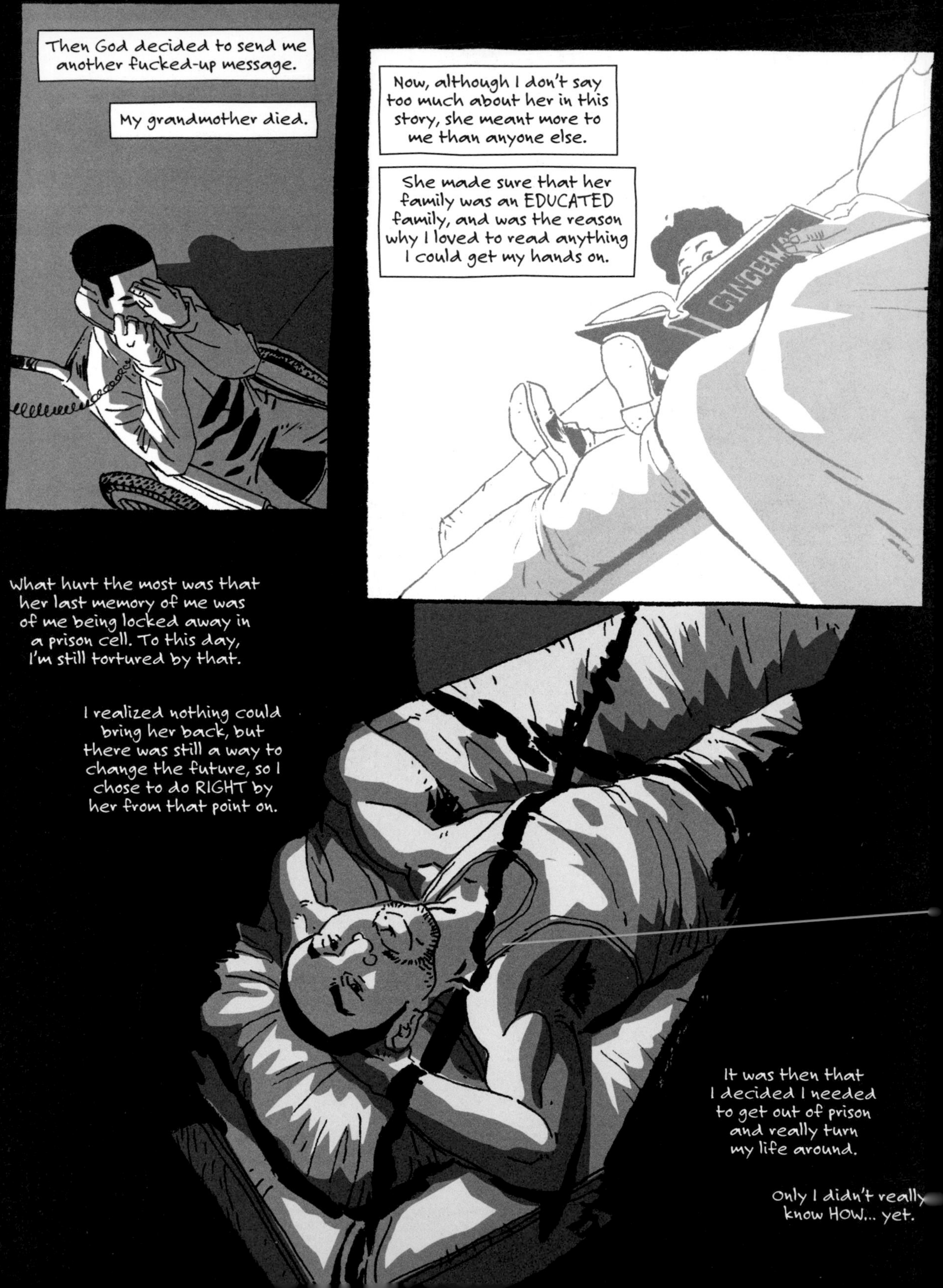
Then God decided to send me another fucked-up message.
My grandmother died.
Now, although I don't say too much about her in this story, she meant more to me than anyone else.
She made sure that her family was an EDUCATED family, and was the reason why I loved to read anything I could get my hands on.
GINGERMAN
What hurt the most was that her last memory of me was of me being locked away in a prison cell. To this day, I'm still tortured by that.
I realized nothing could bring her back, but there was still a way to change the future, so I chose to do RIGHT by her from that point on.
It was then that I decided I needed to get out of prison and really turn my life around.
Only I didn't really know HOW... yet.

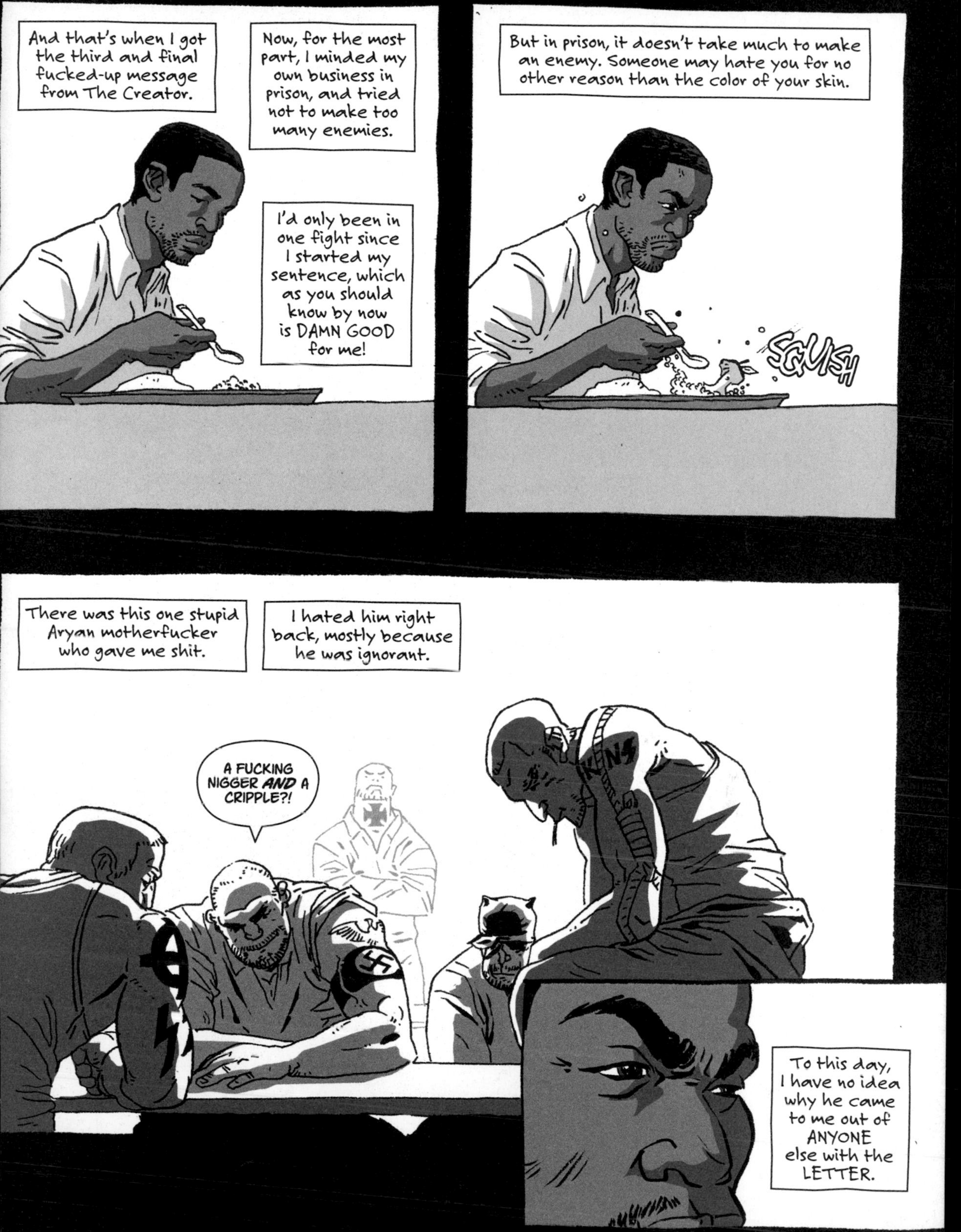

And that's when I got the third and final fucked-up message from The Creator.
Now, for the most part, I minded my own business in prison, and tried not to make too many enemies.
I'd only been in one fight since I started my sentence, which as you should know by now is DAMN GOOD for me!
But in prison, it doesn't take much to make an enemy. Someone may hate you for no other reason than the color of your skin.
SQUISH
There was this one stupid Aryan motherfucker who gave me shit.
I hated him right back, mostly because he was ignorant.
A FUCKING NIGGER *AND* A CRIPPLE?!
To this day, I have no idea why he came to me out of ANYONE else with the LETTER.

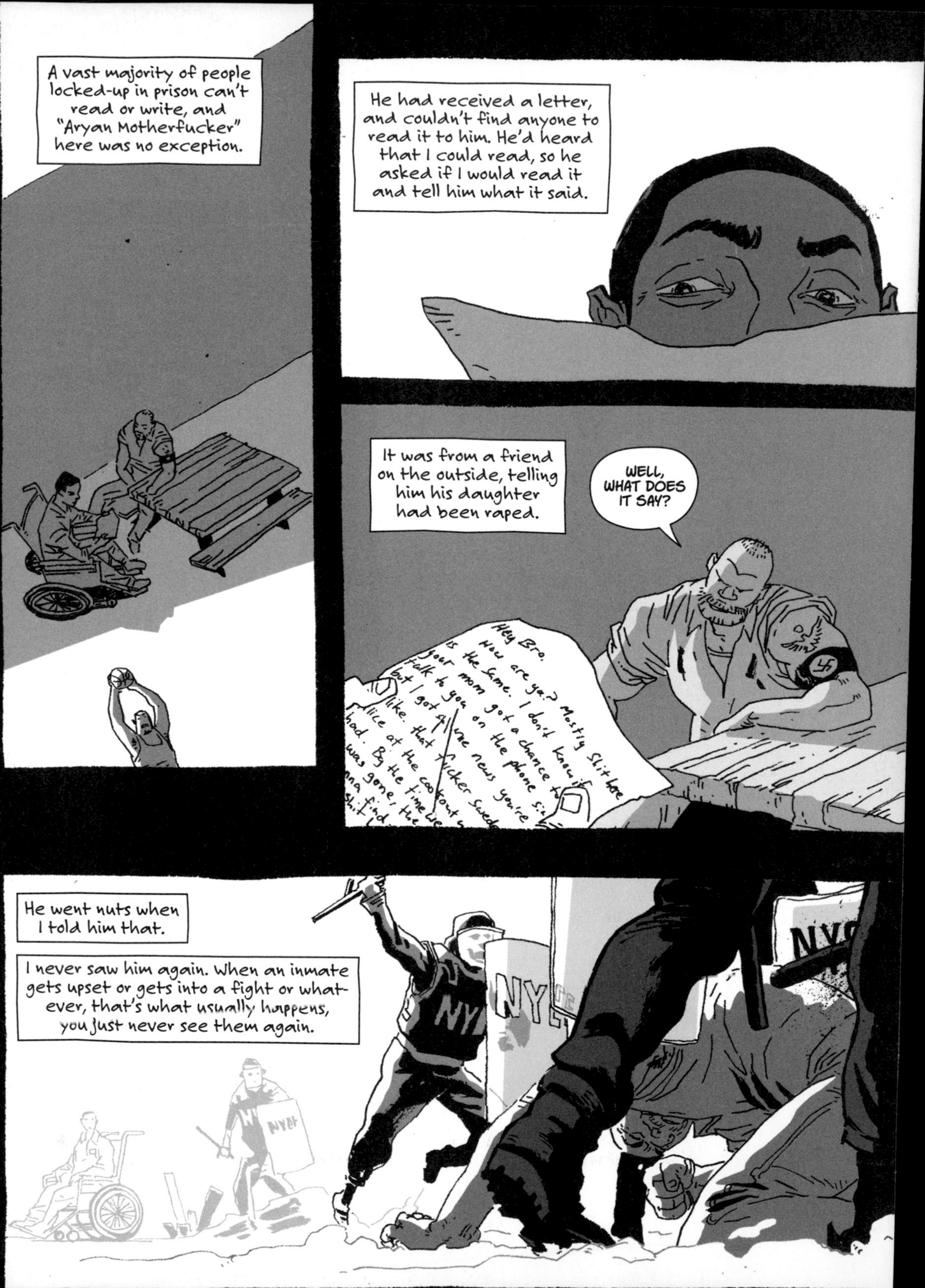
A vast majority of people locked-up in prison can't read or write, and "Aryan Motherfucker" here was no exception.
He had received a letter, and couldn't find anyone to read it to him. He'd heard that I could read, so he asked if I would read it and tell him what it said.
It was from a friend on the outside, telling him his daughter had been raped.
WELL, WHAT DOES IT SAY?
He went nuts when I told him that.
I never saw him again. When an inmate gets upset or gets into a fight or whatever, that's what usually happens, you just never see them again.

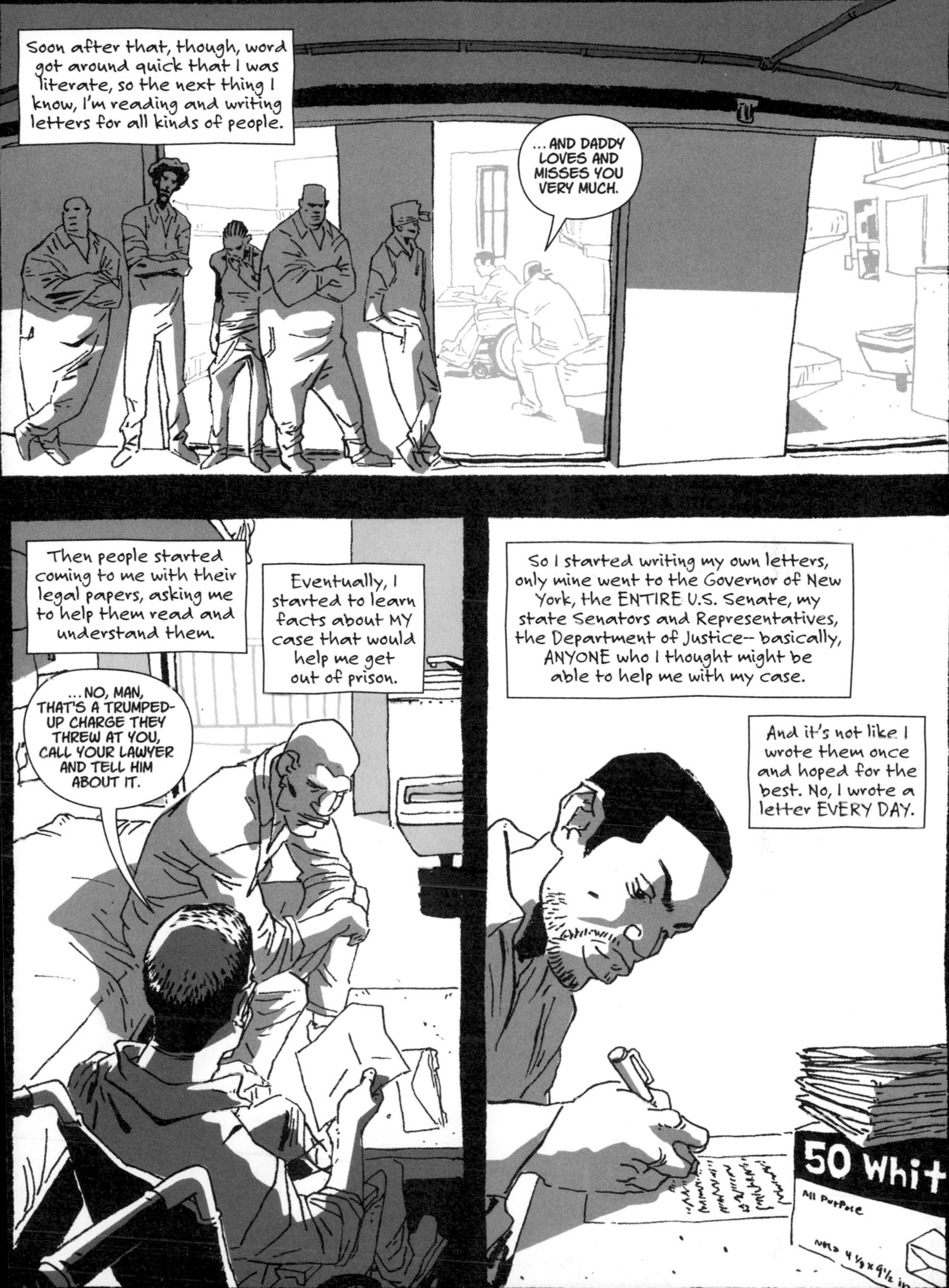

Soon after that, though, word got around quick that I was literate, so the next thing I know, I'm reading and writing letters for all kinds of people.
...AND DADDY LOVES AND MISSES YOU VERY MUCH.
Then people started coming to me with their legal papers, asking me to help them read and understand them.
Eventually, I started to learn facts about MY case that would help me get out of prison.
...NO, MAN, THAT'S A TRUMPED-UP CHARGE THEY THREW AT YOU, CALL YOUR LAWYER AND TELL HIM ABOUT IT.
So I started writing my own letters, only mine went to the Governor of New York, the ENTIRE U.S. Senate, my state Senators and Representatives, the Department of Justice-- basically, ANYONE who I thought might be able to help me with my case.
And it's not like I wrote them once and hoped for the best. No, I wrote a letter EVERY DAY.
50 Whit
All Purpose

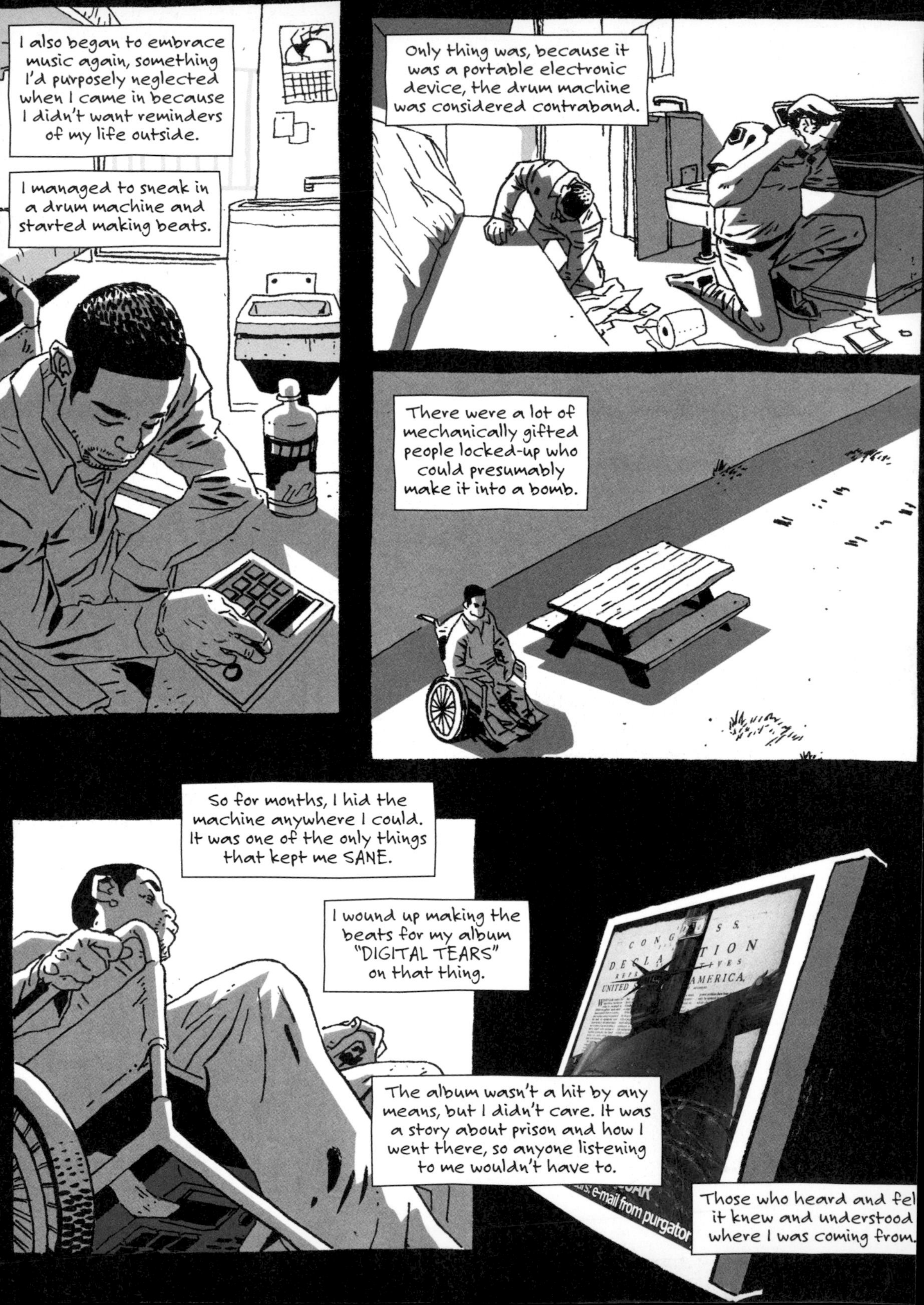
I also began to embrace music again, something I'd purposely neglected when I came in because I didn't want reminders of my life outside.
I managed to sneak in a drum machine and started making beats.
Only thing was, because it was a portable electronic device, the drum machine was considered contraband.
There were a lot of mechanically gifted people locked-up who could presumably make it into a bomb.
So for months, I hid the machine anywhere I could. It was one of the only things that kept me SANE.
I wound up making the beats for my album "DIGITAL TEARS" on that thing.
The album wasn't a hit by any means, but I didn't care. It was a story about prison and how I went there, so anyone listening to me wouldn't have to.
Those who heard and fel it knew and understood where I was coming from.

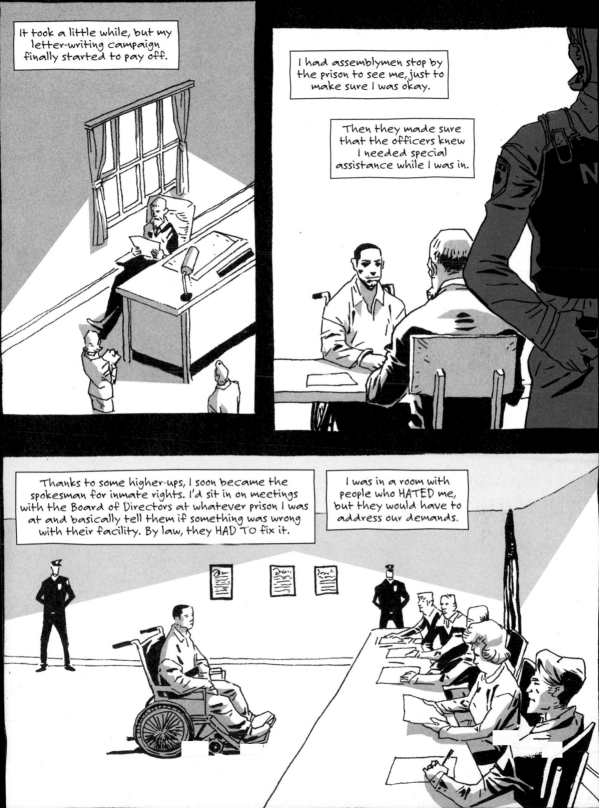

It took a little while, but my letter-writing campaign finally started to pay off.

I had assemblymen stop by the prison to see me, just to make sure I was okay.

Then they made sure that the officers knew I needed special assistance while I was in.

Thanks to some higher-ups, I soon became the spokesman for inmate rights. I'd sit in on meetings with the Board of Directors at whatever prison I was at and basically tell them if something was wrong with their facility. By law, they HAD TO fix it.

I was in a room with people who HATED me, but they would have to address our demands.

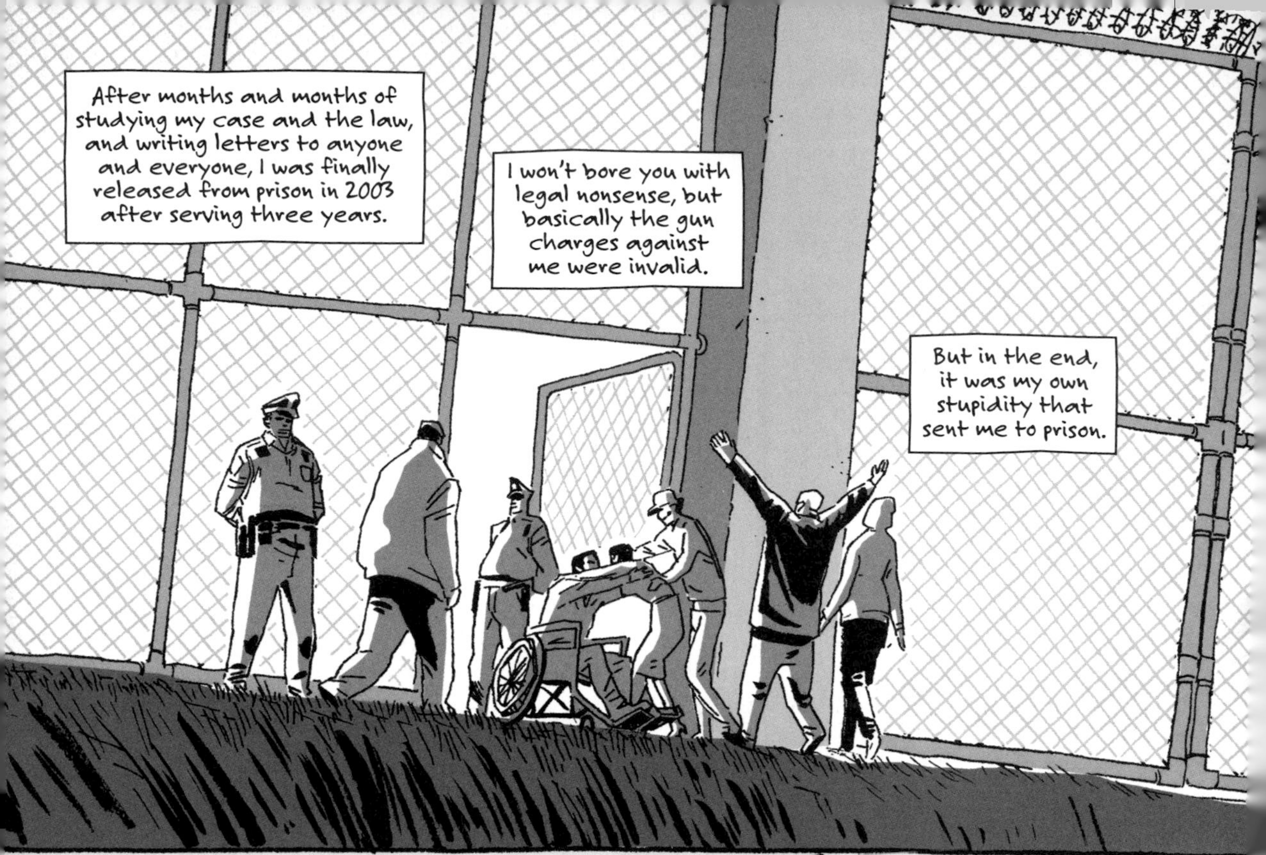
After months and months of studying my case and the law, and writing letters to anyone and everyone, I was finally released from prison in 2003 after serving three years.
I won't bore you with legal nonsense, but basically the gun charges against me were invalid.
But in the end, it was my own stupidity that sent me to prison.

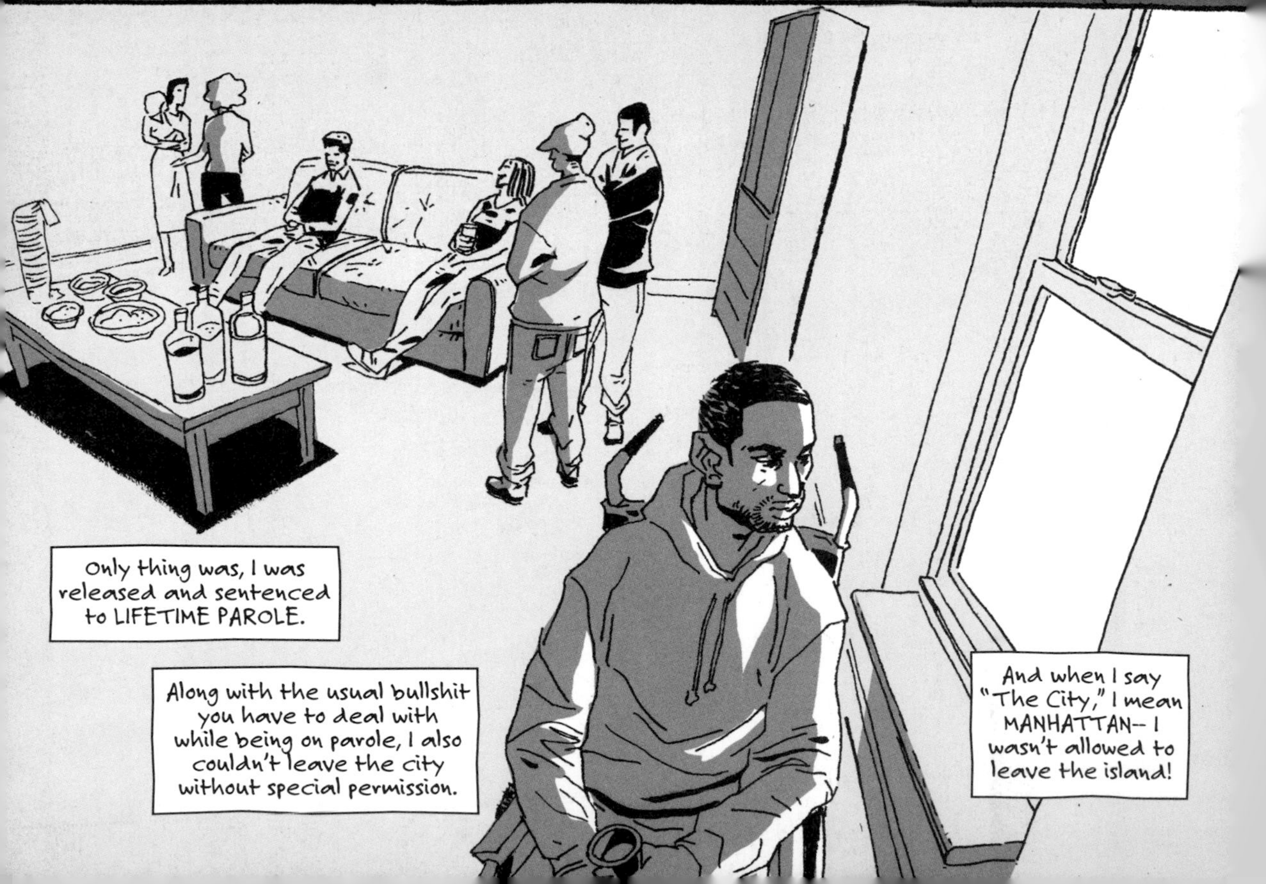
Only thing was, I was released and sentenced to LIFETIME PAROLE.
Along with the usual bullshit you have to deal with while being on parole, I also couldn't leave the city without special permission.
And when I say "The City," I mean MANHATTAN-- I wasn't allowed to leave the island!

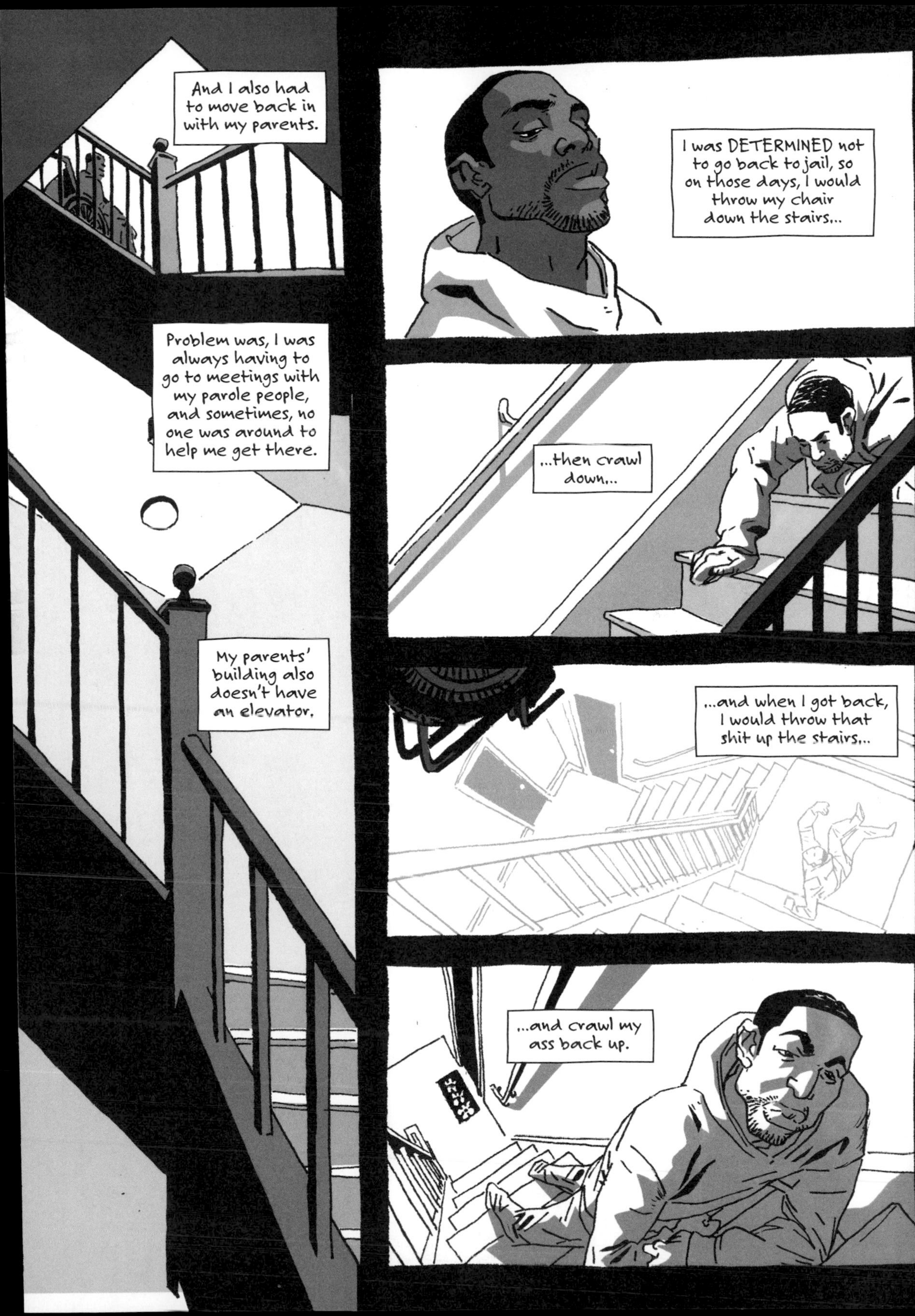
And I also had to move back in with my parents.
Problem was, I was always having to go to meetings with my parole people, and sometimes, no one was around to help me get there.
My parents' building also doesn't have an elevator.
I was DETERMINED not to go back to jail, so on those days, I would throw my chair down the stairs...
...then crawl down...
...and when I got back, I would throw that shit up the stairs...
...and crawl my ass back up.

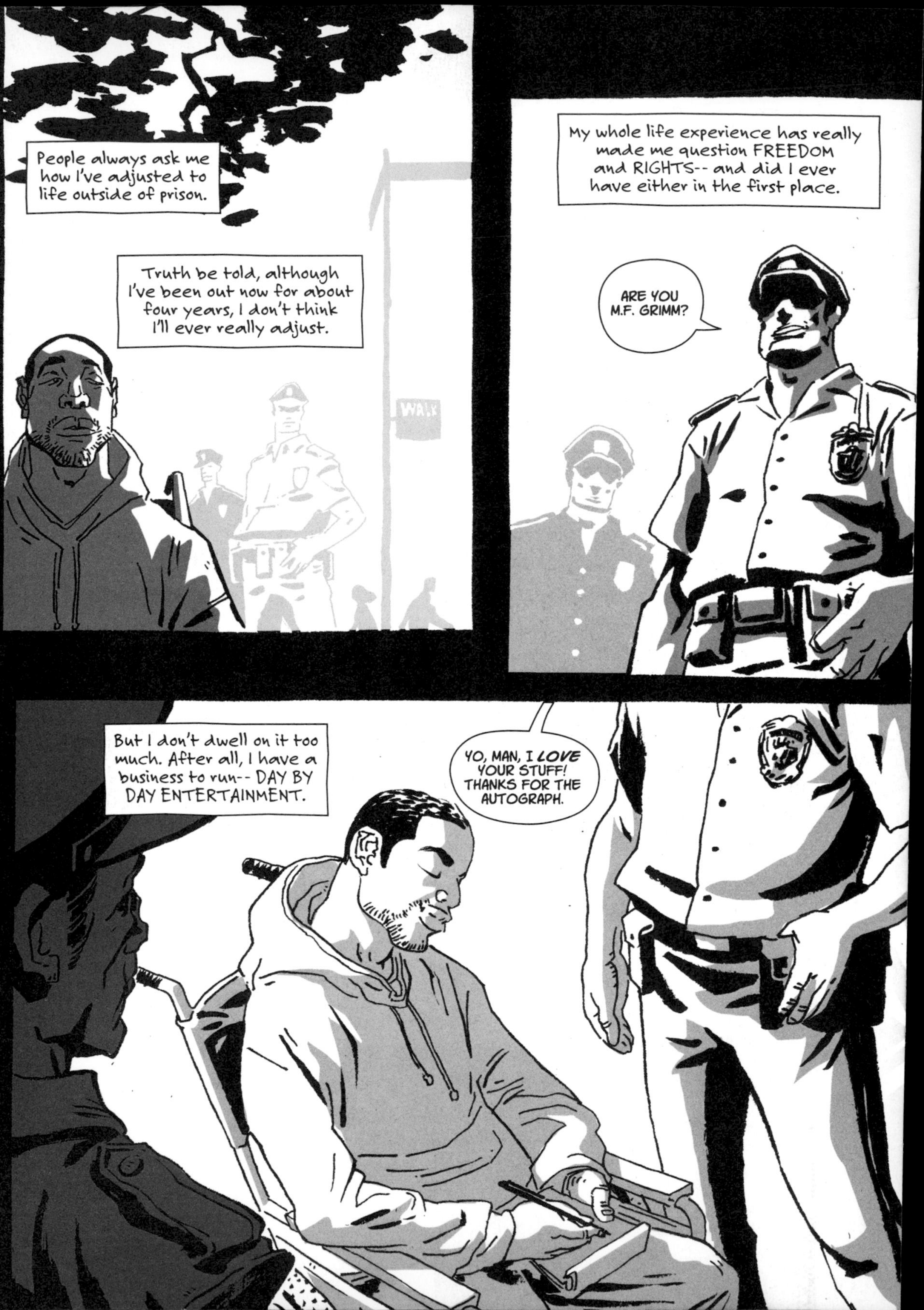
People always ask me how I've adjusted to life outside of prison.
Truth be told, although I've been out now for about four years, I don't think I'll ever really adjust.
My whole life experience has really made me question FREEDOM and RIGHTS-- and did I ever have either in the first place.
ARE YOU M.F. GRIMM?
But I don't dwell on it too much. After all, I have a business to run-- DAY BY DAY ENTERTAINMENT.
YO, MAN, I LOVE YOUR STUFF! THANKS FOR THE AUTOGRAPH.

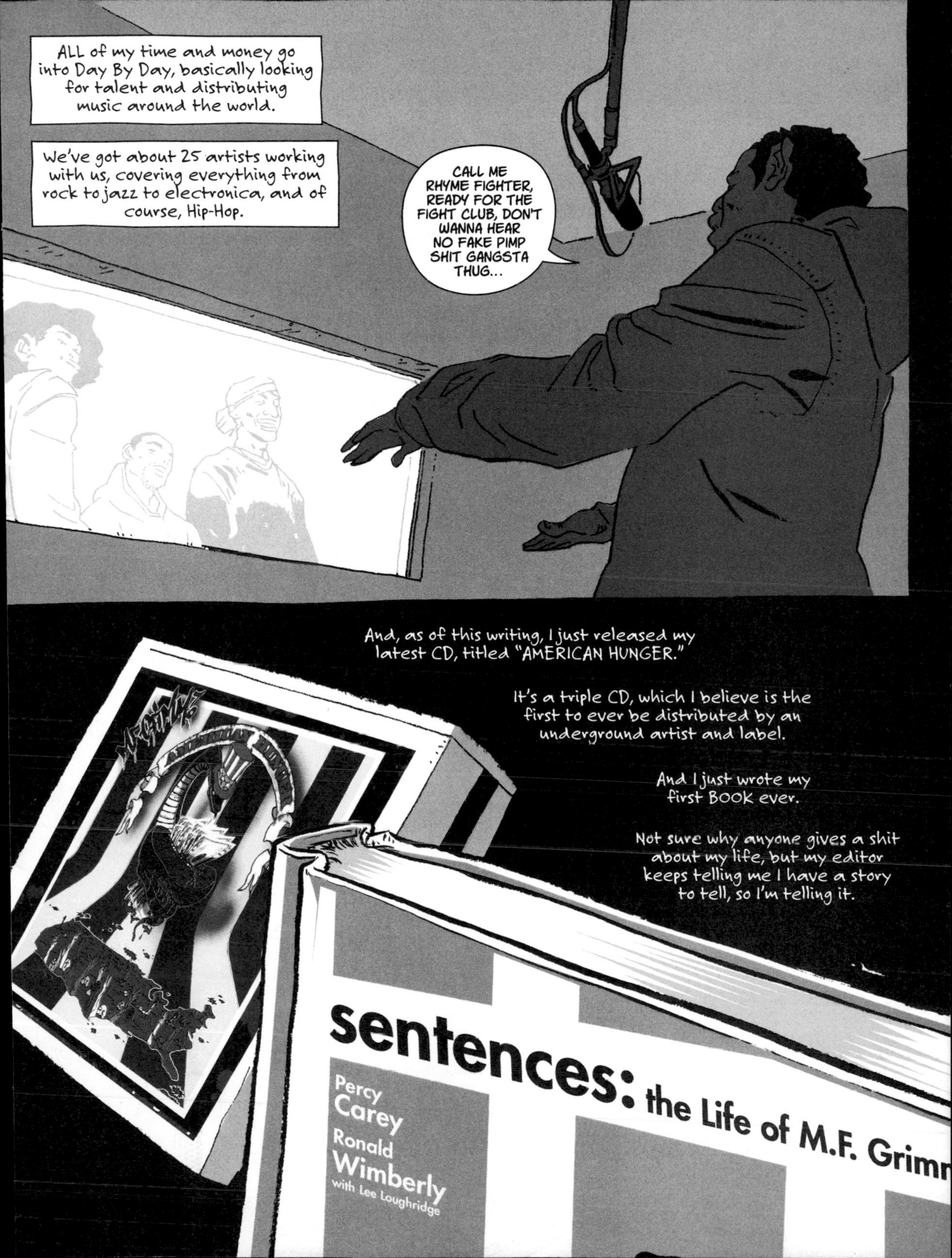
ALL of my time and money go into Day By Day, basically looking for talent and distributing music around the world.
We've got about 25 artists working with us, covering everything from rock to jazz to electronica, and of course, Hip-Hop.
CALL ME RHYME FIGHTER, READY FOR THE FIGHT CLUB, DON'T WANNA HEAR NO FAKE PIMP SHIT GANGSTA THUG...
And, as of this writing, I just released my latest CD, titled "AMERICAN HUNGER."
It's a triple CD, which I believe is the first to ever be distributed by an underground artist and label.
And I just wrote my first BOOK ever.
Not sure why anyone gives a shit about my life, but my editor keeps telling me I have a story to tell, so I'm telling it.
sentences: the Life of M.F. Grimm
Percy Carey
Ronald Wimberly
with Lee Loughridge

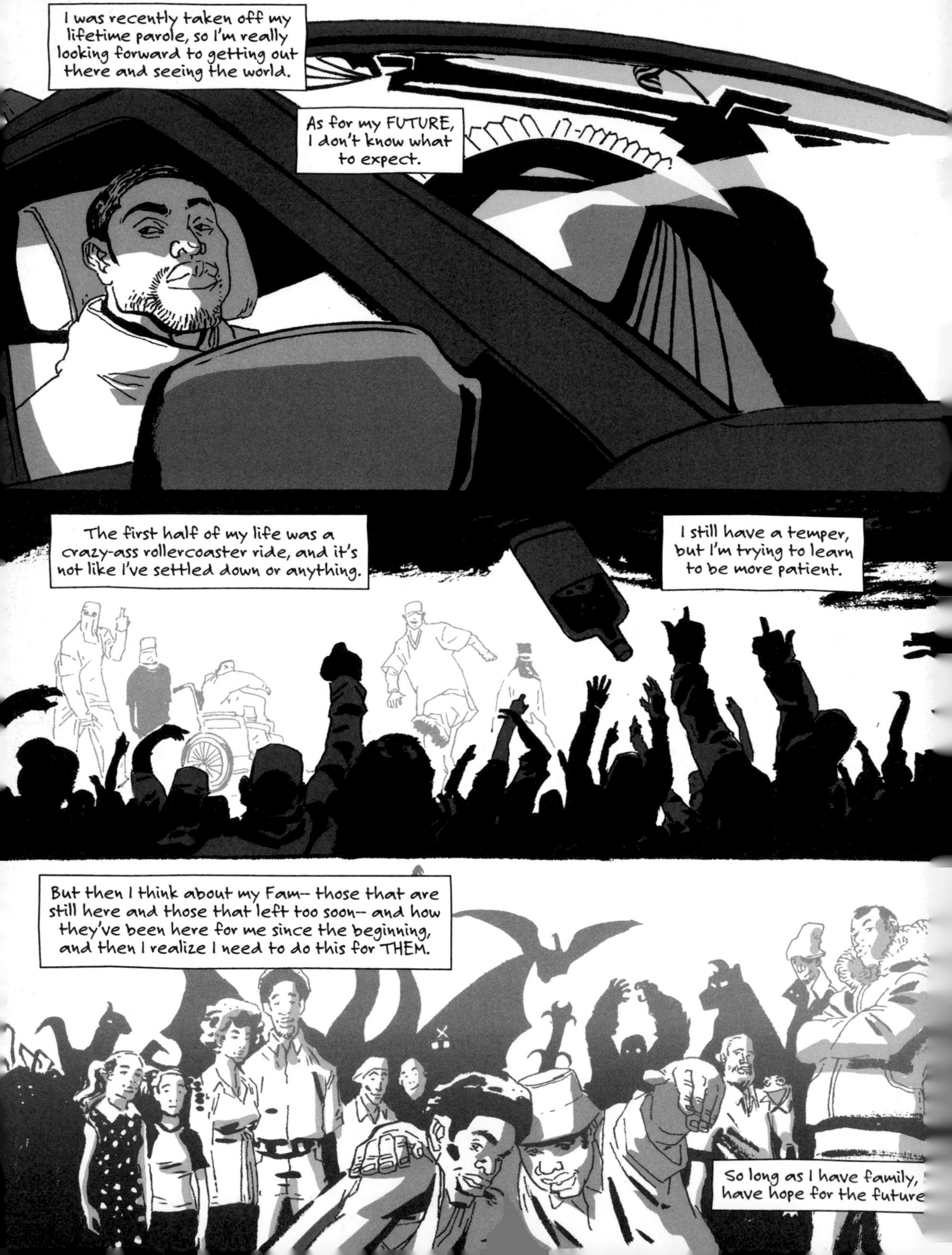
I was recently taken off my lifetime parole, so I'm really looking forward to getting out there and seeing the world.
As for my FUTURE, I don't know what to expect.
The first half of my life was a crazy-ass rollercoaster ride, and it's not like I've settled down or anything.
I still have a temper, but I'm trying to learn to be more patient.
But then I think about my Fam-- those that are still here and those that left too soon-- and how they've been here for me since the beginning, and then I realize I need to do this for THEM.
So long as I have family, have hope for the future

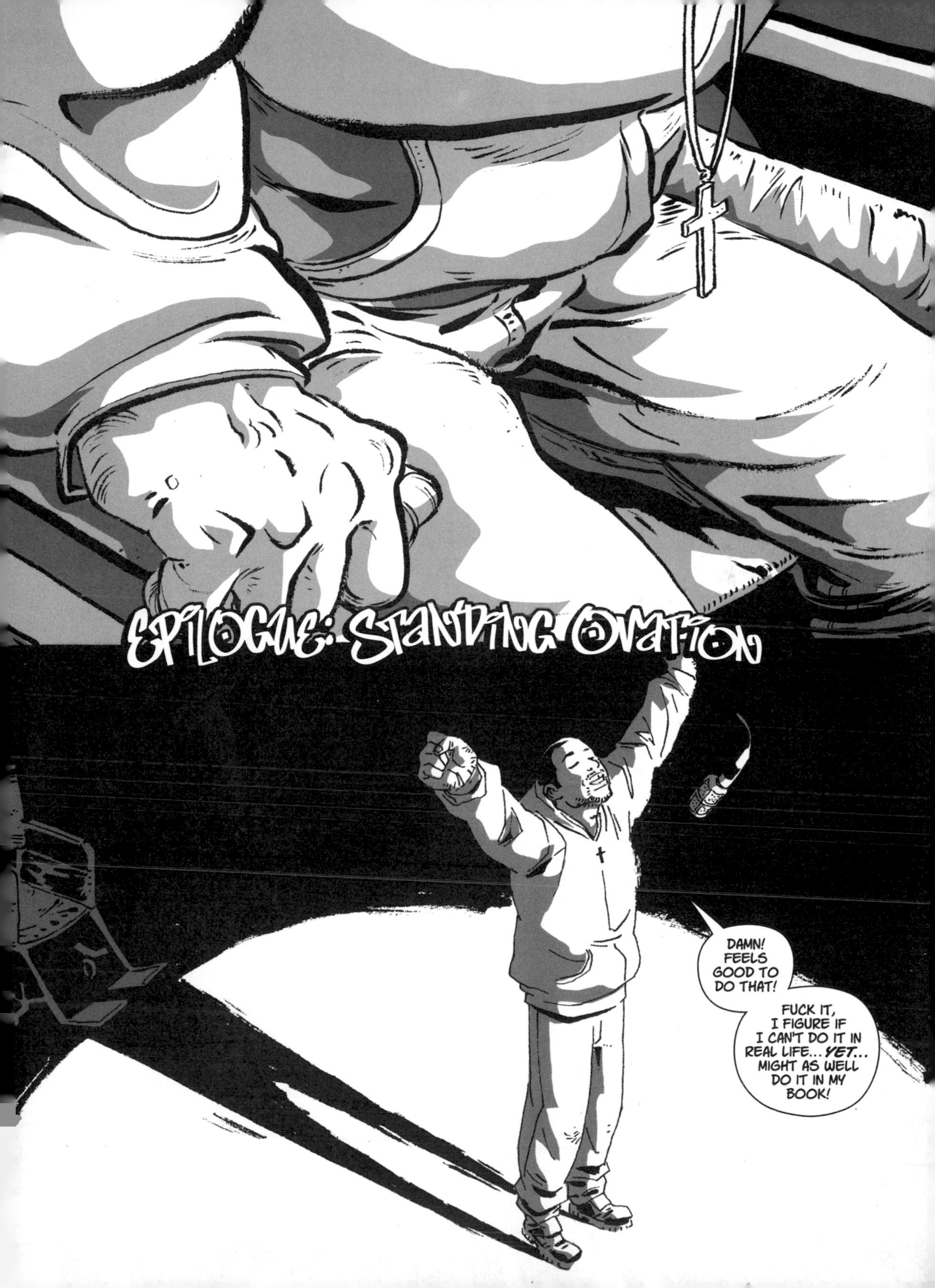
EPILOGUE: STANDING OVATION
DAMN! FEELS GOOD TO DO THAT!
FUCK IT, I FIGURE IF I CAN'T DO IT IN REAL LIFE... YET... MIGHT AS WELL DO IT IN MY BOOK!

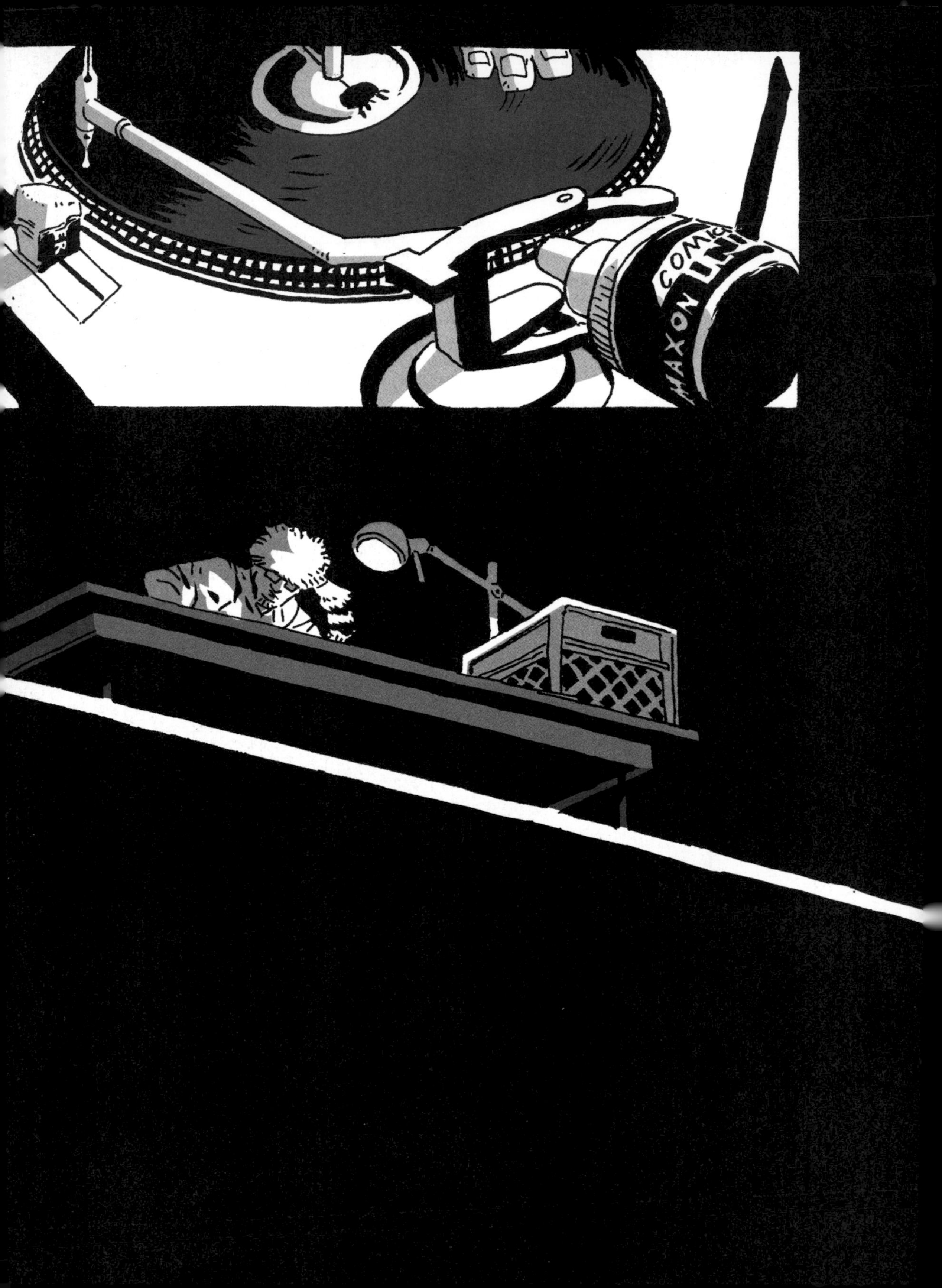
COMIC
MAXON

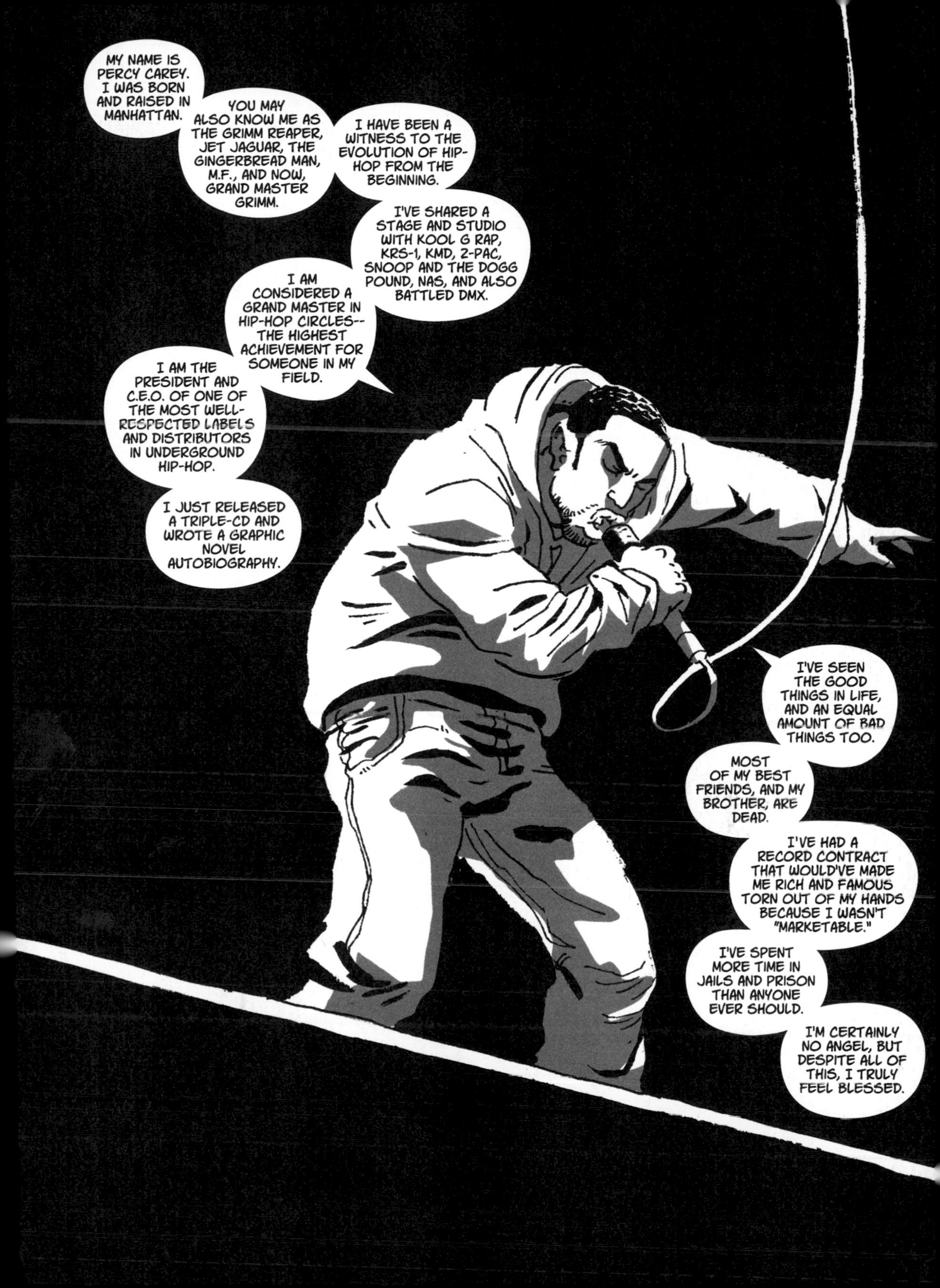
MY NAME IS PERCY CAREY. I WAS BORN AND RAISED IN MANHATTAN.
YOU MAY ALSO KNOW ME AS THE GRIMM REAPER, JET JAGUAR, THE GINGERBREAD MAN, M.F., AND NOW, GRAND MASTER GRIMM.
I HAVE BEEN A WITNESS TO THE EVOLUTION OF HIP-HOP FROM THE BEGINNING.
I'VE SHARED A STAGE AND STUDIO WITH KOOL G RAP, KRS-1, KMD, 2-PAC, SNOOP AND THE DOGG POUND, NAS, AND ALSO BATTLED DMX.
I AM CONSIDERED A GRAND MASTER IN HIP-HOP CIRCLES--THE HIGHEST ACHIEVEMENT FOR SOMEONE IN MY FIELD.
I AM THE PRESIDENT AND C.E.O. OF ONE OF THE MOST WELL-RESPECTED LABELS AND DISTRIBUTORS IN UNDERGROUND HIP-HOP.
I JUST RELEASED A TRIPLE-CD AND WROTE A GRAPHIC NOVEL AUTOBIOGRAPHY.
I'VE SEEN THE GOOD THINGS IN LIFE, AND AN EQUAL AMOUNT OF BAD THINGS TOO.
MOST OF MY BEST FRIENDS, AND MY BROTHER, ARE DEAD.
I'VE HAD A RECORD CONTRACT THAT WOULD'VE MADE ME RICH AND FAMOUS TORN OUT OF MY HANDS BECAUSE I WASN'T "MARKETABLE."
I'VE SPENT MORE TIME IN JAILS AND PRISON THAN ANYONE EVER SHOULD.
I'M CERTAINLY NO ANGEL, BUT DESPITE ALL OF THIS, I TRULY FEEL BLESSED.

What you just read about me is only a little piece of my life in general. We've only really scratched the surface here.

There's a lot of things, people and places that I can't talk about, even off the record.

I didn't do this book to glorify my life, and I certainly hope those of you who read this don't look at me as a model for how to be successful.

God knows I would give this all up to have back those that have died along the way. Not a minute goes by that I don't think of my brothers and sisters who were lost along the way.

But most important, I want to show the youth that there's other options out there that don't involve guns and crime. You CAN make it in this business-- and any business for that matter-- without taking the route I took.

If I can help one person, then this project has been a success.

My name is PERCY CAREY.

Thank you for reading my story.

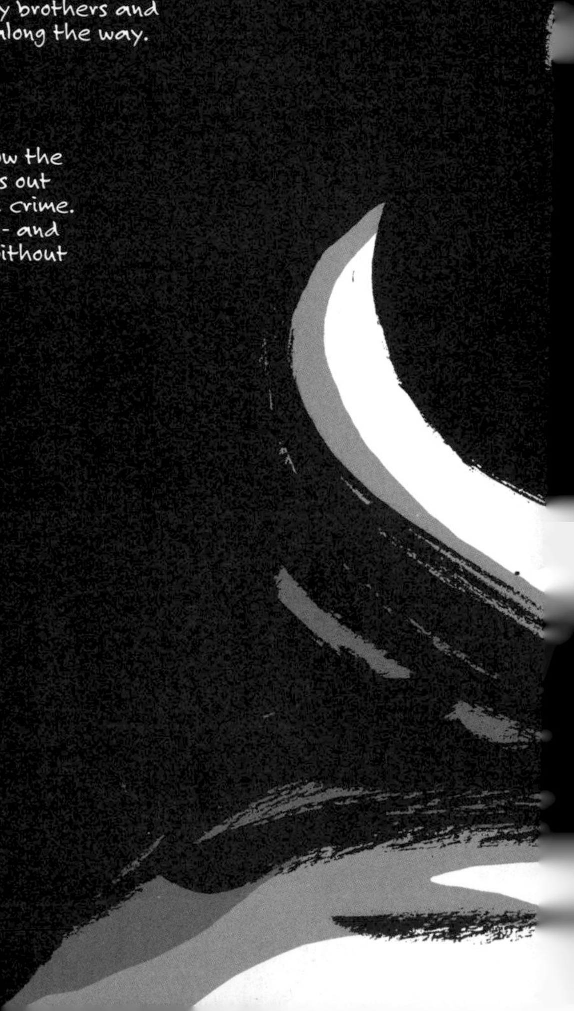

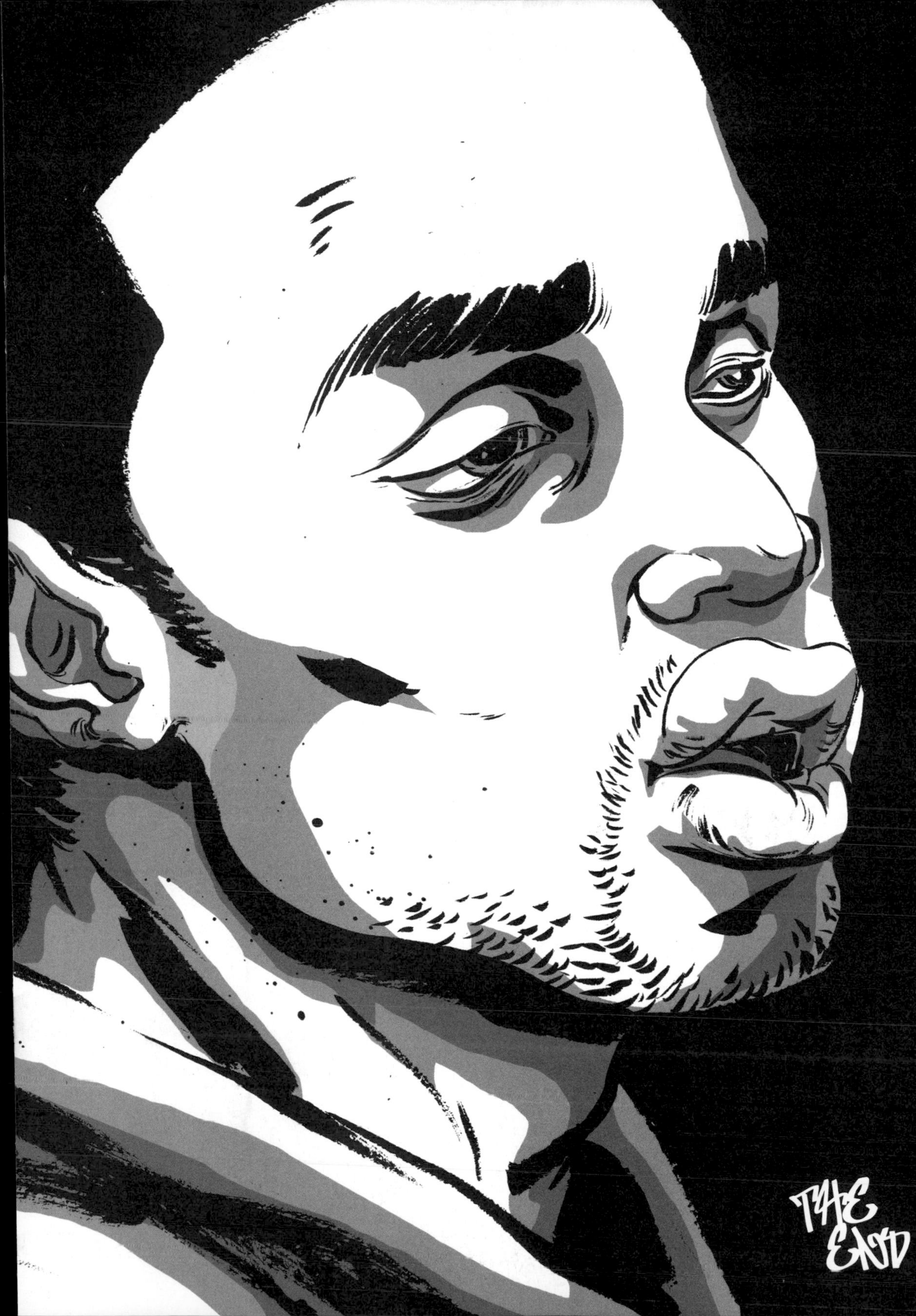
THE
END

Some quote Scriptures but parrots quote
Grimm Scriptures are made from Scratch my mind floats
And I have War Scars and War Scrapes from War Skits
Rhymes Souped up like lentil to show my mental's not accidental
My World Revolves because it's autocratic
My Guns revolve but some are automatic
Vision beyond optical needed when living Prodigal
Sleep with third eye open or get clipped like a cuticle
Conditional choices stable or critical
Who lives? who dies? who strives? is so political
Young Street champs stripped of belts in pistol title shots
Heavyweight division K.O.'s no split decisions
Giuliani referee'd this hellhole but he didn't give a fuck so
There was cuts head butts and elbows
Drug Sweeps, bullets fly blood splat in blotches
Thugs Creep People died Tourtured held hostage
actions brutal beyond belief but authentic
Rhymes are Genuine thoughts are anti-synthetic.
attempt to get Jurassic planted back pre-historic
Roach niggas are morbid from my acid thoughts of boric
kidnapped. Snatched, dragged off, notes of extortion
Shit's creek, they seek demands of financial portions.
Six million dollars nigga like your steve Austin
Cause if they really love you then that's how much love is costing
or death will be puzzled jigsaw fate
chopped up distributed body Parts in different states
Take you to Spots that nobody knows
Curiosity grows as you decompose.

"M."

—From the journal of Percy Carey

# bios

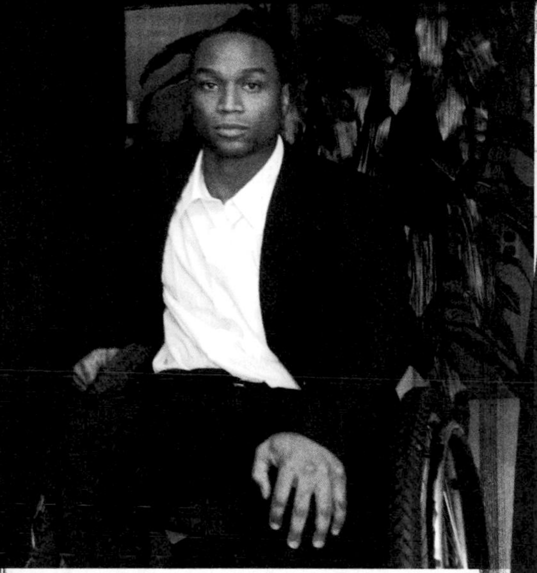

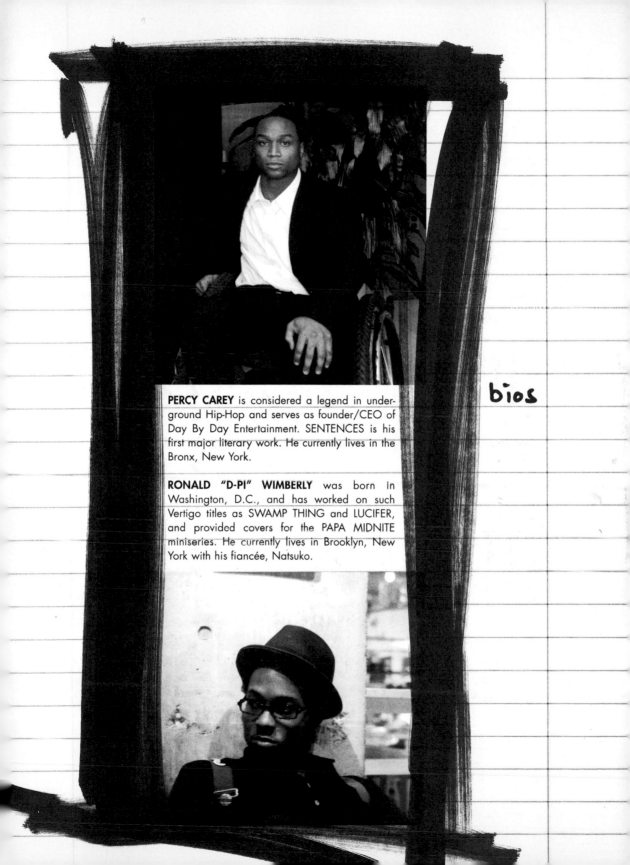

**PERCY CAREY** is considered a legend in underground Hip-Hop and serves as founder/CEO of Day By Day Entertainment. SENTENCES is his first major literary work. He currently lives in the Bronx, New York.

**RONALD "D-PI" WIMBERLY** was born in Washington, D.C., and has worked on such Vertigo titles as SWAMP THING and LUCIFER, and provided covers for the PAPA MIDNITE miniseries. He currently lives in Brooklyn, New York with his fiancée, Natsuko.

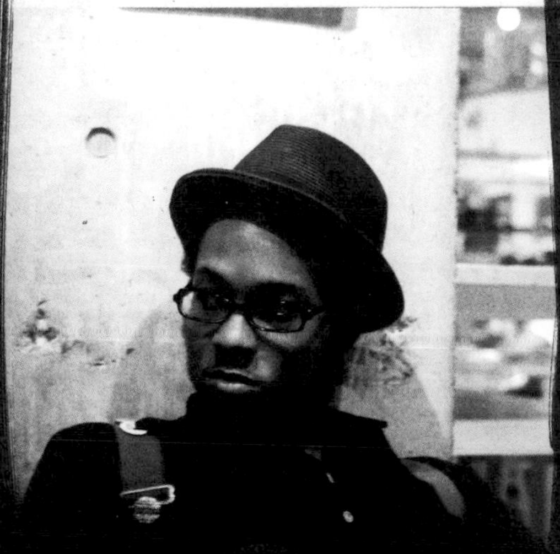

**Be sure to check out these other VERTIGO graphic novels.**
All titles are suggested for mature readers.

## 100 BULLETS
**Brian Azzarello/Eduardo Risso**
With one special briefcase, Agent Graves gives you the chance to kill without retribution. But what is the real price for this chance — and who is setting it?

## SLOTH
**Gilbert Hernandez**
Troubled teenager Miguel Serra becomes a walking urban legend after he wills himself into a coma and wakes up one year later virtually unchanged. Discover how a haunted lemon orchard, a mysterious goatman and murder collide as Miguel, his girlfriend Lita and their friend Romeo take on the teenage wasteland of suburbia.

## THE ORIGINALS
**Dave Gibbons**
For two childhood friends, there's nothing more important than belonging to the Originals. But being a part of the "in" crowd brings its own deadly consequences...

## JOHN CONSTANTINE: HELLBLAZER
**Jamie Delano/Garth Ennis/ Warren Ellis/ Brian Azzarello/Steve Dillon/Marcelo Frusin/various**
Where horror, dark magic, and bad luck meet, John Constantine is never far away.

## PREACHER
**Garth Ennis/Steve Dillon/various**
A modern American epic of life, death, God, love, and redemption — filled with sex, booze, and blood.

## PRIDE OF BAGHDAD
**Brian K. Vaughan/Niko Henrichon**
Inspired by true events, this riveting adventure tells the story of four lions roaming the war-torn streets of Baghdad. A heartbreaking look at the cost of war and price of freedom.

## THE SANDMAN
**Neil Gaiman/various**
One of the most acclaimed and celebrated comics titles ever published — a rich blend of modern myth and dark fantasy by the *New York Times* best-selling author.

## Y: THE LAST MAN
**Winner of multiple Eisner Awards**
**Brian K. Vaughan/Pia Guerra/José Marzán, Jr.**
An unexplained plague kills every male mammal on Earth — all except Yorick Brown and his pet monkey. Will he survive this new, emasculated world to discover what killed his fellow men?

## THE QUITTER
**Harvey Pekar/Dean Haspiel**
The creator of *American Splendor* reveals his troubled teen years as the neighborhood bully.

## THE LOSERS
**Andy Diggle/Jock**
A hard-hitting crime/espionage series that mixes real-world scenarios with widescreen action.

## V FOR VENDETTA
**Alan Moore/David Lloyd**
One of the accomplishments that cemented Alan Moore's reputation — now a major motion picture. A powerful story about loss of freedom and individuality, that takes place in a totalitarian England following a devastating war that changed the face of the planet.

Search the Graphic Novels section of vertigocomics.com for art and info on every one of our hundreds of books. To purchase any of our titles, call 1-888-COMIC BOOK for the comics shop nearest you or go to your local book store.